European sculpture from Bernini to Rodin

David Bindman

general editor David Herbert

studio vista|dutton pictureback

For Susan, Catherine and Julia

© David Bindman 1970
Designed by Gillian Greenwood
Published in Great Britain by Studio Vista Limited
Blue Star House, Highgate Hill, London N19
and in the USA by E. P. Dutton and Co. Inc.
201 Park Avenue South, New York, NY 10003
Set in 8D on 11 pt Univers 689
Made and printed in Great Britain by
Richard Clay (The Chaucer Press), Ltd, Bungay, Suffolk

SBN 289 79703 9 (paperback)
      289 79704 7 (cased)

The 300 years spanning the time between the work of Bernini and that of Rodin form an age both exceptionally fertile in the field of sculpture and surprisingly little documented. In this book David Bindman has written a brief but scholarly and lucid account of the history of European sculpture in this period; from the classical background of Bernini's Baroque naturalism through the Rococo, the Neoclassical reaction and nineteenth-century Romanticism to Rodin. The general discussion achieves its depth and balance from a perceptive examination of particular works, 120 of which are illustrated—sculptures by Bernini, Algardi, Bouchardon, Pigalle, Canova, Préault, Rodin and more than twenty others. His account of nineteenth-century sculpture, a subject still almost untouched by serious research, is particularly valuable in its originality.

David Bindman is a lecturer in art history at Westfield College, University of London. He has written mainly on the work of William Blake and his contemporaries and is currently preparing a catalogue of the Blake collection in the Fitzwilliam Museum, Cambridge, and the Blake entry for the Paul Mellon Dictionary of British Art.

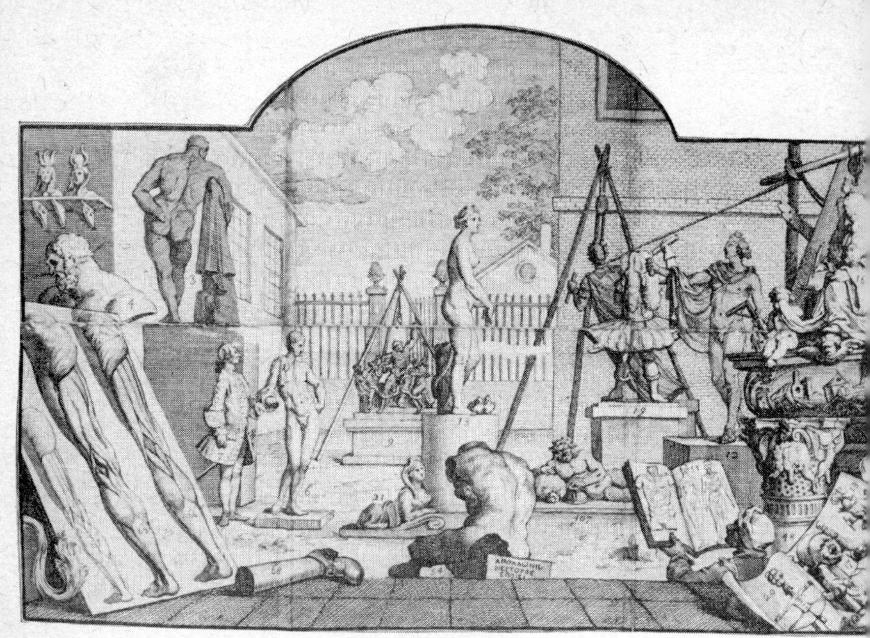

William Hogarth *The Sculptor's Yard*
from *The Analysis of Beauty* 1753

Key

3 Farnese Hercules

4 Head of Farnese Hercules

6 Antinous

9 Laocöon

12 Apollo Belvedere

13 Venus de Medici

Contents

Acknowledgements

The author and publishers wish to thank the following who supplied photographs. Where no separate acknowledgement is made the photographs were provided by the owners of the works.

The Courtauld Institute of Art, London: frontispiece, 27, 29, 46, 58, 72, 78, 79, 84, 85, 104–5, 110, 111, 117, 118, 131, 138, 141
The Mansell Collection, London: 10–13, 17, 19, 20, 24–5, 26, 28, 30, 32–40, 41, 43, 45, 58, 90, 93, 96, 109
Editions Bulloz, Paris: 122, 147
Photographie Giraudon, Paris: 52, 55, 57, 95, 118, 120, 129
Photographie Roger-Viollet, Paris: 54, 61, 62–3, 121
All photographs from the Victoria and Albert Museum, London, 14, 15, 42, 50, 74, 80, 81, 92, 99, 101, 103, 114, 115, 130, 141, and from the Wallace Collection, London, 53, 60, 70, 71, are Crown Copyright Reserved.

Preface

The period of 300 years from the early period of Bernini to the
death of Rodin was exceptionally fertile in the field of sculpture.
A book of this length, if it is not to degenerate into a list of names,
can only hope to mention a few of the important figures. I have
tried, therefore, to draw as straight a line as possible between
Bernini and Rodin, giving only the briefest mention to schools outside the mainstream—however interesting they may be. I have also
eliminated the great painter-sculptors of the nineteenth century,
like Degas and Gauguin, because they have been adequately
covered elsewhere, while the professional sculptors of that period
have been correspondingly neglected.

Sculpture has always been something of a Cinderella amongst
the arts, and in this period only Bernini has been treated in English
with the full resources of modern scholarship; there is as yet no
monograph even on so great an artist as Puget. The nineteenth
century is still a *tabula rasa* as far as serious research is concerned,
and the work of artists like Préault and Rude is hardly known outside France. In the meantime it is hoped that the illustrations to this
book will provide an introduction to, or reminder of, a diverse and
fascinating period in the history of sculpture.

I would like to thank Mrs Franklin for typing the manuscript, and
my colleagues at Westfield College, especially Alistair Whyte, for
their constant help and advice.

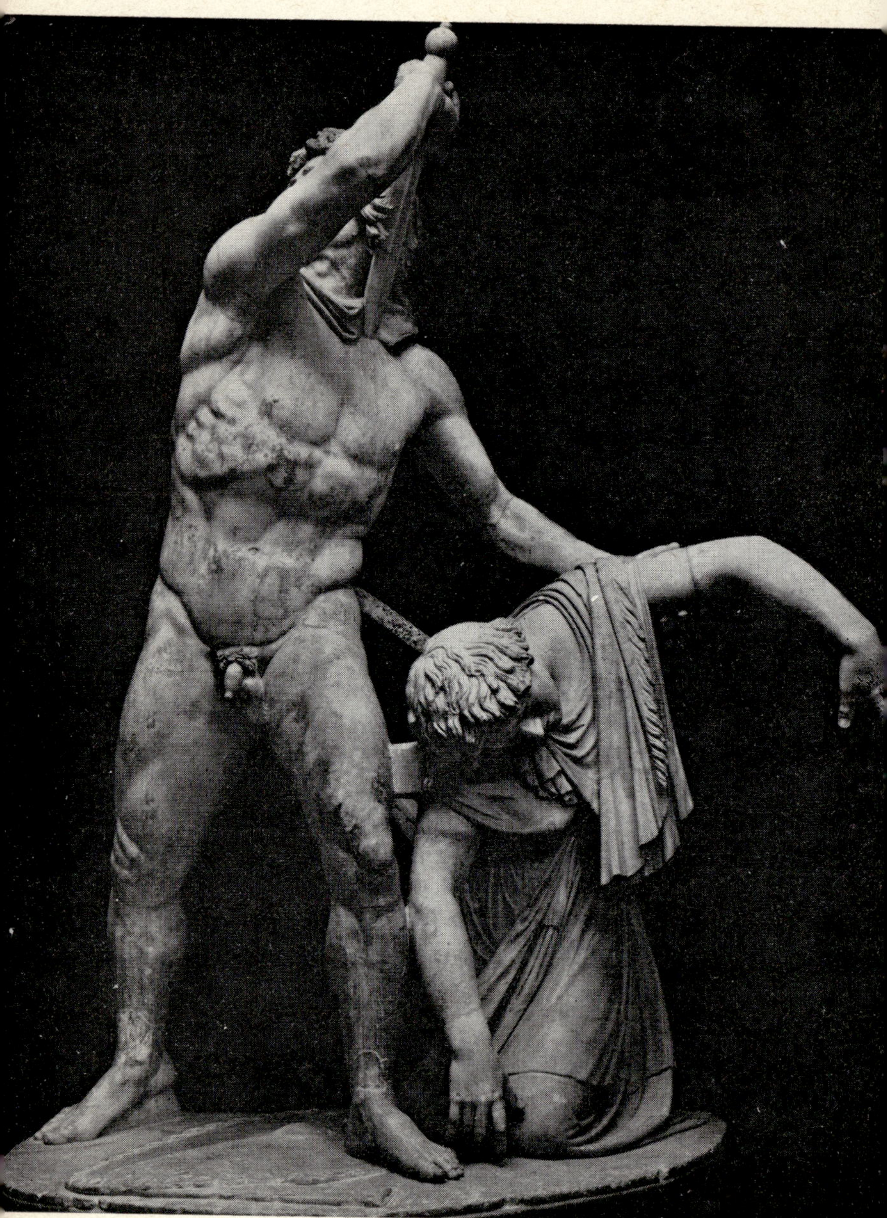

Bernini and the baroque

Artists and theorists in the seventeenth and eighteenth centuries believed that a small number of sculptures of the very highest quality had survived from antiquity, and that these alone provided a standard for their contemporaries. Little attempt was made to separate the different styles or periods of antiquity until the second half of the eighteenth century, when it was gradually realized that many of the canon were in fact Roman copies of Greek originals, or of the later Hellenistic period: however, even before they made formal distinctions sculptors showed an instinctive preference for one style or another, or interpreted the same object according to their own leanings. Bernini, for example, was attracted to the dramatic naturalism of what is often called the Hellenistic baroque style of Pergamese groups of the second and first century BC, like the *Vanquished Gaul Killing Himself and his Wife*, while the classical sculptor Duquesnoy was drawn towards the Vatican *Antinous* or *Hermes*, a Roman imitation of a Greek original of probably the fifth century BC. On the other hand, the *Apollo Belvedere* was the prototype for works as different in style as the figure of Apollo in Bernini's *Apollo and Daphne*, and Canova's *Perseus.*

Like the words 'gothic' and 'rococo', 'baroque' was originally a term of abuse, meaning grotesque, deformed or over-elaborate. It carried with it the implication that the baroque style stood in opposition to the true classical principles of art and sought meretricious and transitory effects that appealed to man's meaner desires. The academies of art that had grown up in the sixteenth and seventeenth centuries saw themselves as the custodians of the true classical tradition, whose principles were being threatened by the pursuit of a virtuosity that lured artists and patrons away from more demanding and elevated conceptions. The academies felt themselves to be the guardians of eternal values that had found their highest expression in antiquity, and they stood for an art which was restrained, simple and austere. Baroque artists, on the other hand, would have argued that the initial function of both painting and sculpture was to seduce the eye of the beholder by convincing him of the reality of the scene before him.

Vanquished Gaul Killing Himself and his Wife c. 240–200 BC
National Museum, Rome

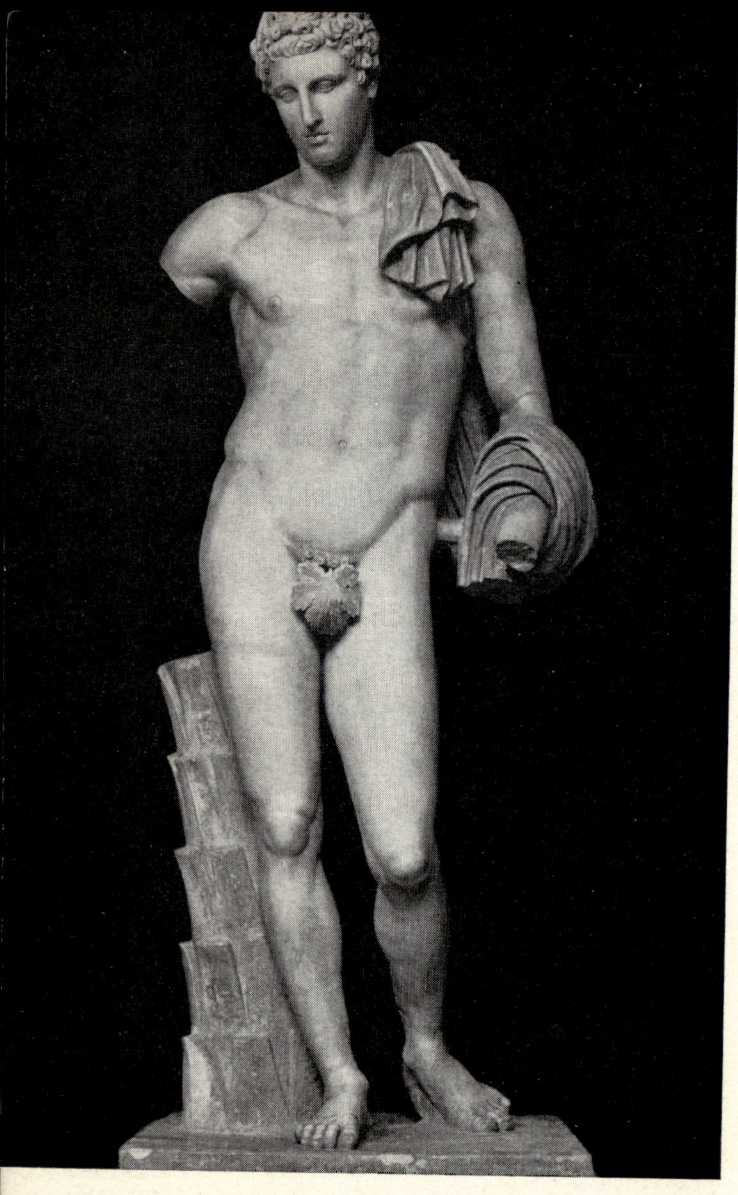

Antinous or *Hermes* 1st century AD
Vatican

10

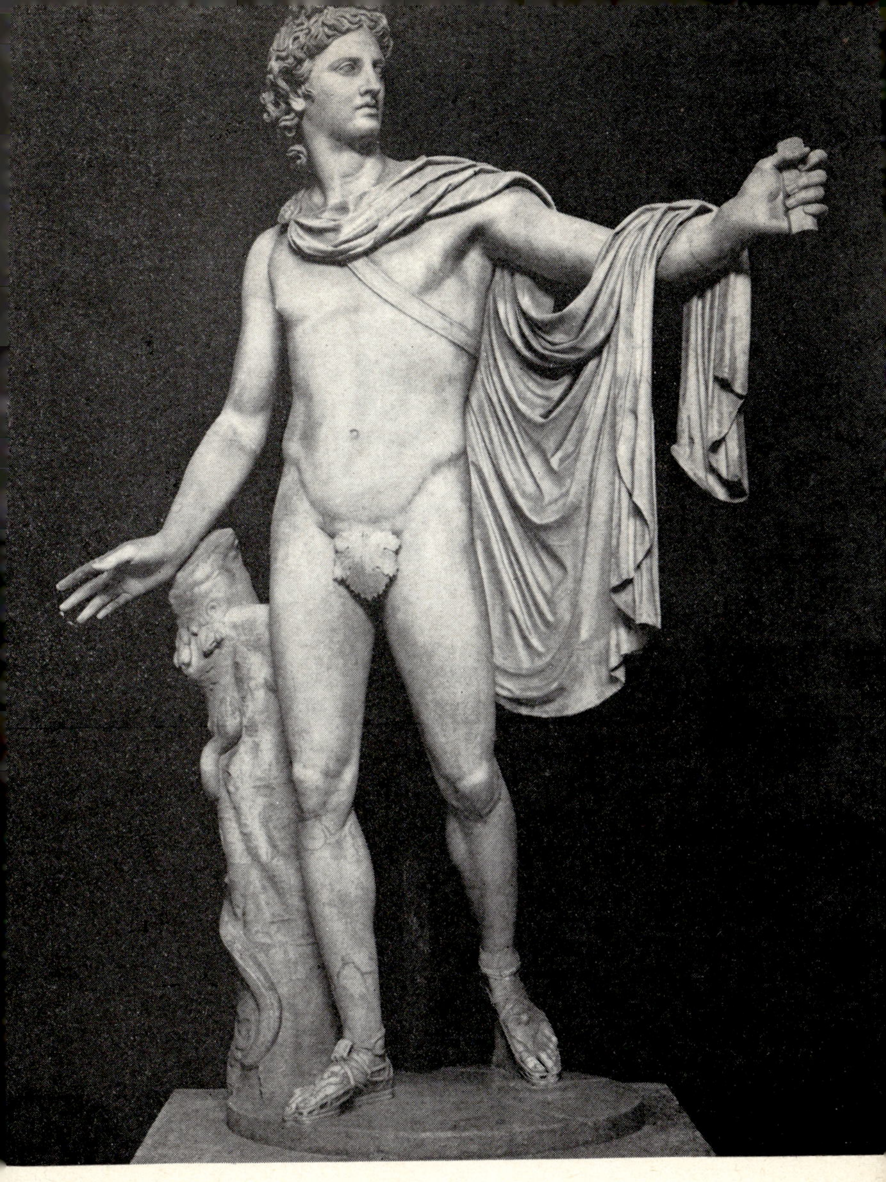

Apollo Belvedere 1st century AD
Vatican

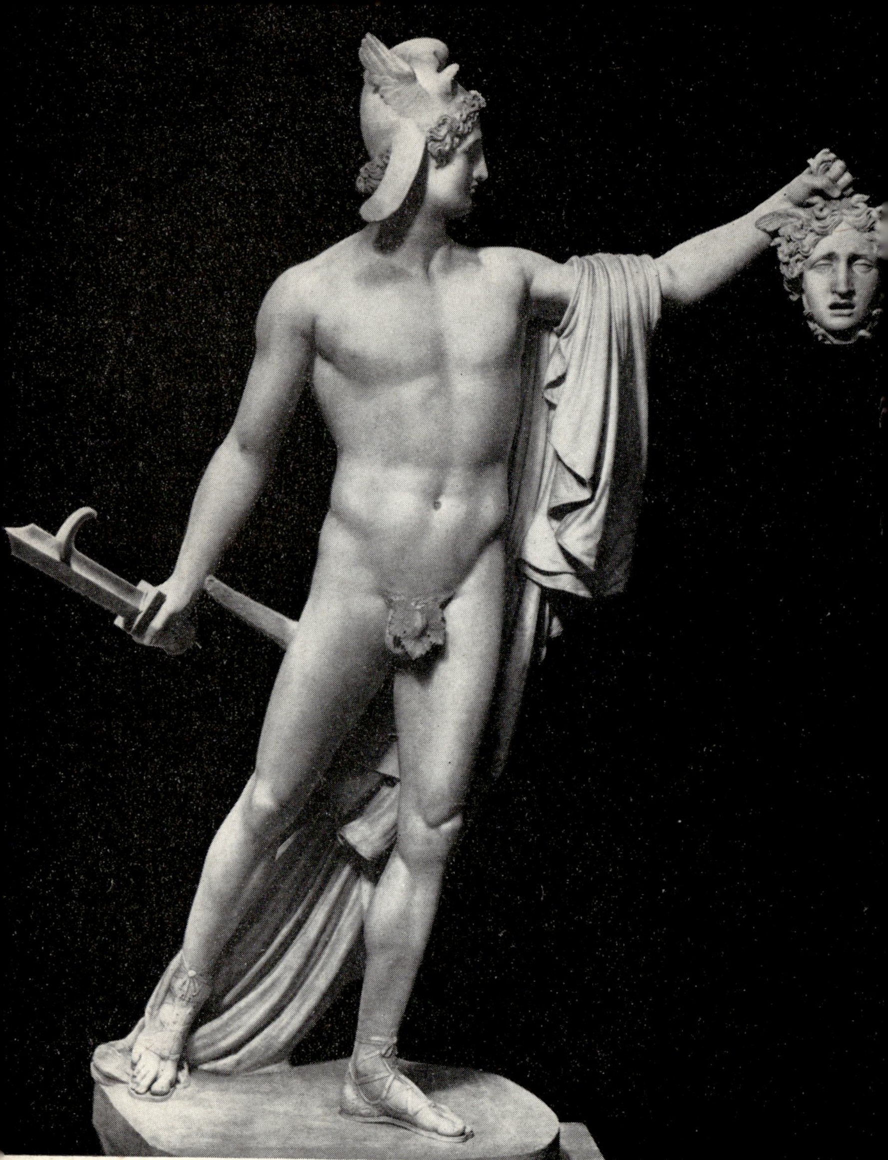

A. Canova *Perseus c.* 1800
Vatican

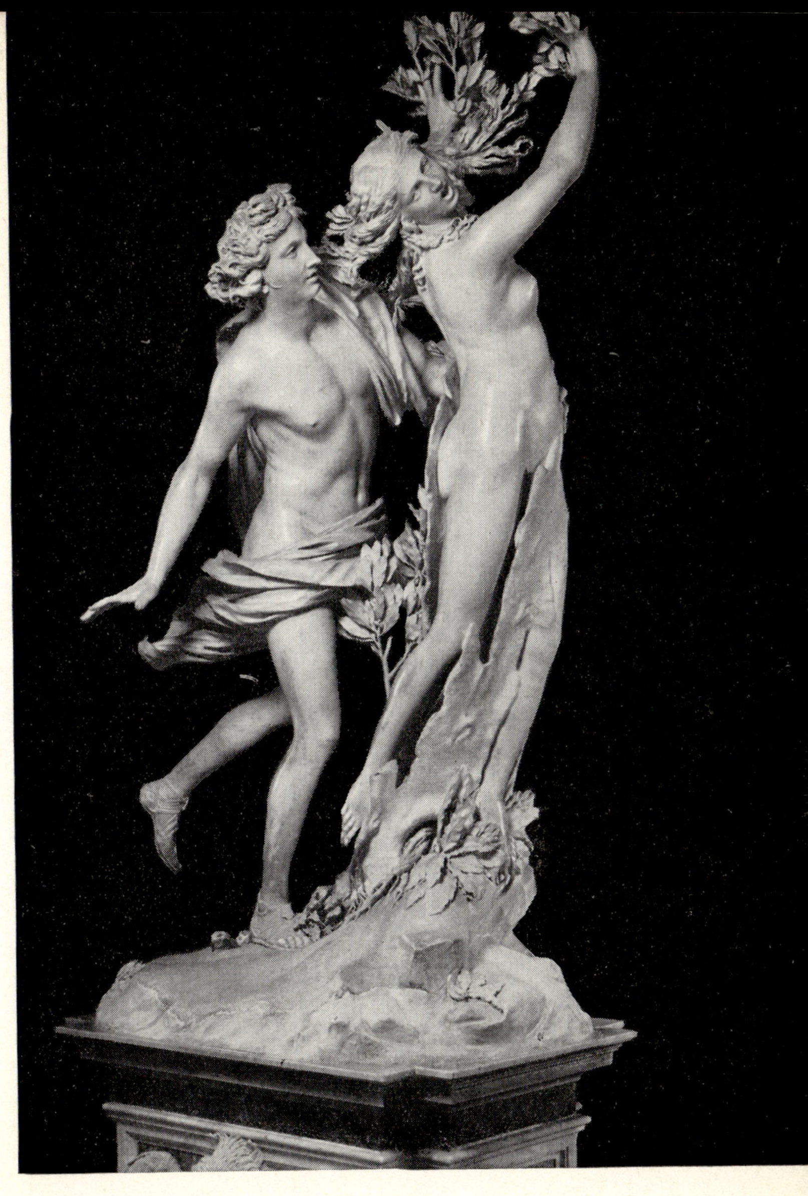

G. L. Bernini *Apollo and Daphne* 1622–5
Borghese Gallery, Rome

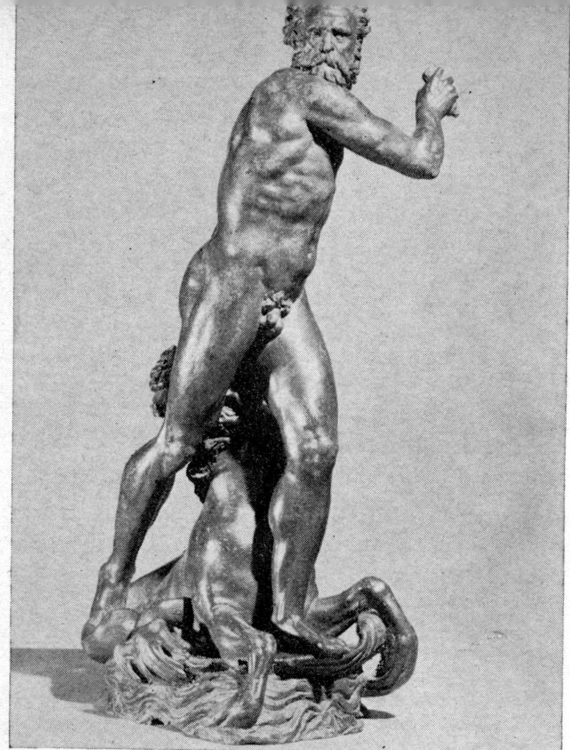

A. Vittoria *Neptune c.* 1580–85
Victoria and Albert Museum, London

In practice the distinction between classical and baroque artists is less clear-cut, and even Bernini believed himself to be working in the tradition of Michelangelo and antiquity. His baroque naturalism is more a reaction against the aestheticism of mannerist sculpture than against the classical ideal; his work repudiates the elegant curves and balletic grace of his predecessors by an aggressive concreteness and naturalism. The contrast can be seen by comparing the figure of *Neptune* (*c.* 1580–85) by Alessandro Vittoria, one of the best of the later mannerist sculptors, with

14

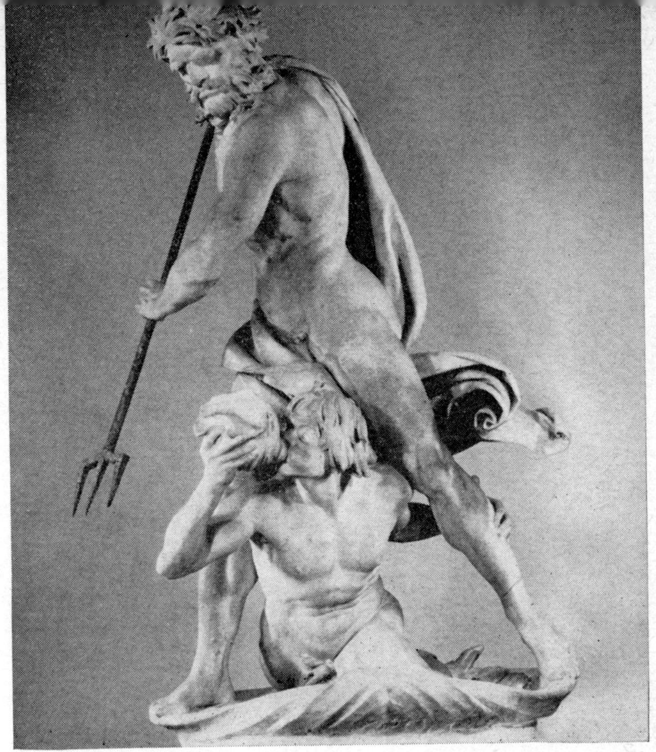

G. L. Bernini *Neptune and Triton c.* 1621
Victoria and Albert Museum, London

Bernini's *Neptune and Triton* (*c.* 1621). The *contraposto*, or turning movement, of Vittoria's figure makes the sculpture 'work' from all angles, and it is clearly an object to be handled and admired for its changing contours. The movement is confined within one plane and there is no thrust in any one direction, while the modelling is more delicate than powerful. Bernini's version still retains something of the mannerist *contraposto*, but the thrust of the figure is behind the trident which carries the impetus of the action beyond the plane of the pedestal, as if calming the waters of the pond

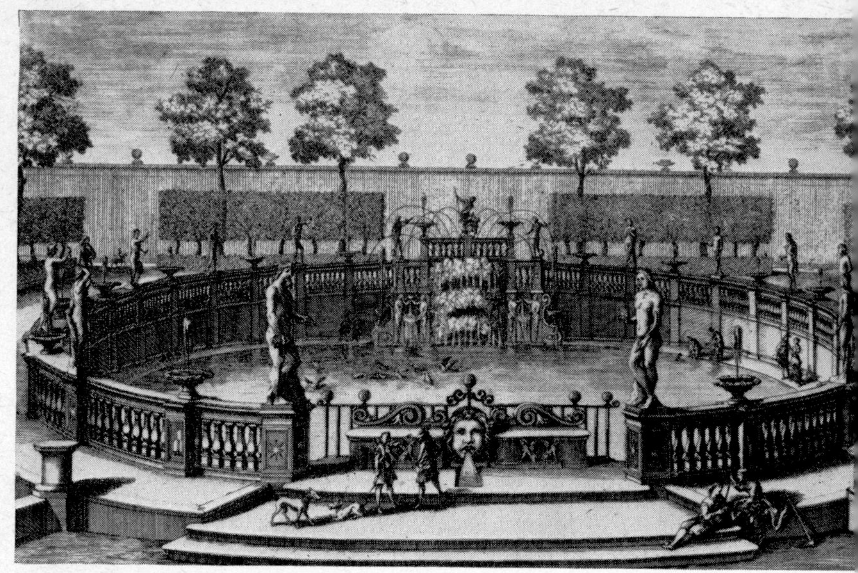

G. F. Venturini *Fishpond in the Garden of the Villa Montalto*
from G. B. Falda *Le Fontane di Roma,* vol. III, pl. 17, mid 17th century

which it was originally intended to surmount, as can be seen
from a seventeenth-century engraving of Cardinal Montalto's garden. Vittoria's *Neptune* was, therefore, designed as a statue complete in itself, while Bernini's group was intended to be an active
part of its setting, bringing the pond into an allegorical conceit.

Bernini's most important achievement was to destroy the autonomy of sculpture by attempting to create an illusion of reality
that had previously been considered within the province of
painting. Painting by its nature was suited to deceiving the eye,
and to achieve a comparable effect in sculpture required a virtuosity that Bernini was almost alone in possessing. He had the
facility, in Sir Joshua Reynolds's words, to make stone 'sport and
flutter in the air', and he brought into the range of sculpture the
depiction of a moment in time, gestures in transition and a
pictorial background to the figures, by treating the relatively
intractable materials of sculpture as if they were entirely malleable.
Posterity dealt harshly with his facility and the argument against
Bernini which was to condemn him to unpopularity until the
beginning of this century was succinctly expressed by Reynolds in

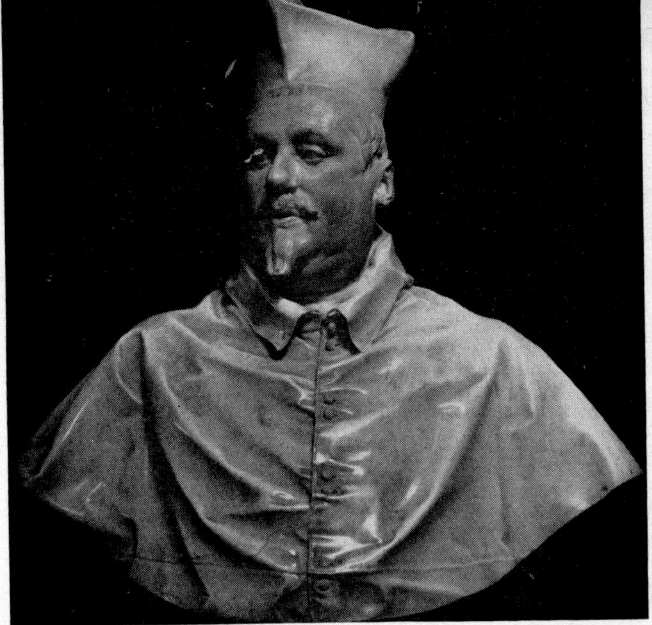

G. L. Bernini *Cardinal Scipione Borghese* 1632
Borghese Gallery, Rome

his *Discourse on Sculpture* * : 'Instead of pursuing the study of that ideal beauty with which he had so successfully begun, he turned his mind to an injudicious quest of novelty; attempted what was not within the province of the Art, and endeavoured to overcome the hardness and obstinacy of his materials : which even supposing he had accomplished, so far as to make this species of drapery appear natural, the ill-effect and confusion occasioned by its being detached from the figure to which it belongs, ought to have been a sufficient reason to have deterred him from that practice.' Only with the twentieth century has the classical prejudice against the 'impurity' of his methods been overcome, and he can now take his place amongst the greatest of all artists.

Giovanni Lorenzo Bernini was born in 1598, his father being a sculptor who had worked on many projects in Rome. Bernini's gifts revealed themselves even in his early teens and by the age of twenty he had established himself as the foremost sculptor in Rome. He was taken up by Cardinal Scipione Borghese, the Pope's nephew, who was engaged, in the years 1613–15, in building the

* Sir J. Reynolds, *Discourses* No. 10.

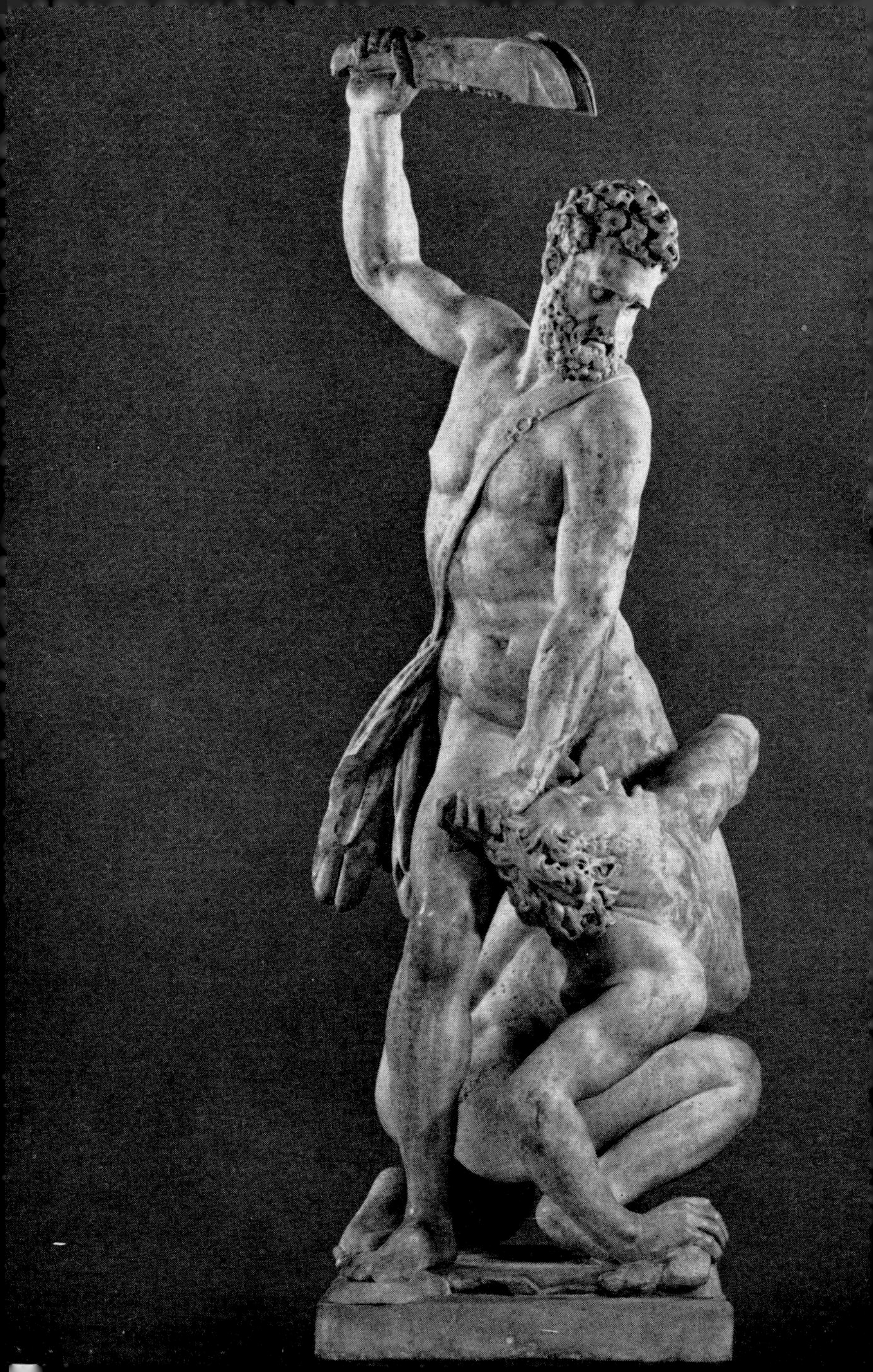

Villa Borghese and filling it with antiquities. Scipione Borghese was typical of the Roman connoisseurs who emerged at the beginning of the seventeenth century: aristocratic, aesthetic in inclination and of wide classical learning. He epitomizes the relaxed feeling in Rome after the early austerity of the Counter-Reformation, as Church Militant became Church Triumphant.

Bernini's sculptures for Scipione Borghese form a clearly defined phase in his work, and they show a rapid development from the late mannerist style of his father Pietro, who probably helped him with some of his earliest works, to a complete mastery of movement and gesture. The first of the series, the *Aeneas and Anchises*

G. da Bologna *Samson Slaying a Philistine c.* 1565–6
Victoria and Albert Museum, London

G. L. Bernini *Aeneas and Anchises* 1617–19
Borghese Gallery, Rome

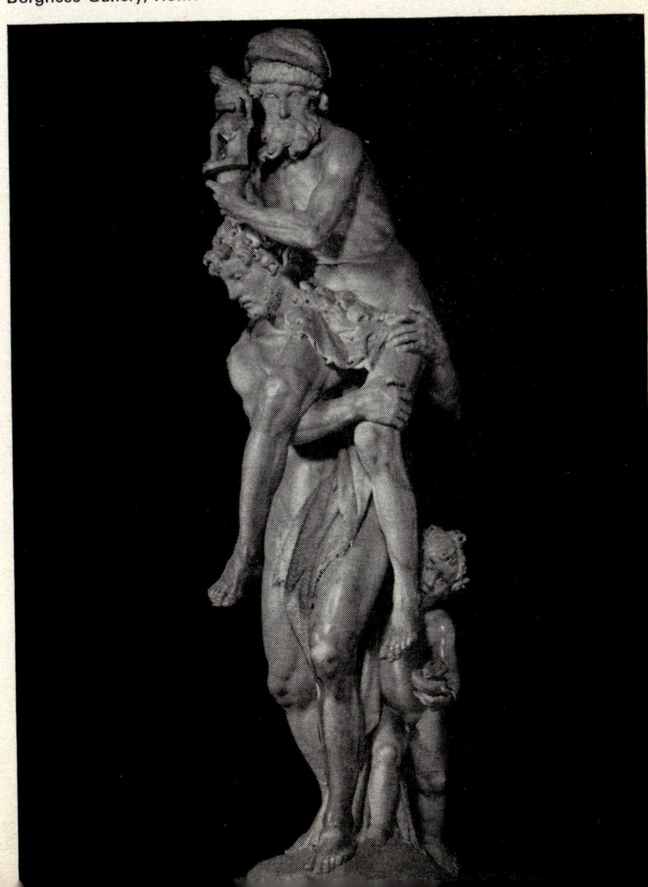

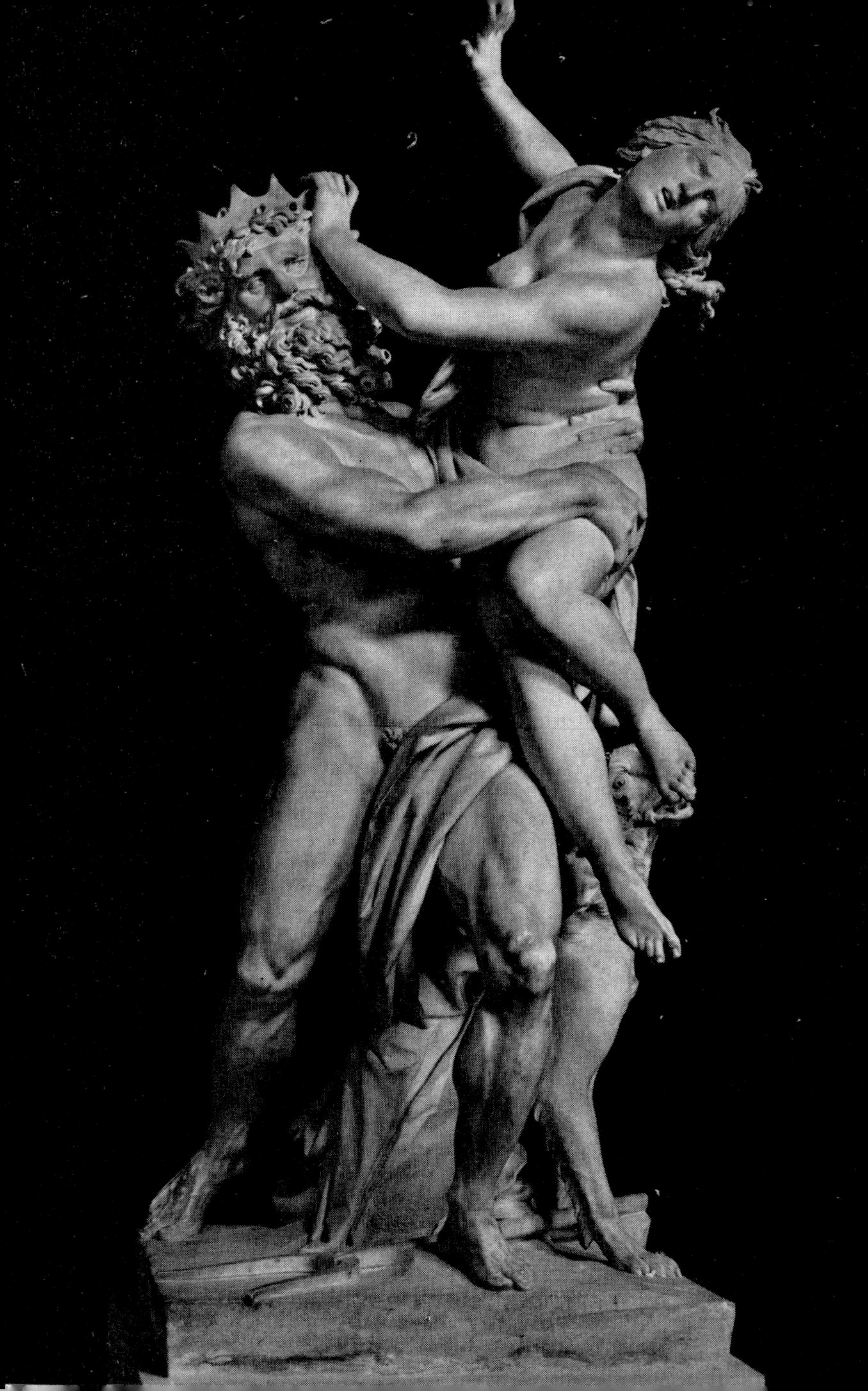

of 1617–19, has the serpentine movement of Giovanni da Bologna, but it is rather uncertain in conception, perhaps because its original placing against the wall as a relief inhibited its movement in space. This was followed by the *Neptune and Triton* (see page 15), a transitional work to the full-blooded baroque of the *Pluto and Proserpine*. As with the *Aeneas and Anchises*, the composition of the *Pluto and Proserpine* depends upon its being placed against a wall so that the beholder comes upon it directly from the front; the figure of Pluto is then seen to be advancing towards him. But now the group stands arbitrarily in the centre of the room where it was moved in the late eighteenth century. Unlike the *Neptune and Triton*, which is raised on a plinth to dominate the Montalto pond, the *Pluto and Proserpine* was intended to be seen at eye level, and the god appears to be stepping boldly off the pedestal while Proserpine struggles helplessly, looking outside the group for help. The composition depends not on an abstract movement but on the relationship between the figures of Pluto and Proserpine; the purposeful strength of the former is contrasted with the latter's discordant gestures, through the counterpoint of balance against unsteadiness, and firmness against softness.

The explanation for Bernini's astonishing transformation in these years is perhaps to be found in the painting of the period; indeed the very feebleness of the sculpture of the period in Rome led him to look at the achievements of painters, such as Annibale Carracci's spectacular ceiling of the Farnese Gallery, which surpassed the Sistine Chapel in its illusionistic complexity. Bernini borrowed motifs from the Farnese ceiling, but it was more important to him as an example of the reconciliation of convincing naturalism with heroic monumentality. Carracci reveals his debt to Michelangelo and the sculptors of antiquity in his figures, but they are modelled with a greater attention to colour and texture, while his use of painted caryatids and pictures-within-pictures legitimized Bernini's experiments with illusion. It is also evident that Bernini had taken the opportunity to study Hellenistic works like the *Vanquished Gaul Killing Himself and his Wife* (see page 8), the *Dying Gaul* and the *Laocöon*.

In the *David* (1623), the beholder is brought further within the orbit of the sculpture, for in contrast to Michelangelo's version, David is seen at the point of releasing the stone, which he aims, if the beholder is positioned correctly, directly at or above him. As an example of dramatic naturalism it is striking, but it lacks the

on pages 24 *and* 25
Annibale Carracci *Polyphemus* 1595–1604
Farnese Gallery, Rome

Laocöon c. 150 AD
Vatican

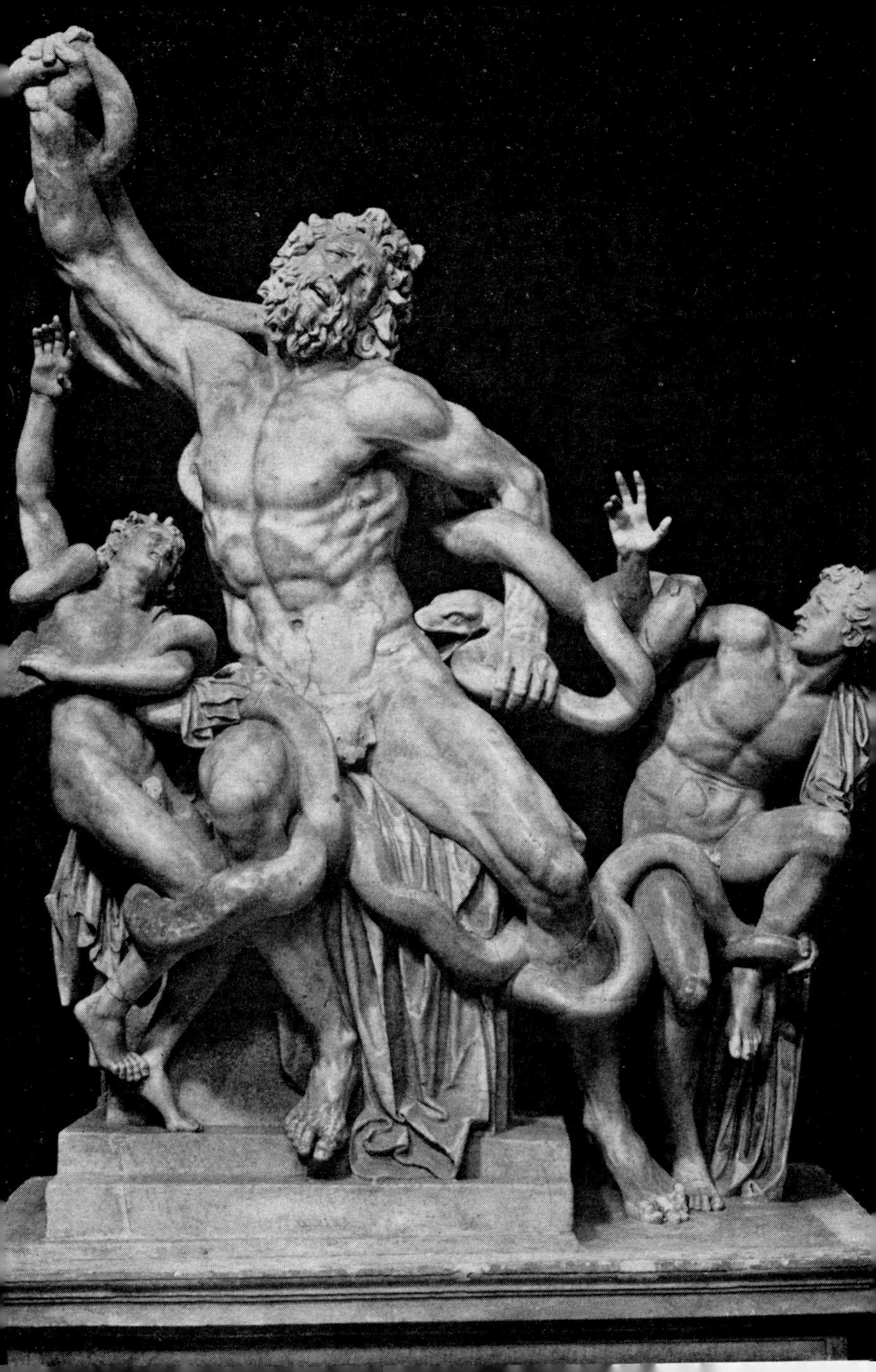

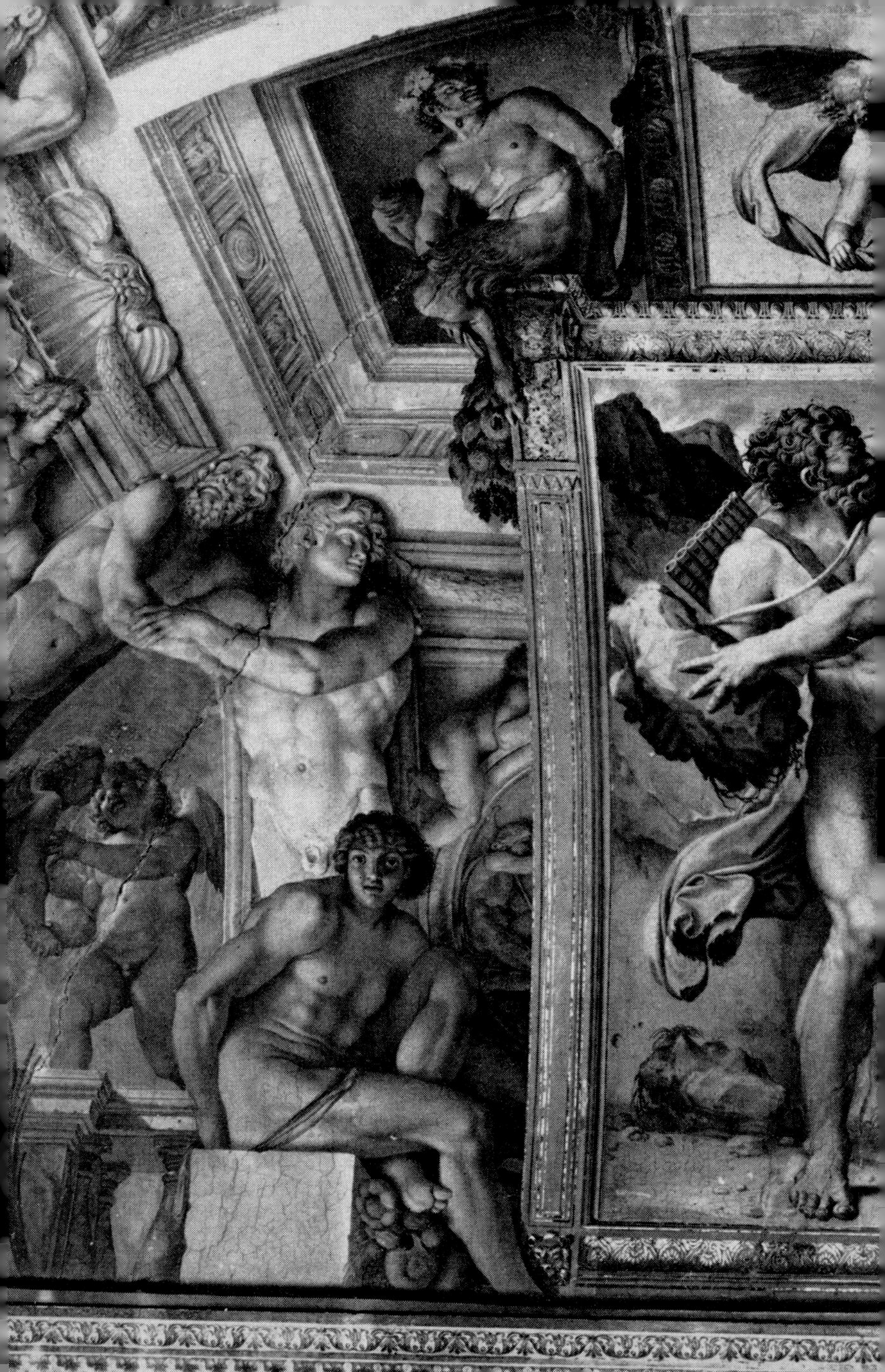

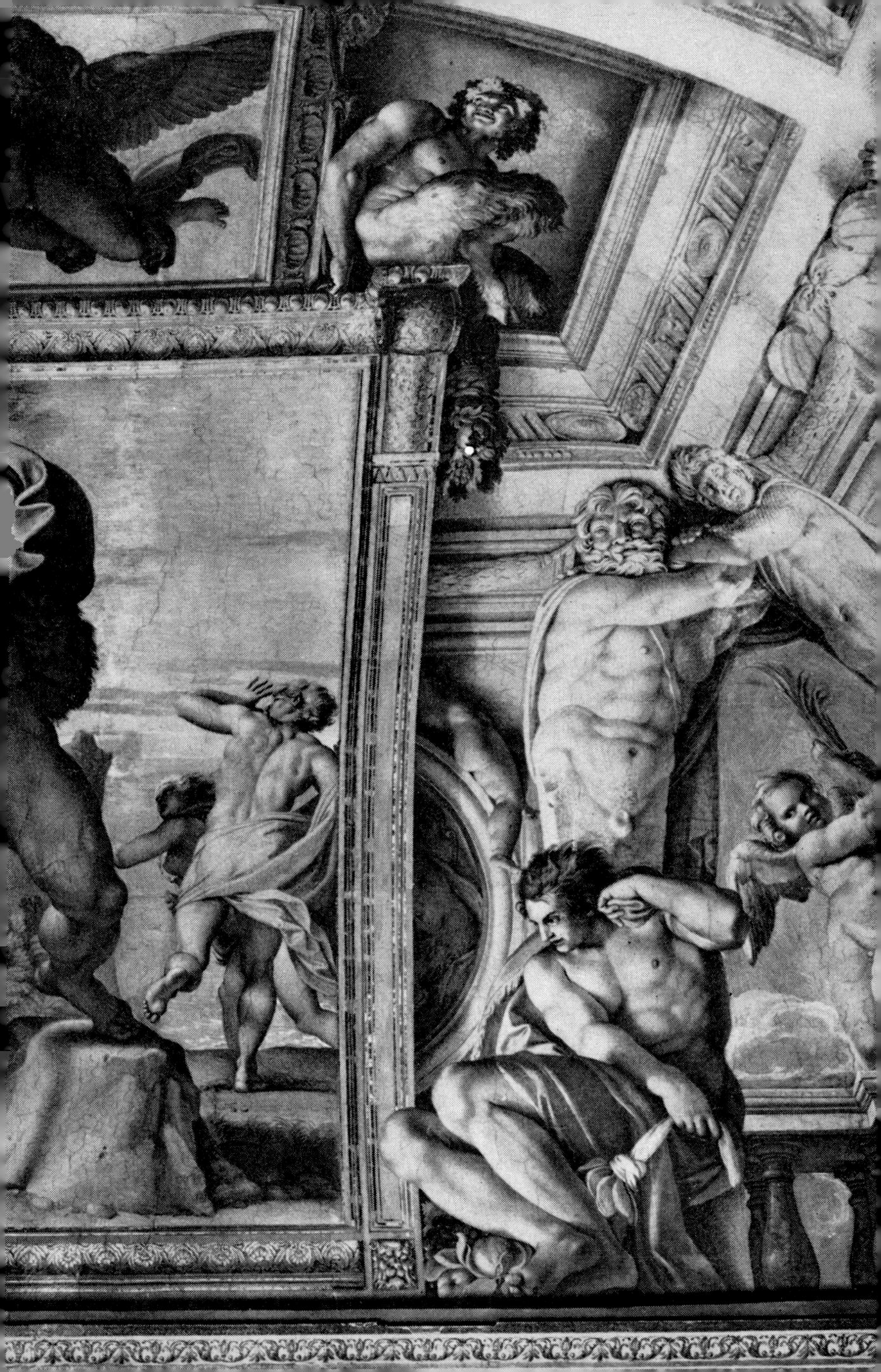

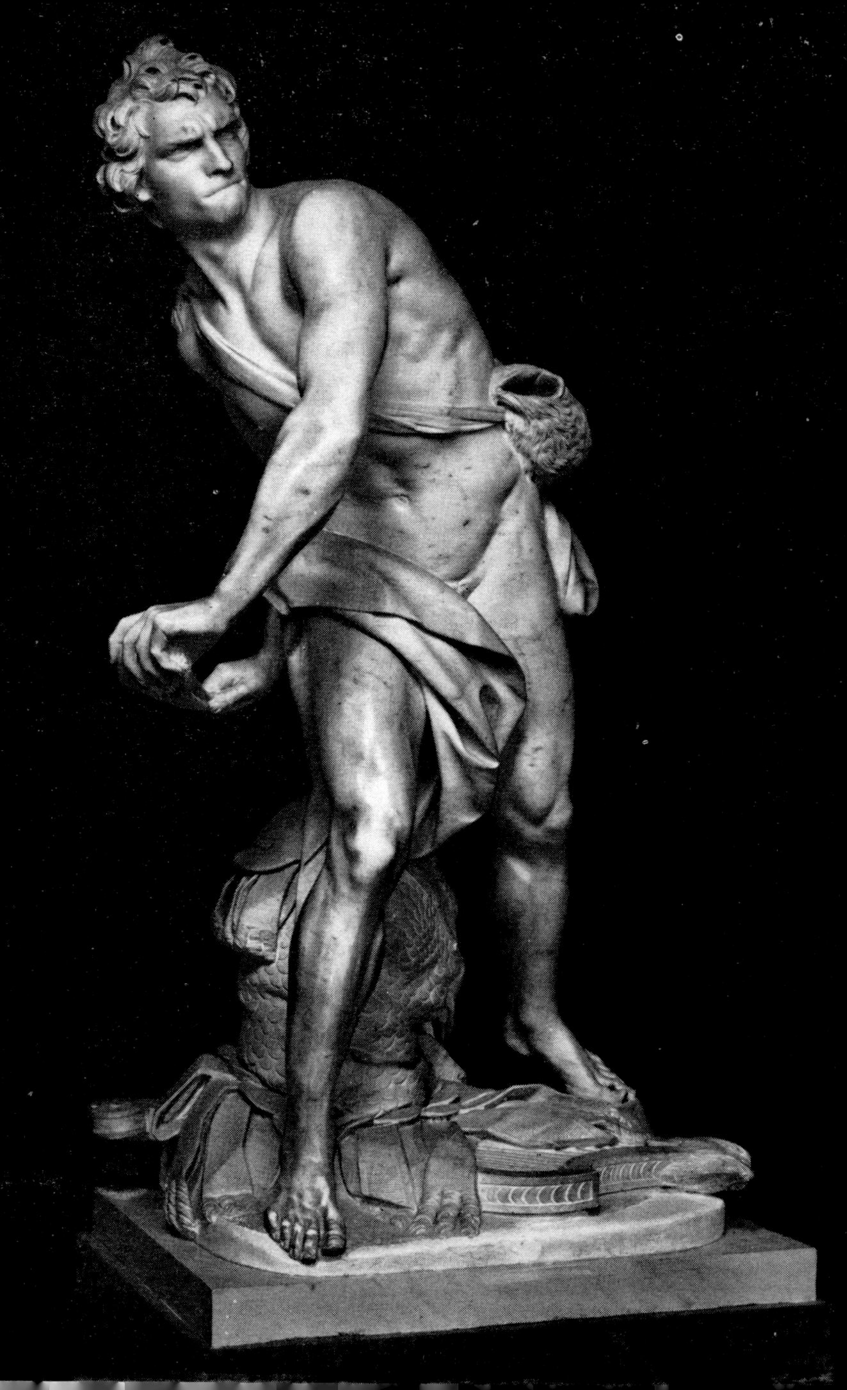

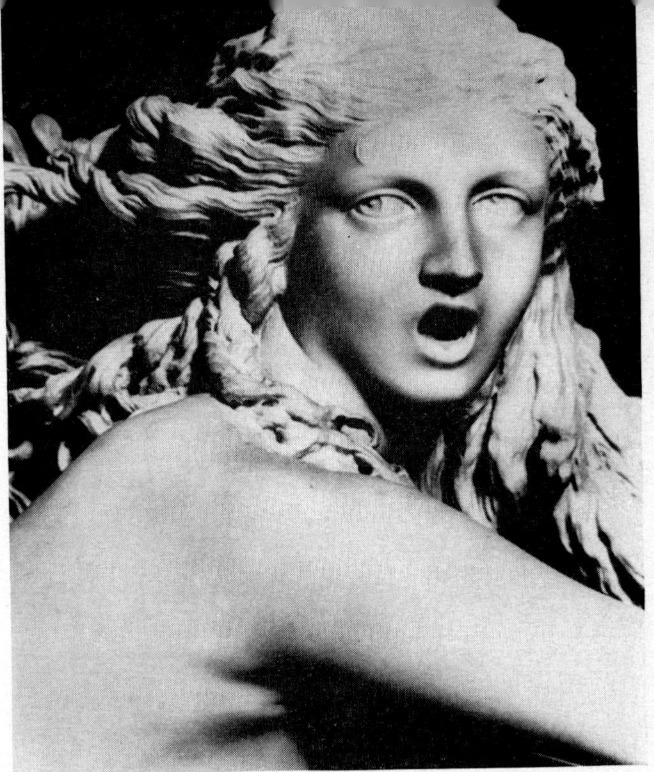

G. L. Bernini *Apollo and Daphne* 1622–5
Detail. Borghese Gallery, Rome

G. L. Bernini *David* 1623
Borghese Gallery, Rome

poetic feeling of the masterpiece of the Borghese series, the *Apollo and Daphne* (1622–5) (see page 13), where virtuosity is subordinated to the poetic rendering of metamorphosis. The transformation of Daphne is shown taking place as if Apollo were still in hot pursuit, and Bernini has shown with remarkable sensitivity Daphne's terror and Apollo's sudden bewilderment.

With the completion of the Borghese sculptures Bernini was to move away from the circle of the aristocratic connoisseurs into the service of the papal policy. The Roman Church was in the throes of reform in the early seventeenth century, and Bernini's entry into its service was to coincide with the final victory of the progressives, who were sympathetic to the popular teachings of

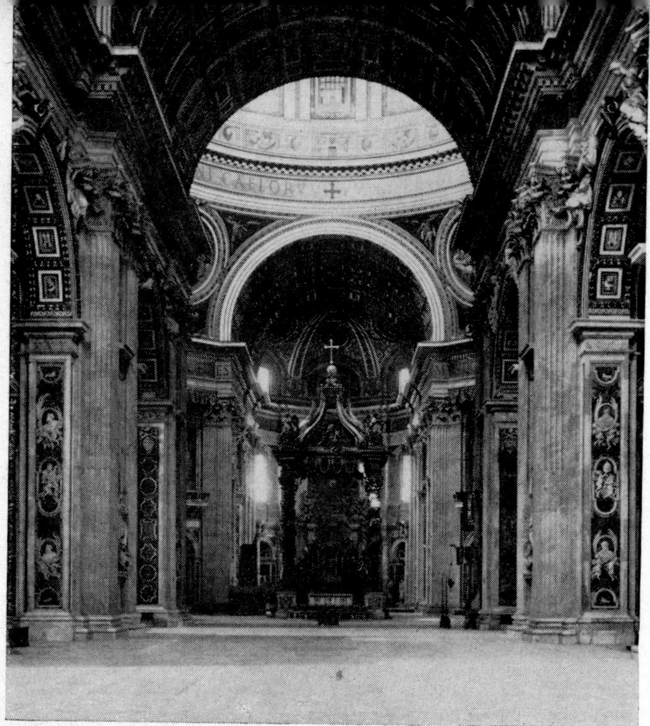

St Peter's View towards the High Altar
Rome

Ignatius Loyola and the Jesuits. Ignatius Loyola and Teresa of Avila were both canonized in 1622, a year which marks not only the beginning of a fully baroque religious style, but also of a new iconography based on the lives of more recent saints and martyrs. The text book of this phase was Ignatius Loyola's *Spiritual Exercises*, which Bernini is known to have used. It advocated a concrete form of religious experience, based on the tangibility of punishment and suffering. The religious man had to cleanse his soul by reliving the Passion of Christ and forcing his body to undergo the torments of hell through all his senses, so that he should be continually aware of his own mortality. His models of conduct were to be not only the modern saints but the holy men of the early Church who had achieved wisdom through self-denial. It is hard for us to reconcile this self-denying ethic with the ostentation of the high baroque, but Bernini would have seen no contradiction, for artists revealed the divine to men through their senses, regardless of their education or language.

28

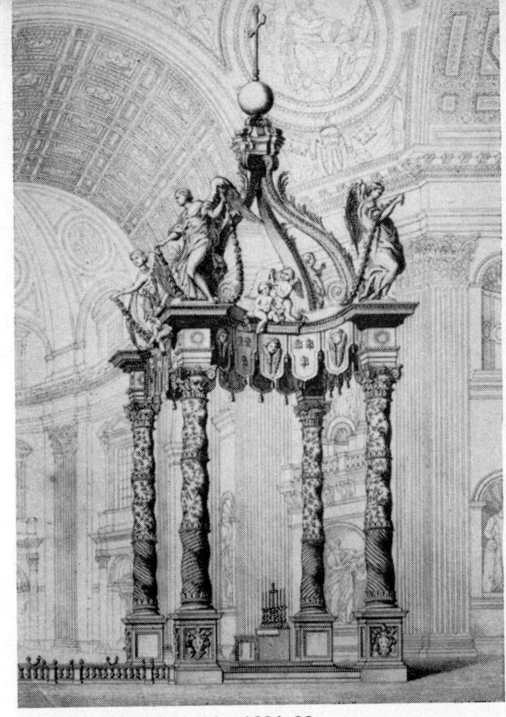

G. L. Bernini *Baldacchino* 1624–33
St Peter's, Rome

Urban VIII, who ascended to the pontificate in 1623, inherited the traditional papal role of developing the city of Rome in a manner worthy of the centre of Christendom, and in particular the problem of St Peter's which was still far from complete. Urban VIII was the ideal patron for Bernini, for he was sympathetic to the religious fervour of the Jesuits, while at the same time he saw the value of a magnificent display of temporal power. He took Bernini into service in 1624, and from then on the sculptor was permanently employed by the papacy under successive popes until his death. His work in St Peter's did not allow him to return to the Ovidian subjects of his youth, and it caused a fundamental shift in the formal basis of his work. He extends his concern for pictorial illusion into a total manipulation of the environment. In the *Cathedra Petri* and the Cornaro Chapel for example, the sculptural groups are enclosed within a new order of reality, which controls the light that falls upon them and the space they inhabit. The transition to a scenographic conception of

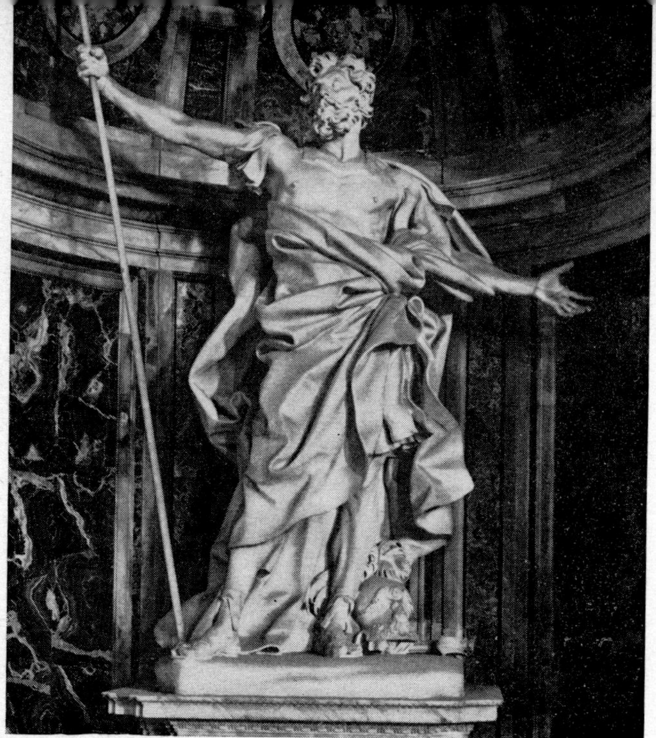

G. L. Bernini *St Longinus* 1632–8
St Peter's, Rome

sculpture can be seen in one of his earliest commissions in St Peter's, the *baldacchino* (1624–33), or canopy, which has both an architectural and symbolic function, acting as a kind of frame for the high altar of the *Cathedra Petri* (1657–66), which was planned at the same time as the *baldacchino* but not begun until twenty-four years after the latter was completed. With the *baldacchino* the boundary between sculpture and architecture in Bernini's work becomes indeterminate, and later even painting was incorporated into Bernini's conception. In the words of his contemporary Baldinucci, it was 'Common knowledge that he was the first who undertook to unite architecture, sculpture and painting in such a way that they together make a beautiful whole'.

Not all of Bernini's commissions for St Peter's required such a complex solution and in the colossal figure of *St Longinus* he

30

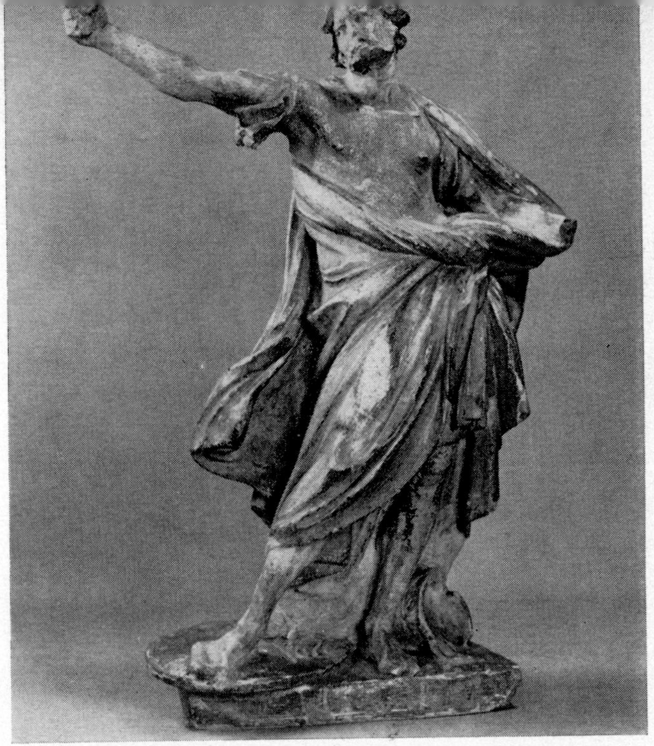

G. L. Bernini Bozzetto for *St Longinus c.* 1632
Fogg Art Museum, Harvard University, Cambridge, Mass.

returned to the Renaissance problem of placing a figure within a niche. Just as the *Apollo and Daphne* shows the moment of Daphne's metamorphosis, so the *St Longinus* shows the Roman soldier's moment of conversion, his sudden vision of divine light. The figure is contained within the niche, but is placed frontally with arms spread out, creating a jagged silhouette. The draperies play a vital part in the expression of emotion and they are carved with a largeness of form that allows them to be seen clearly from far away. The one surviving bozzetto shows the first idea to have been more classical, with the out-flung arm balanced by the curve of the body away from it, but the final work is more dramatic and original. A study of Bernini's preliminary sketches shows that he very frequently used a classical pose as a starting point for the development of the composition, although the final solution may bear little trace of the original idea.

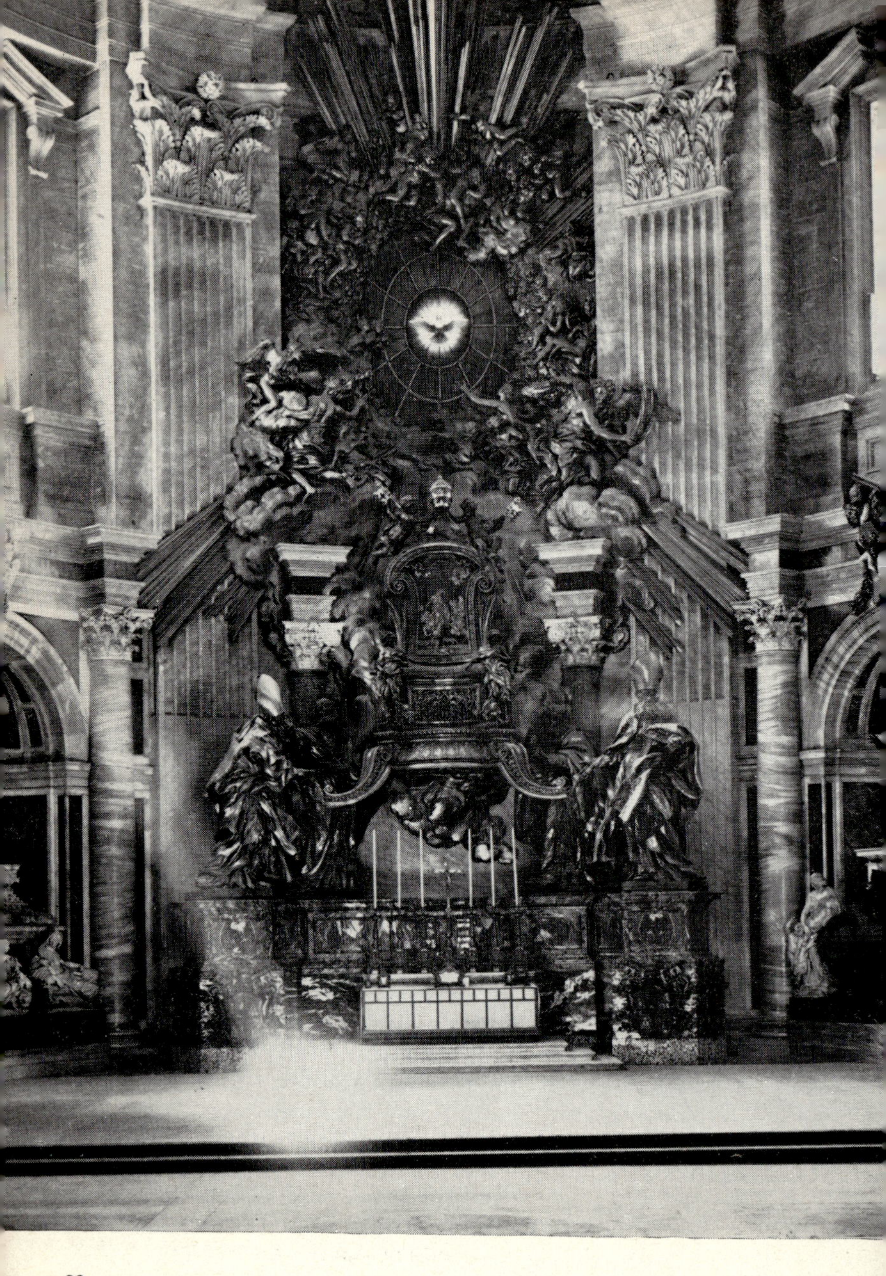

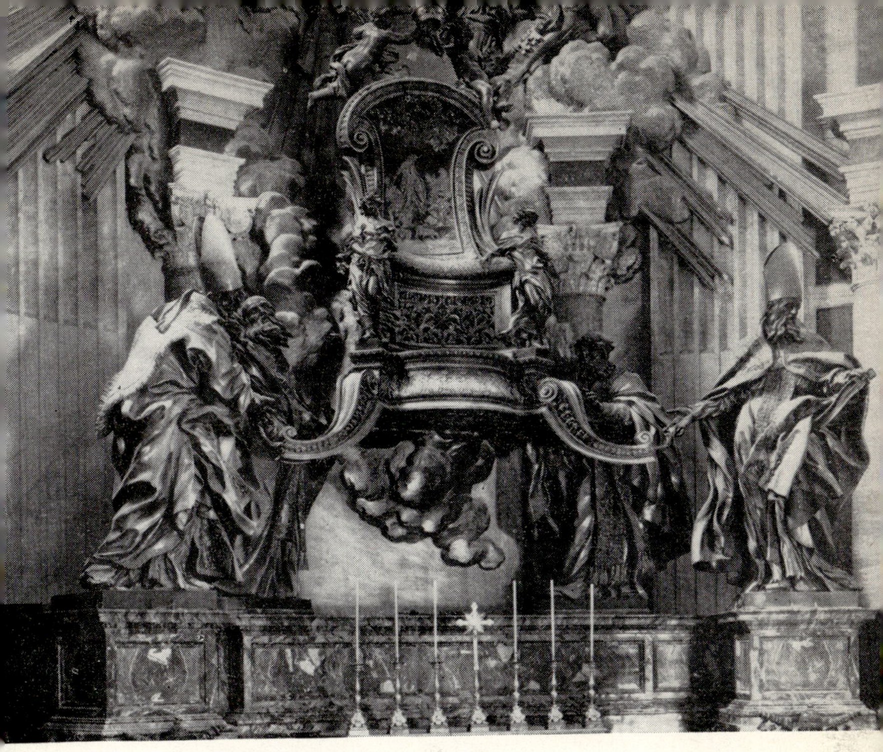

G. L. Bernini *Cathedra Petri* 1657–66
Detail. St Peter's, Rome

G. L. Bernini *Cathedra Petri* 1657–66
St Peter's, Rome

By contrast with the *Longinus*, the *Cathedra Petri* is so complex in its interaction of media that it is best described in Baudelaire's words as a 'mise-en-scène'. The architectural structure that frames the altar is dissolved by a symbolic vision of the elevation of the chair of St Peter. The window at the top is transformed into the divine light that bursts with a sudden radiance through the clouds, as the four fathers of the Church elevate St Peter's throne. As a solution to the problem of creating a climax grand enough for the immensity of the interior, it is a stunning achieve-ment, but, in itself, it is too bombastic to be wholly satisfactory as a work of art.

The most successful of Bernini's scenographic works is the earlier Cornaro Chapel (1647–52), which shows the conversion of St Teresa, watched by members of the Cornaro family. This work should be seen not as a sculptured altar, but as a completely unified side-chapel, in which the donors are shown as participants in the sacred drama. St Teresa and the angel are shown as if suspended on a cloud above the altar, the whole scene within the niche being illuminated from heaven by a concealed window. In the chapel itself, in side-boxes, the Cornaro family, past and present, sit discussing the vision as if they were watching a theatrical performance. The architecture of the chapel is surfaced with different coloured marbles, and an illusionistic painted ceiling,

G. L. Bernini *St Teresa* 1647–52
Detail
S. Maria della Vittoria, Rome

G. L. Bernini *St Teresa* 1647–52
Detail, members of the Cornaro family
S. Maria della Vittoria, Rome

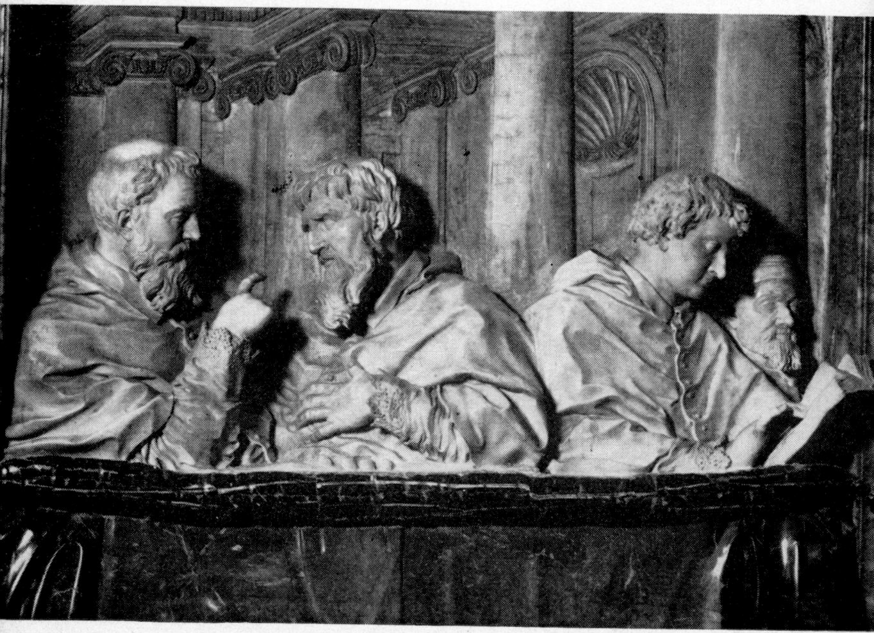

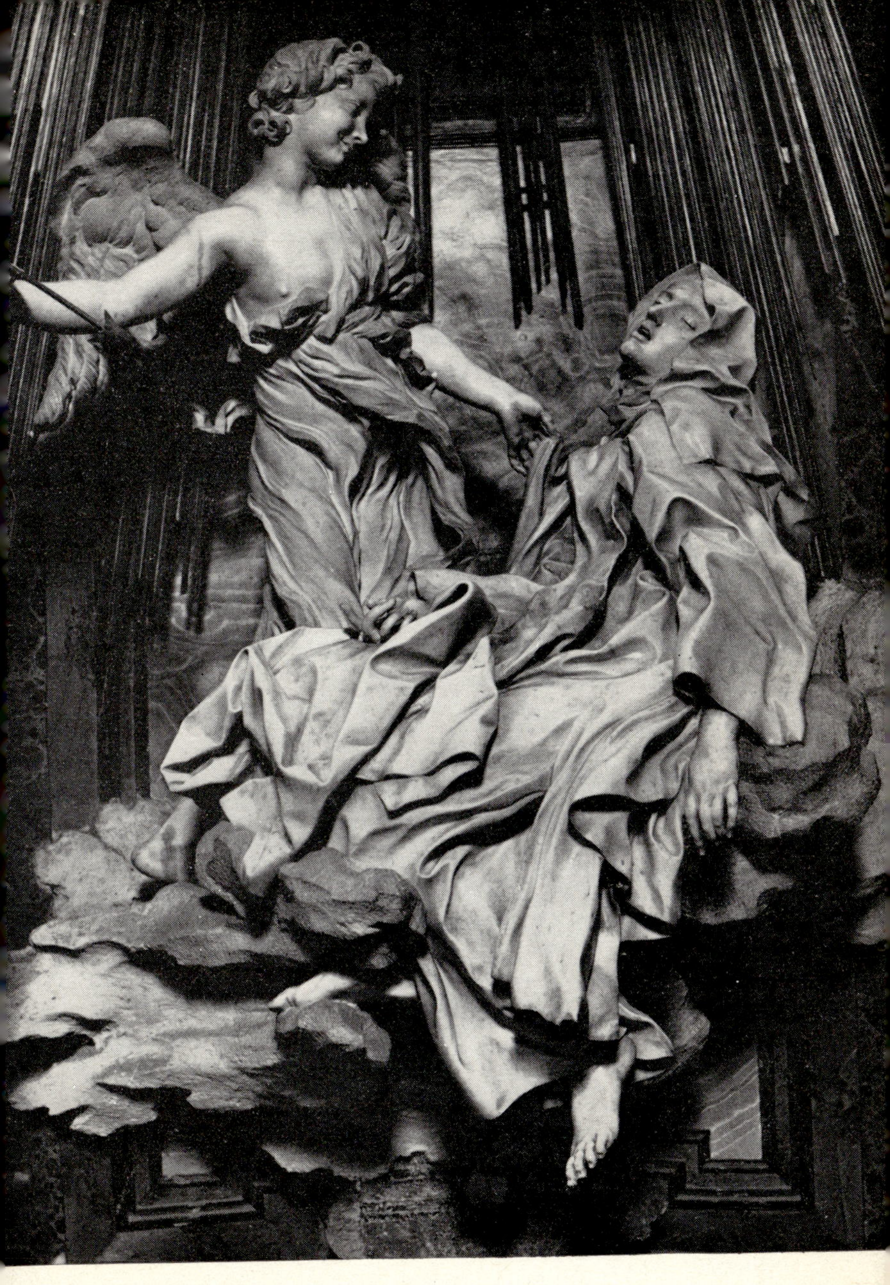

made under Bernini's supervision, adds another order of reality to the scene below. It has been remarked many times since the eighteenth century that Teresa's ecstasy seems to be more sexual than spiritual, but this misapprehension only serves to underline the concrete physical nature of St Teresa's description of her revelation.

G. L. Bernini *St Teresa* 1647–52
S. Maria della Vittoria, Rome

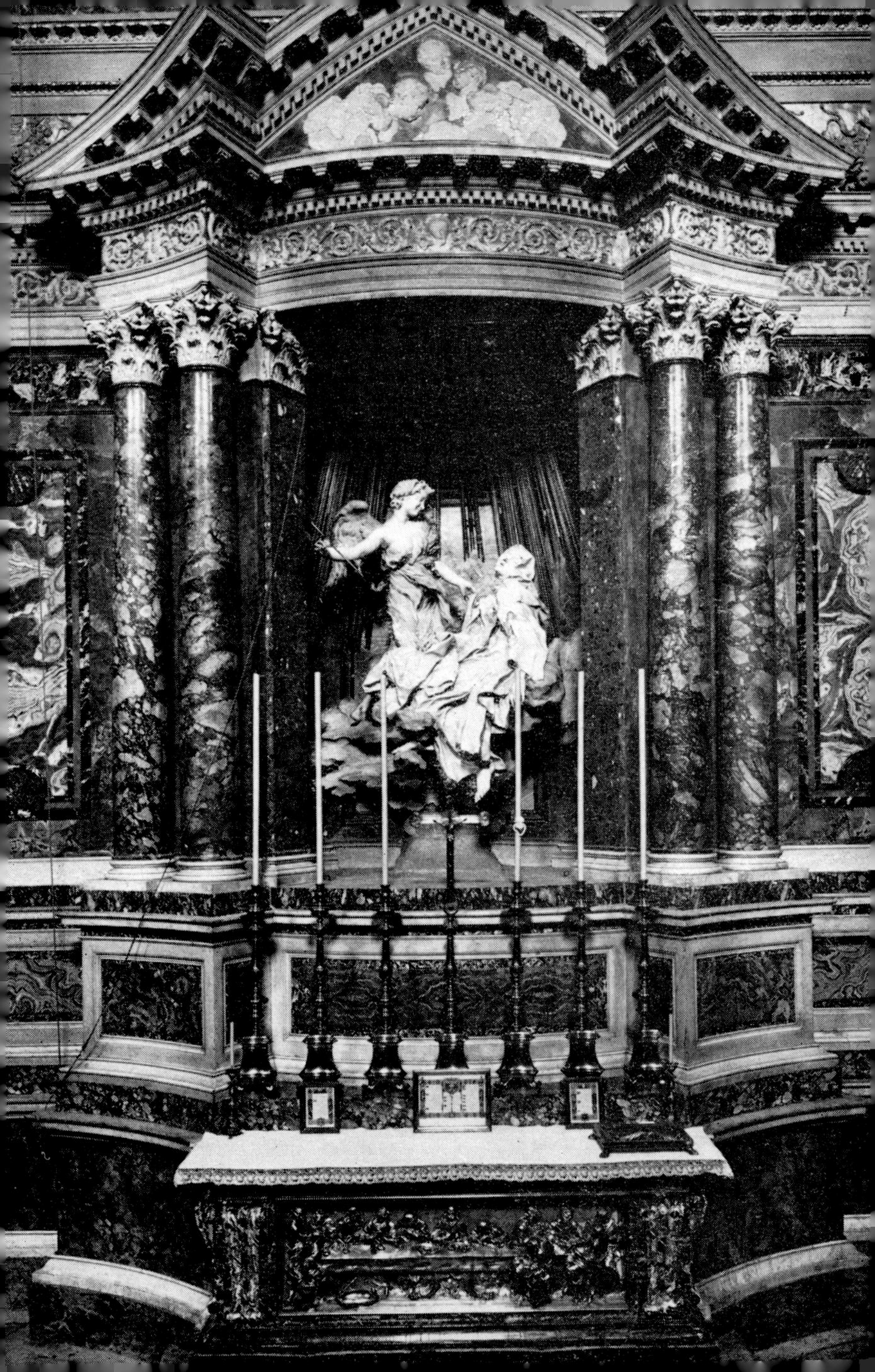

The *Cathedra Petri* (if we can dissociate it from the *bald-acchino*, or indeed from the total concept of the interior of St Peter's), and the Cornaro Chapel represent the full exuberance of Bernini's middle years, when every project was a challenge to his ingenuity and to the vast resources he had available to him. As with many great artists his final years were more contemplative in mood and in his last works his virtuosity is tempered by a

G. L. Bernini *Death of the Blessed Lodovica Albertoni* 1671–4
S. Francesco a Ripa, Rome

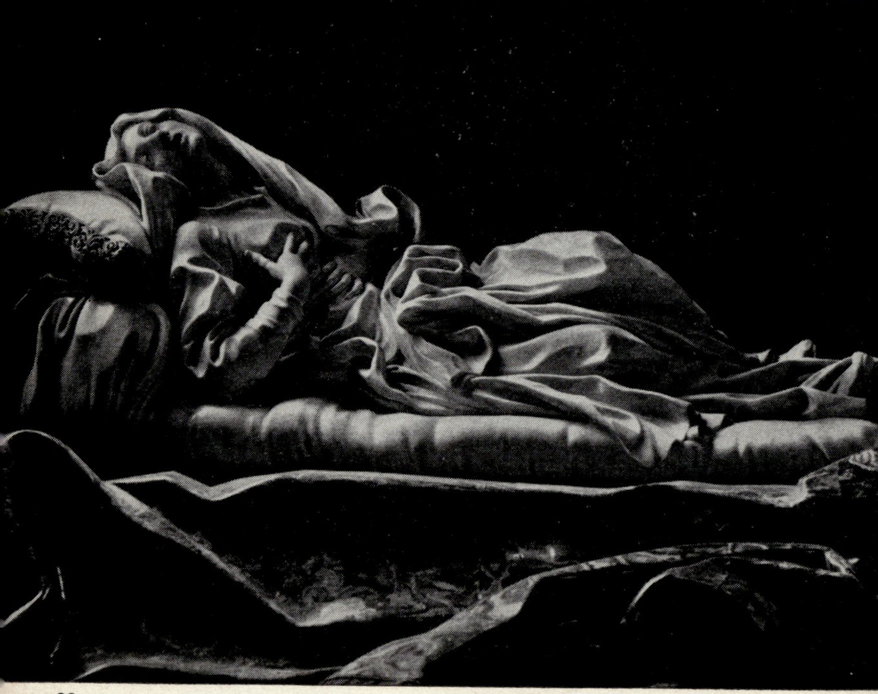

more subtle and profound human feeling. In the *Death of the Blessed Lodovica Albertoni* (1671–4) in the Altieri Chapel of S. Francesco a Ripa, Bernini still uses a concealed light source but the tortured angularity of the drapery has a delicacy that reminds one of his early sculptures, and the pose recalls the classical *Ariadne* in the Vatican which was greatly admired by Poussin.

Ariadne 1st century AD
Vatican

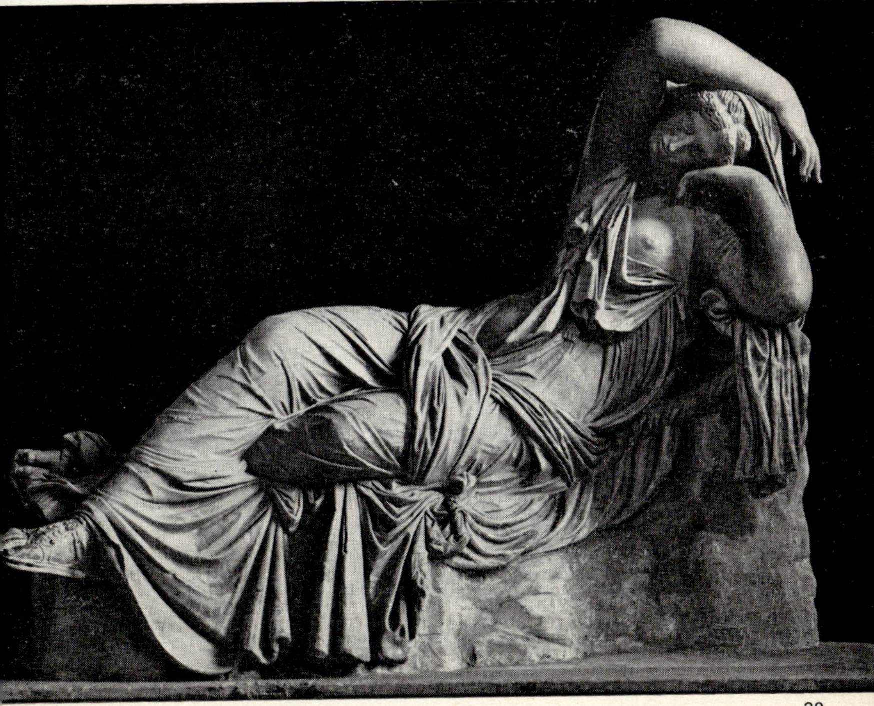

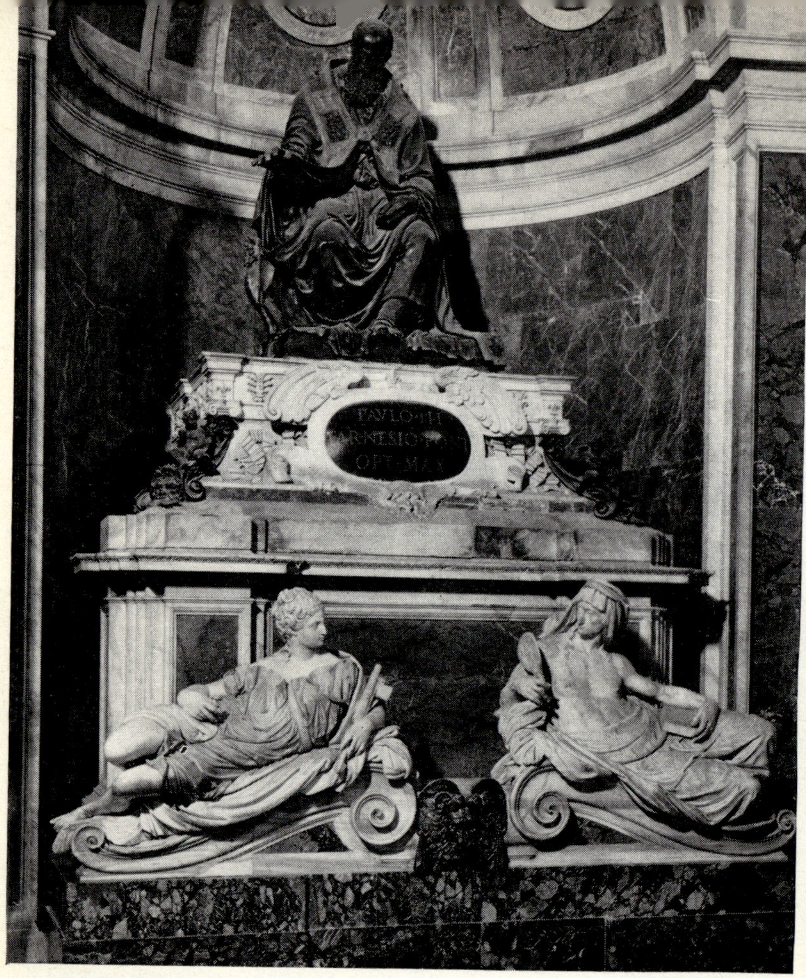

G. della Porta *Paul III Monument* 1550–75
St Peter's, Rome

Bernini was not the only major sculptor in Rome and he had rivals who practised a more restrained style that found favour amongst the more conservative patrons in Rome. Bernini was regarded by them as an extremist who carried his exuberance to the point of bad taste, while outside the papal court there were circles which were devoted to the study of antiquity, such as that of Cassiano del Pozzo. Bernini's relationship to his contemporaries

40

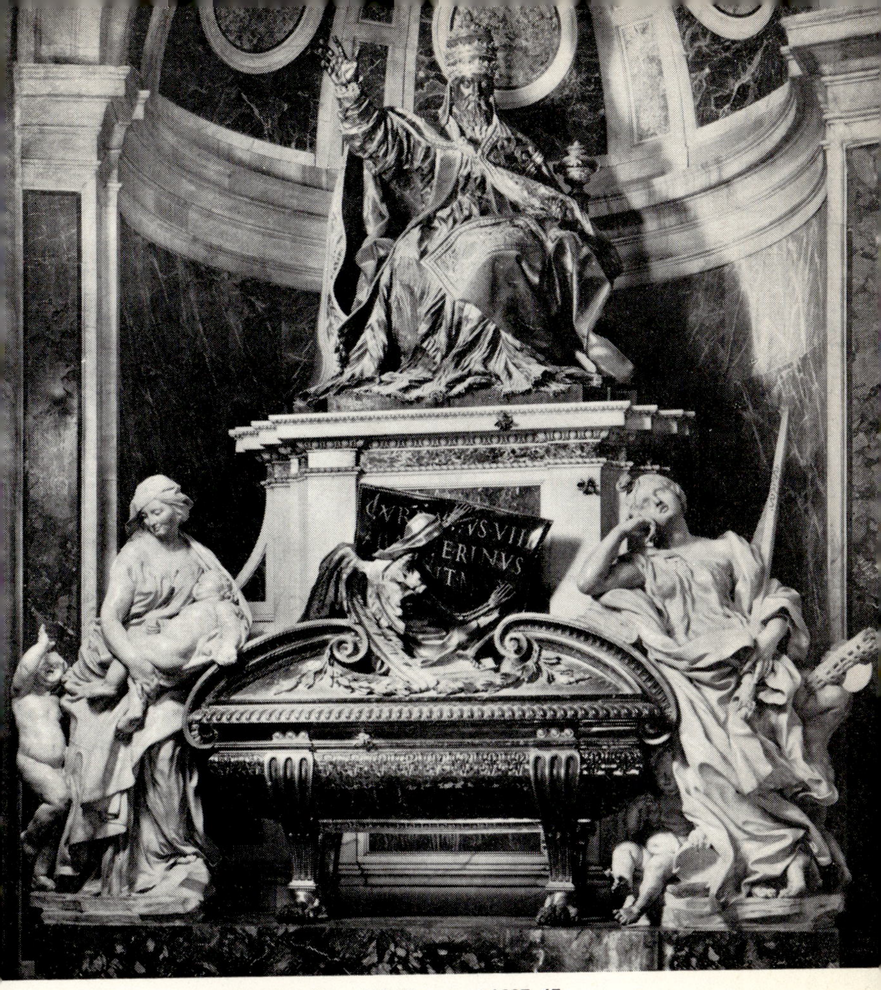

G. L. Bernini *Urban VIII Monument* 1627–47
St Peter's, Rome

—and indeed his successors—can best be seen by looking at the great series of papal tombs in St Peter's, to which he contributed two examples. The immediate predecessor to Bernini's first papal tomb of Urban VIII, was Guglielmo della Porta's tomb of Paul III, which owes its present arrangement to Bernini's alterations. The tomb of Urban VIII was to occupy the opposite niche, and its over-all format is dictated by the need for it to correspond to the

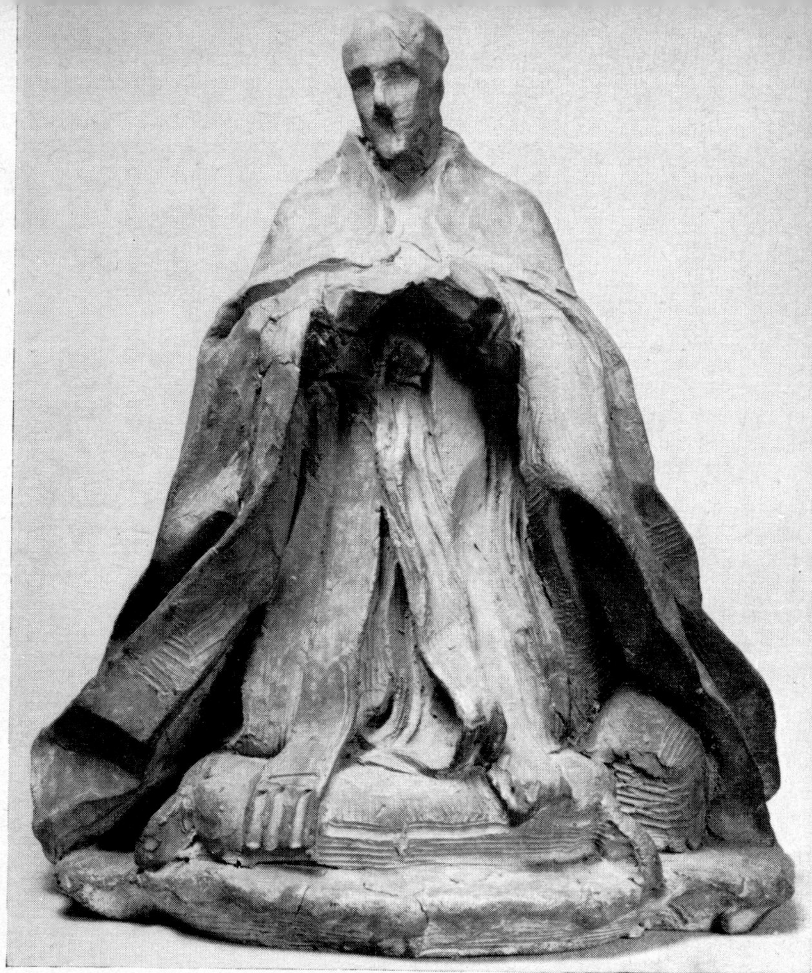

G. L. Bernini Bozzetto for figure of *Alexander VII c.* 1671
Victoria and Albert Museum, London

pyramidal composition of della Porta's work. Bernini worked on
the tomb for twenty years until 1647, and many additions, such as
the bronze skeleton, clearly belong to a later stage in its development. In the place of della Porta's emblematic Virtues, which
derive from Michelangelo's Medici Chapel, Bernini makes the
Virtues contribute to the theme of the loss to humanity caused by
the death of the pope. Both the figure of the pope and the sar-
cophagus beneath are in bronze, contrasting with the marble of

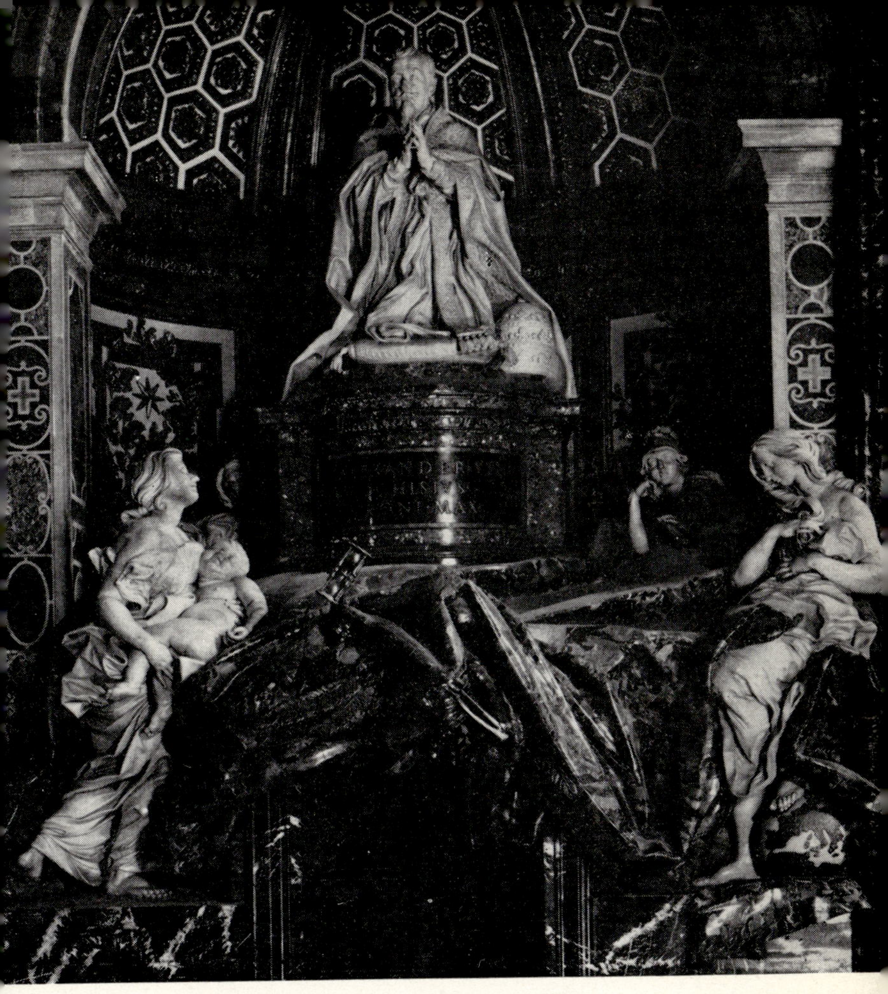

G. L. Bernini *Alexander VII Monument* 1671–8
St Peter's, Rome

the Virtues, the whole group being set against a background of coloured marble. The use of colour and contrasting materials is an important development, but the concept for Bernini's second tomb, of Alexander VII, is more far-reaching, and was to be the prototype for the dramatic imagery of later baroque tombs. The pyramidal composition is retained but the separate elements are now unified by a dramatic conceit, in which the Virtues are animated by reaction to the advent of Death in the form of a skeleton emerging from a door beneath the tomb. The figure of Death pushes his way through a shroud made of Sicilian jasper towards the praying figure of the pope, who remains unaware of Death's approach, while the Virtues react with horror and dismay.

Alessandro Algardi's (1595–1654) monument to Pope Leo XI (1634–52) avoids the dramatic devices of Bernini; but its classical restraint was to make it, despite its relative feebleness, an even greater influence than Bernini's papal tombs. Algardi was the only sculptor who could be regarded as a serious rival to Bernini and who could have been considered for the honour of making a papal tomb during Bernini's lifetime. He had studied in the Carracci Academy of Bologna and had practised as a restorer of antique sculpture in Rome before slowly working his way to eminence. The tomb of Leo XI was begun shortly after Bernini's Urban VIII monument, and Algardi's tomb is, therefore, of great importance in the development of baroque sculpture because it is the first major work to attempt to reconcile the naturalism of Bernini with a more classical style and as such is the forerunner of many monuments in Italy, France and Flanders. While the debt to Bernini can be seen in the full and animated folds of the drapery, Algardi has not attempted to exploit the dramatic possibilities of the traditional elements of the tomb. The work is executed totally in marble, the subtle variations of tone and colour which animate the surfaces of Bernini's sculptures yielding to a polished and natural surface that accentuates the monumentality of the figures.

A. Algardi *Leo XI Monument* 1634–52
St Peter's, Rome

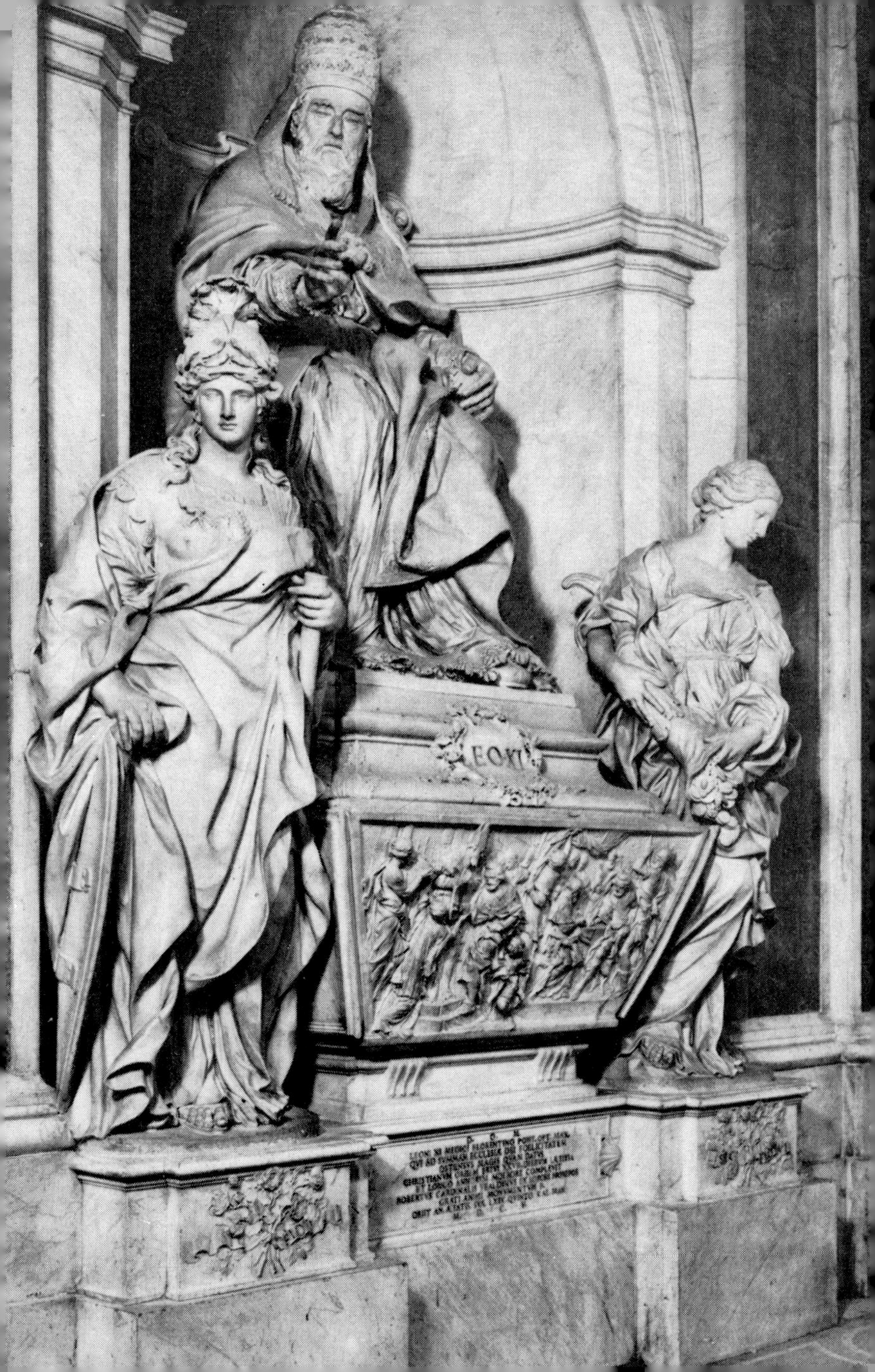

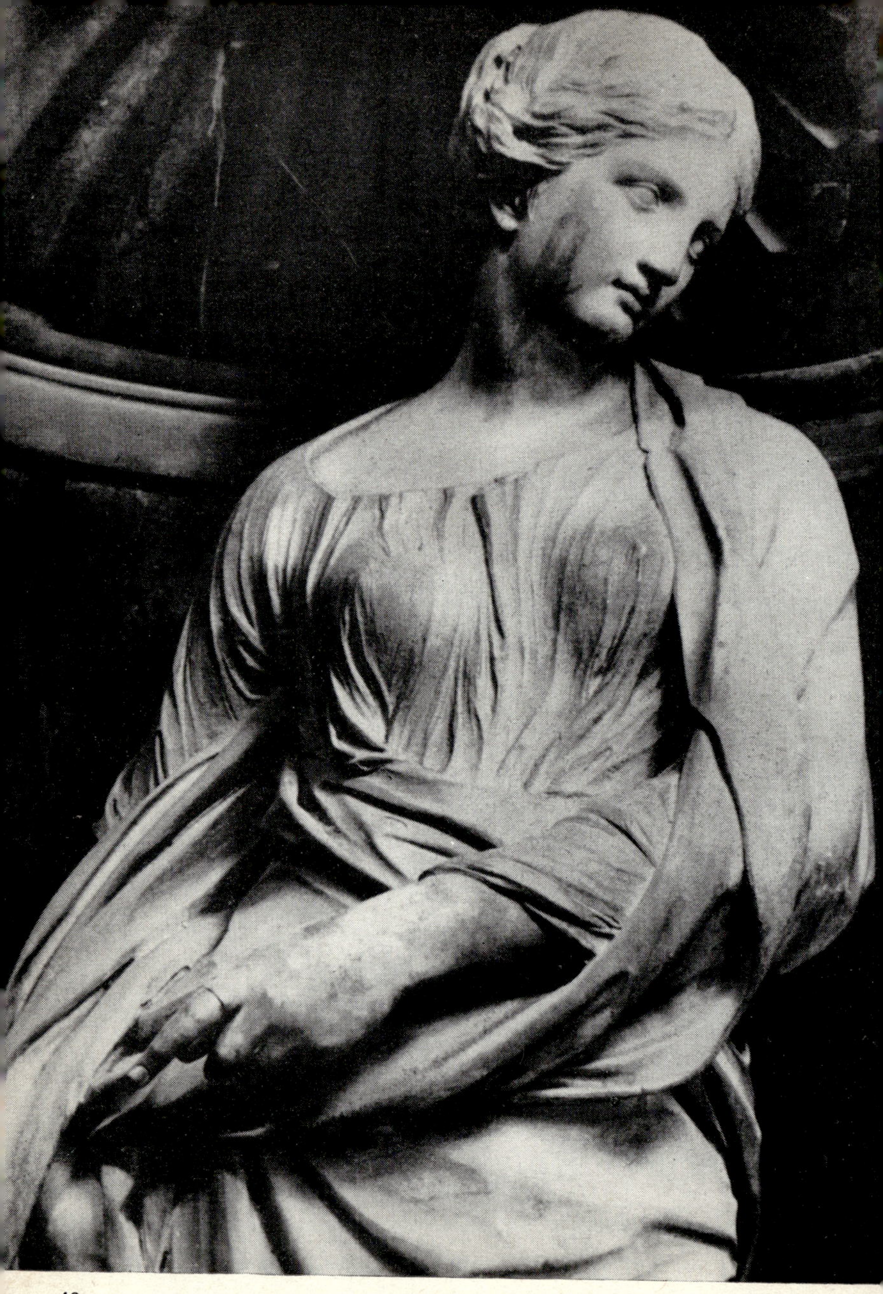

Algardi is the principal sculptor of the style known as high baroque classicism, and this term accurately characterizes his half-way position between Bernini and the classicist François Duquesnoy (1594–1643), known as Il Fiammingo, a Fleming who frequented the circle of Cassiano del Pozzo and shared a house at one time with Nicholas Poussin. Duquesnoy is a shadowy figure who left very few works, but his studies of children were highly prized and he was later regarded as the only 'modern' who could be compared with the 'ancients'. Like Poussin, he was instinctively drawn to the more classical of antique sculptures, and the knowledge of classical remains that he gained from work on Cassiano del Pozzo's corpus of antiquities led him to make a distinction between Greek and Roman styles more than a century before Winckelmann, who is usually given credit for that discovery. The *St Susanna* of S. Maria di Loreto is the principal example of his severe style, and its clarity and decorum were regarded by the academic writers as demonstrating the most perfect synthesis of nature and the antique. The draperies flow elegantly, following the shape of the body, while the figure is balanced in perfect grace and repose, exhibiting no emotion but only 'un aria dolce di grazia purissima' (Bellori). Nonetheless, it is not a completely self-contained statue, for the turn of the head away from the body and the gently pointing hand are conceived in relation to the architecture of the church, and these gestures gently draw the spectator's attention towards the holiness of the setting in an essentially baroque manner.

F. Duquesnoy *St Susanna* 1626–30
Detail
S. Maria di Loreto, Rome

Baroque to rococo

No sculptors of powerful originality emerged in Rome in the second half of the seventeenth century and Bernini's pupils and assistants, Ercole Ferrata for instance, who had actually modelled most of his major works, added little to the elements of his style in their own work. The influence of Algardi and Duquesnoy was perhaps greater than that of Bernini, and their work was the basis of the predominant mode of sculpture in Europe until the end of the seventeenth century. Under Louis XIV Paris began to supersede Rome as the artistic capital of Europe, while French artists had developed a self-confidence that owed much to the reputation of Nicholas Poussin, and the growing authority of their Academy in Rome, which had been founded in 1666. Yet the international style of the late seventeenth century owes almost everything to Roman sculpture of the early part of the century, and the French contribution was less to the development of the baroque as a style than to the achievement of competence and adaptability, through centralization of commissions and uniformity of instruction. Most of the important French sculptors studied at the French Academy in Rome, but even those who did not were able to form an idea of the antique from small bronzes which could be easily transported. Works from Italian centres outside Rome also helped to disseminate the influence of the early baroque and the two superbly finished bronzes of *Apollo Flaying Marsyas* and *Mercury Binding Prometheus* by Foggini in the Victoria and Albert Museum, provide an example of the way in which Italian influence spread to France. Giovanni Battisto Foggini (1652–1725) was a Florentine sculptor who worked for the Medici family and these two pieces were a gift from Cosimo III, Grand Duke of Tuscany, to the court painter Hyacinthe Rigaud in exchange for the latter's self-portrait in 1716. The works probably date from some years before then and they show the lasting influence of even Bernini's early work. The figure of Apollo derives from Bernini's *Apollo and Daphne* (see page 13) and Foggini has also adopted some of Bernini's formal principles; he preserves a relief-like frontality, but the gestures are restrained and classical.

Bernini himself had made a triumphal visit to Paris to submit designs for the Louvre (subsequently rejected) and to carve the great bust of Louis XIV (see page 52), recorded in great detail

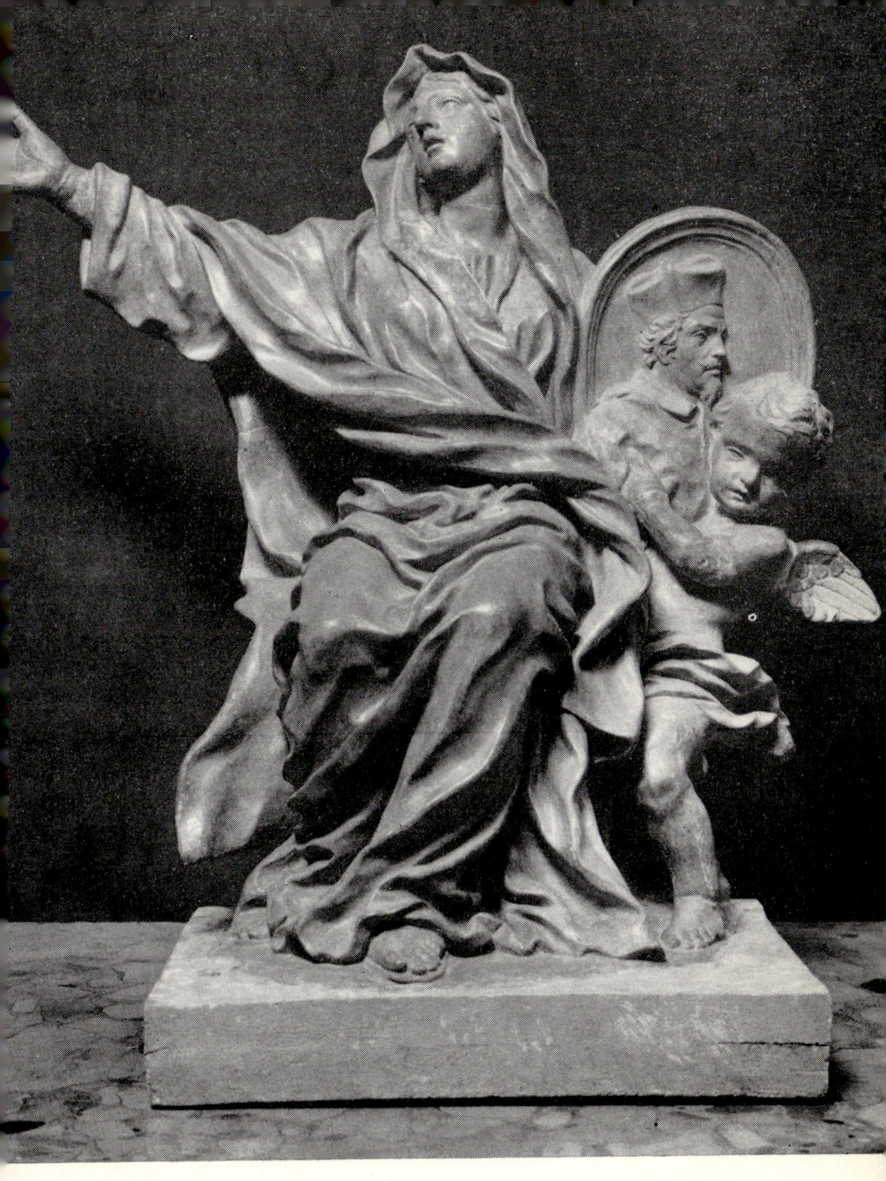

E. Ferrata Figure of *Faith* 1670–80
Heim Gallery, London

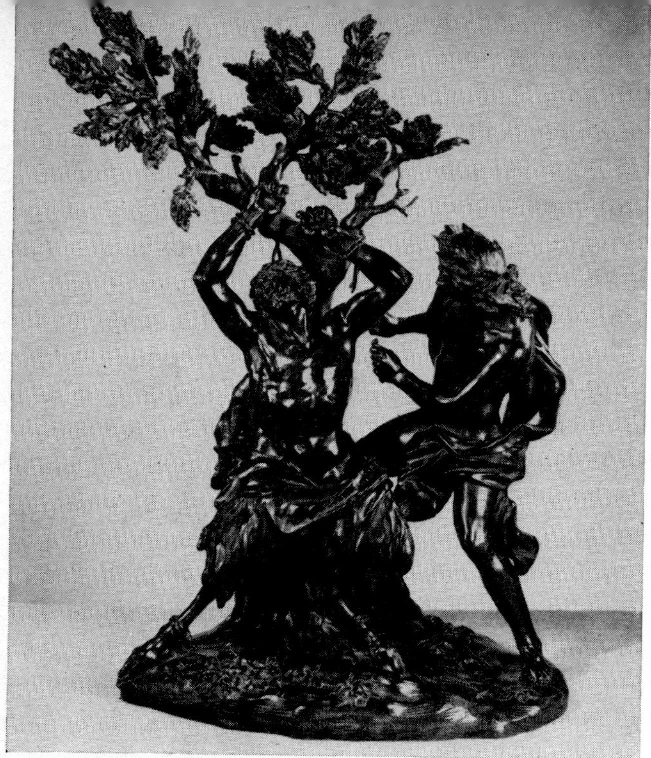

G. B. Foggini *Apollo Flaying Marsyas* late 17th century
Victoria and Albert Museum, London

in the Journal of Chantelou. Although the greatness of Bernini compelled admiration in France, his ideas were not sympathetically received by the French court, which, under Colbert's guidance, had set up a rigidly centralized system for the production of all kinds of works of art. Under Colbert's rule, which lasted until 1683, the painter Lebrun was in absolute control of all commissions, and the greatest sculptural project of the age, the ornamentation of the gardens of Versailles, owes everything to the principles that he imposed on painting and the decorative arts as well. The sculpture at Versailles forms a part of Louis XIV's gigantic scheme of self-glorification, in which the reality of centralized absolutism is enshrined in the cult of Louis XIV as Apollo or sun-god. Sculpture played an important role in the realization of this concept, and most of the works in Versailles were intended to be both allegorical and decorative.

50

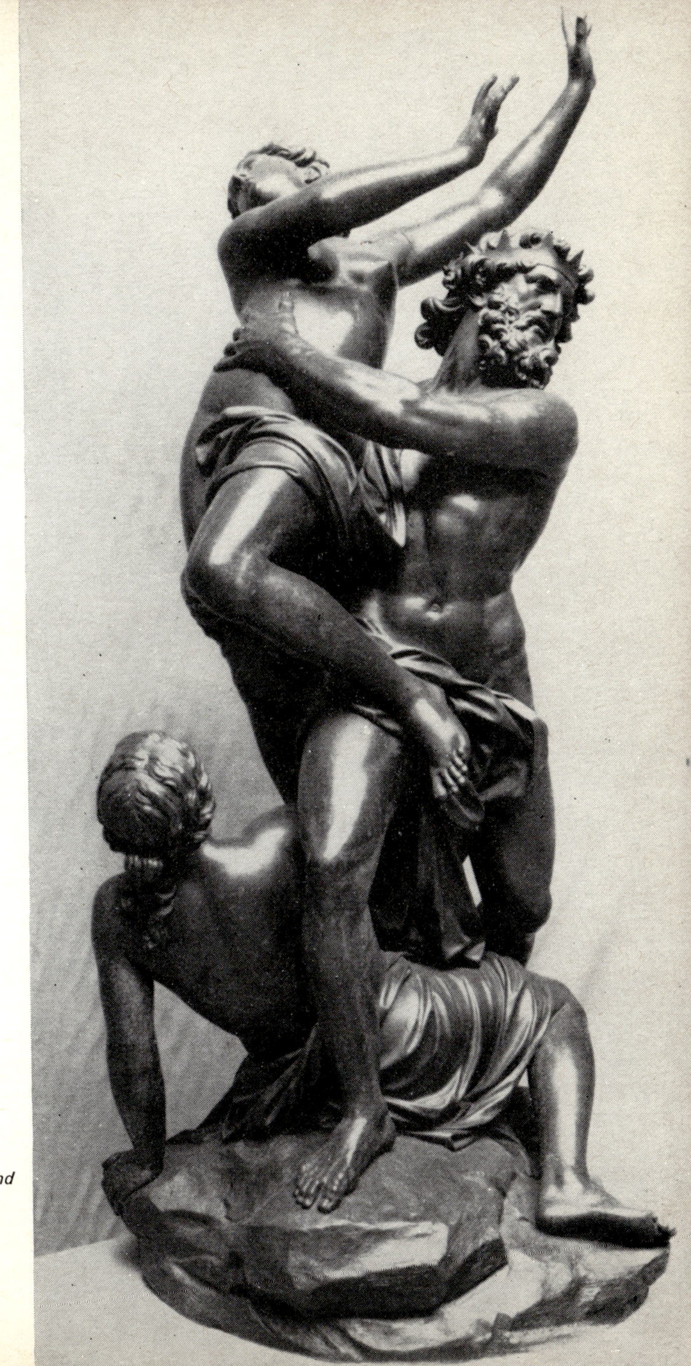

F. Girardon *Pluto and Proserpine* 1677–99
Bronze version of
marble group at
Versailles
Strasbourg Museum

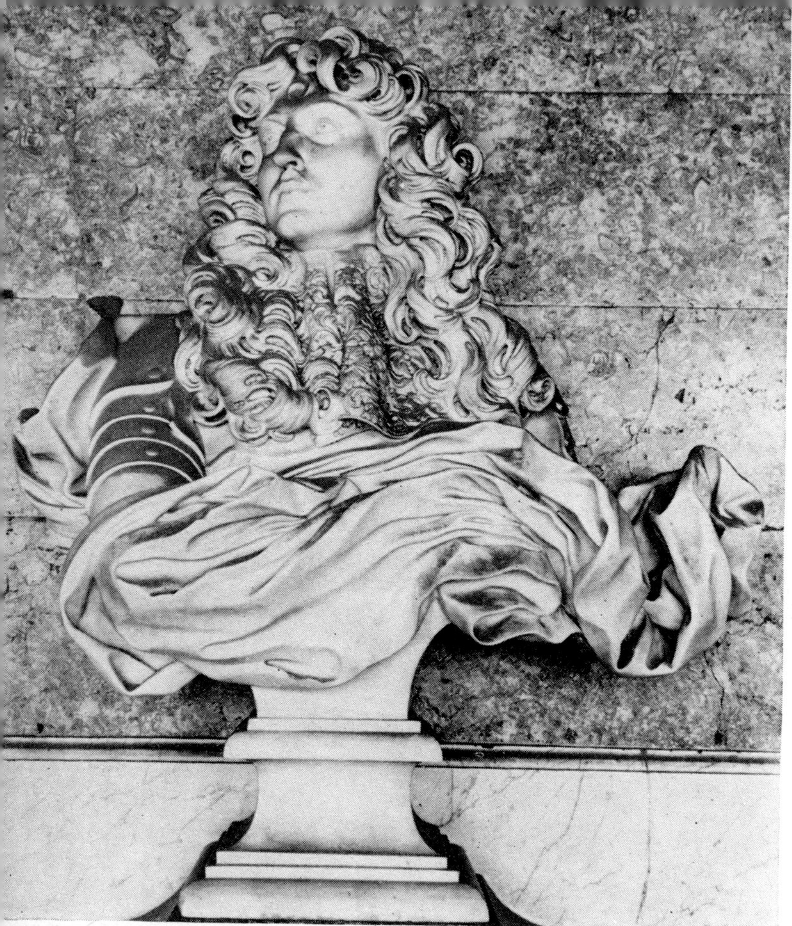

G. L. Bernini *Louis XIV* 1665
Versailles

François Girardon (1628–1715), was not the greatest sculptor
to work for Louis XIV, but he embodies the style of the Lebrun
period from about 1652 to 1683, when the fall of Colbert heralded
a more baroque phase. The elements of his style can be seen in the
Pluto and Proserpine in the gardens of Versailles (bronze version
shown here). The directness and illusionism of Bernini's version
of the same subject (see page 20) has been subtly neutralized in
Girardon's group. Pluto and Proserpine avoid the beholder's eyes,
and the action of the group, instead of encroaching on our space,

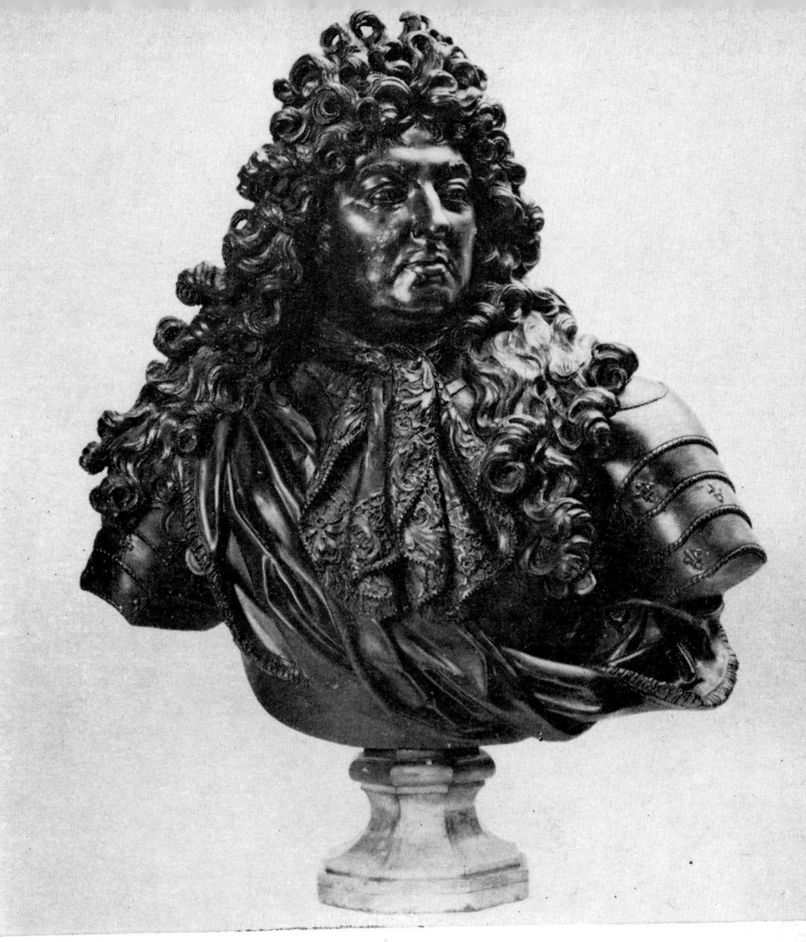

A. Coysevox *Louis XIV* 1680
Wallace Collection, London

seems contained within a series of graceful curves, while the figure of Proserpine's mother is shown within the composition instead of being the object of Proserpine's search as in Bernini's version.

Girardon's principal rival in the service of Louis XIV was Antoine Coysevox (1640–1720) whose growing success in the 1680s was symptomatic of a move in taste at the court towards a looser, more baroque style. Nonetheless, Coysevox's style is still relatively restrained compared to Bernini, as can be seen by

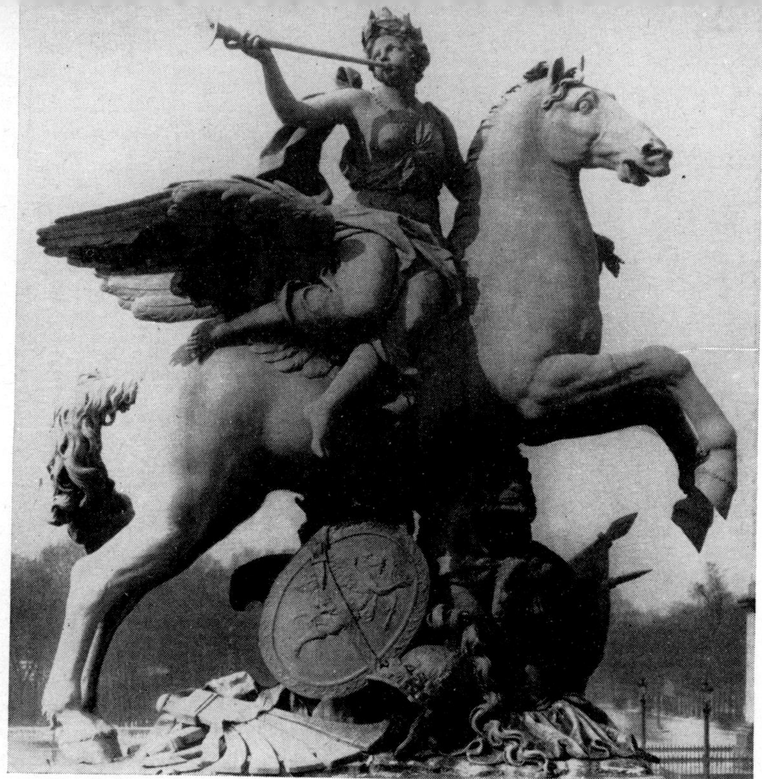

A. Coysevox *Fame* 1700–1702
Tuileries, Paris

comparing Coysevox's bust of Louis XIV with the earlier version
by Bernini in Versailles, of which Coysevox must have been aware.
That the shift towards the baroque in the 1680s was not a
dramatic change of taste is also attested to by the sad fate of
Bernini's equestrian statue of Louis XIV, which had been commissioned as early as 1667, but was not finally delivered to the
court until 1685. The king disliked it so much that he had it
banished to a remote corner of the garden at Versailles, and in
1688 it was transformed by Girardon from an allegory of Louis
XIV as Hercules reaching the summit of the hill of virtue and
glory, into Marcus Curtius leaping the Gulf. The 1680s, however,
also saw a brief period of favour for the great Pierre Puget (1620–
94). Colbert had banished him from Versailles for political and
artistic reasons, but after 1683 the way was clear for Colbert's

54

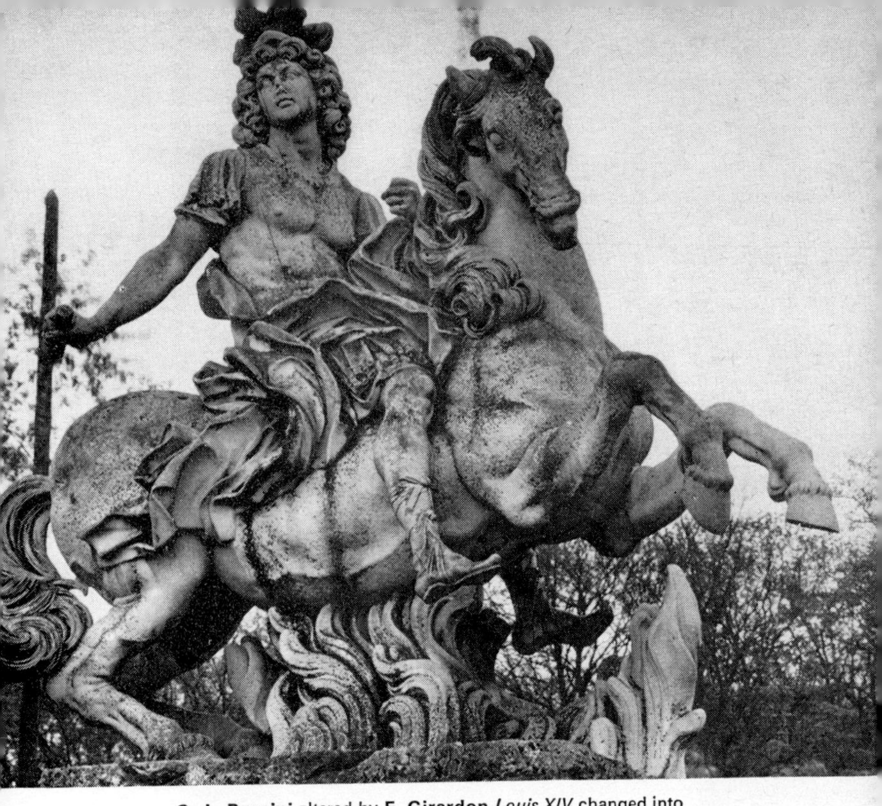

G . L. Bernini altered by **F. Girardon** *Louis XIV* changed into
Marcus Curtius 1688. Versailles

successor, Louvoir, to approve the acceptance of Puget's famous
Milo of Crotona.

Puget was one of the very few sculptors to recapture the immediacy of Bernini's best work, yet ironically he was seen as almost anything but a baroque sculptor; he was regarded in France successively as a classical sculptor and as an ancestor of romanticism, one of Baudelaire's 'les Phares'. In a sense, both these elements are to be found in Puget's work. With no other artist in this book has the legend so coloured the perception of his work. To Delacroix he was a tragic genius who, like himself, had been misunderstood by his contemporaries, 'harcelé de son vivant par les envieuses passions des artists, ses rivaux, méconnu et délaissé par les grands et les ministres', while to the realists of the later nineteenth century he was a son of toil who had

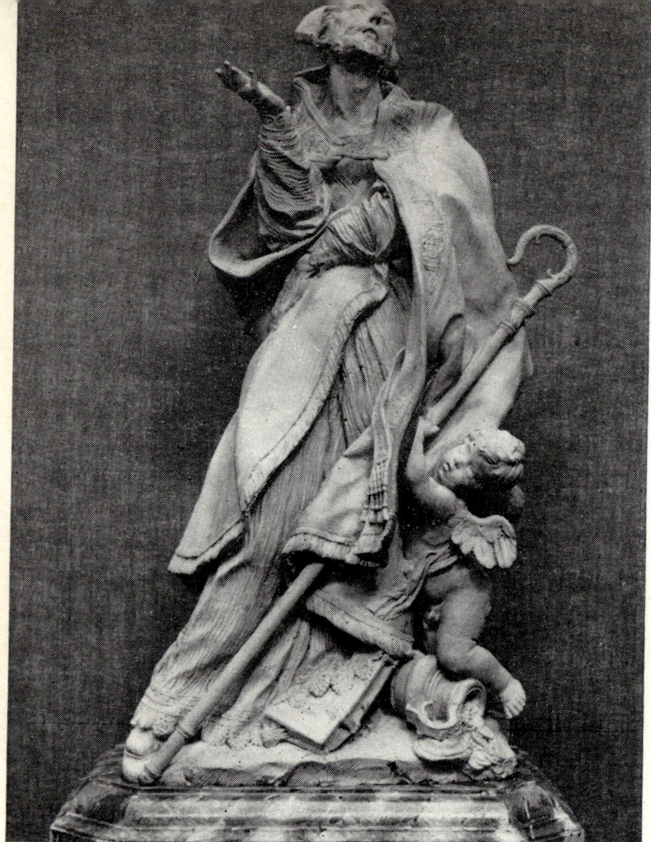

P. Puget *The Blessed Alessandro Sauli as St Ambrose c.* 1660
Formerly Heim Gallery

rejected the tyrannical culture of Louis XIV. The historian Michelet
called him, 'un grand artiste en qui fut l'âme souffrante d'un siècle
malade'. These verdicts are perhaps more evocative of his personality than his art, for despite his labour in the dockyards of
Toulon and his neglect by his contemporaries, his sculpture shows
a full awareness of Michelangelo, Bernini and antiquity.

Puget was born in 1620 in Marseilles, and his work for Pietro da
Cortona as a painter in Florence brought him into direct contact
with the Italian baroque at an early age. He returned to France in
1643, and his two caryatids for the Hotel de Ville in Toulon of
1656 established him as an artist of originality who was able to
combine a knowledge of baroque movement with a tragic

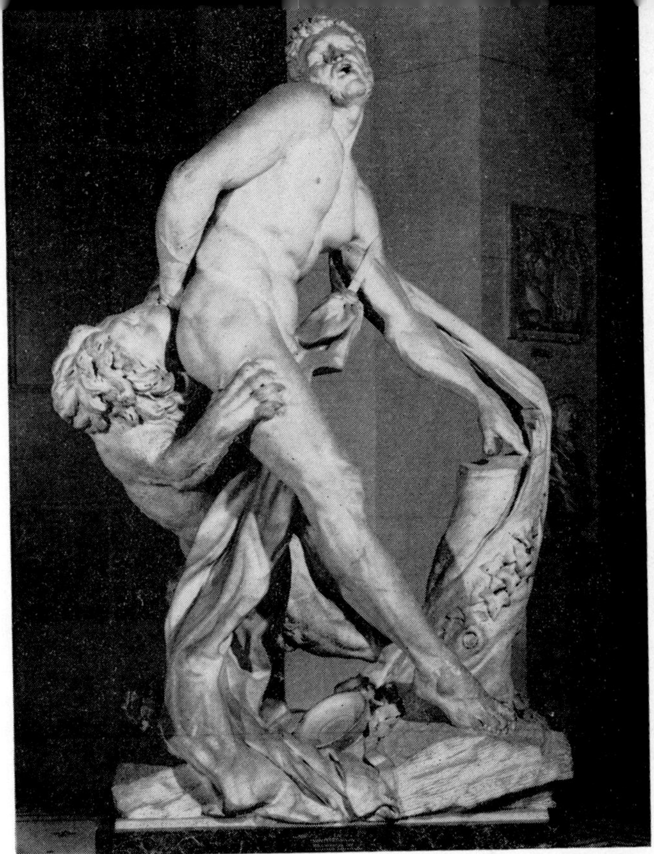

P. Puget *Milo of Crotona* 1671–83
Louvre, Paris

intensity that recalls the 'gothic' qualities that Rodin was to find in Michelangelo. He began to receive commissions in France, but his work for Fouquet, the banker, at Vaux-le-Vicomte was curtailed after the fall of his patron, and he stayed on in Genoa where he had gone to get some marble for Fouquet and established himself as a local sculptor about 1660. From this period dates the bozzetto of the *Blessed Alessandro Sauli*, which shows his mastery of the idiom of Bernini combined with an elegance and religious intensity that looks forward to the German baroque of the eighteenth century. On his return to France in 1667, he worked in the dockyards of Toulon and Marseilles until in 1670 he was given permission to work on two sculptures, one of which

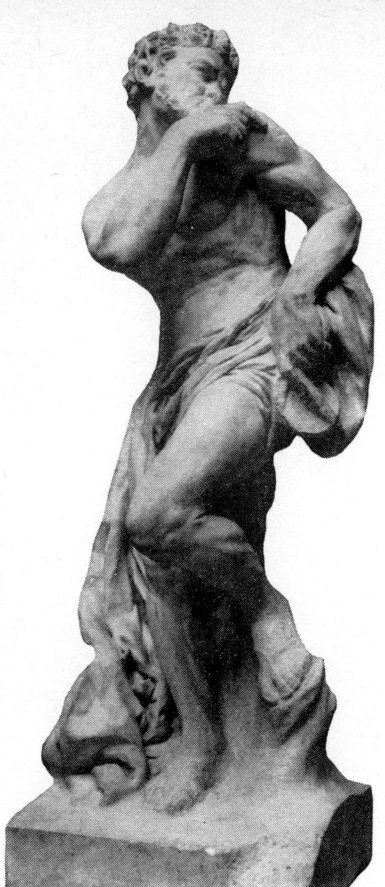

P. Puget *Faun* late 17th century
Marseilles Museum

was to be the *Milo of Crotona*. The figure of Milo, whose hand is caught in a tree, clearly owes a lot to the *Laocöon* (see page 23), but at the same time the composition is more formal than the earlier baroque. The movement is contained within a structure of parallel lines rather than curves, giving a sense of restraint to the figure, and heightening the sense of inner anguish. Although the figure should be seen from the front, it is contained within the space defined by the pedestal. Thus, Puget's emotional power is held in check by a classical framework, and it is a measure of the strength of these contradictory forces that Puget should have

58

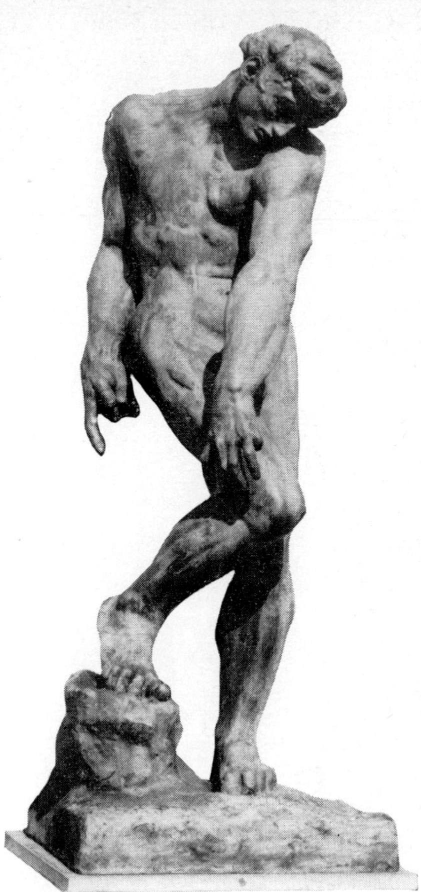

A. Rodin *Adam* 1880
Philadelphia Museum of Art

been acceptable to the baroque taste of the court and yet he was the only sculptor of his age to be admired for his classical 'correctness' by the followers of Jacques-Louis David.

The success of the Milo was only a temporary triumph, for he was to die embittered after summary treatment from the court, to which his bad temper and arrogance contributed. But Puget was not a man of his own time; the strength of his individuality can be seen in his figure of a *Faun*, whose closest cousin is Rodin's *Adam*—a resemblance noted by Rodin's contemporaries though he himself disclaimed direct influence.

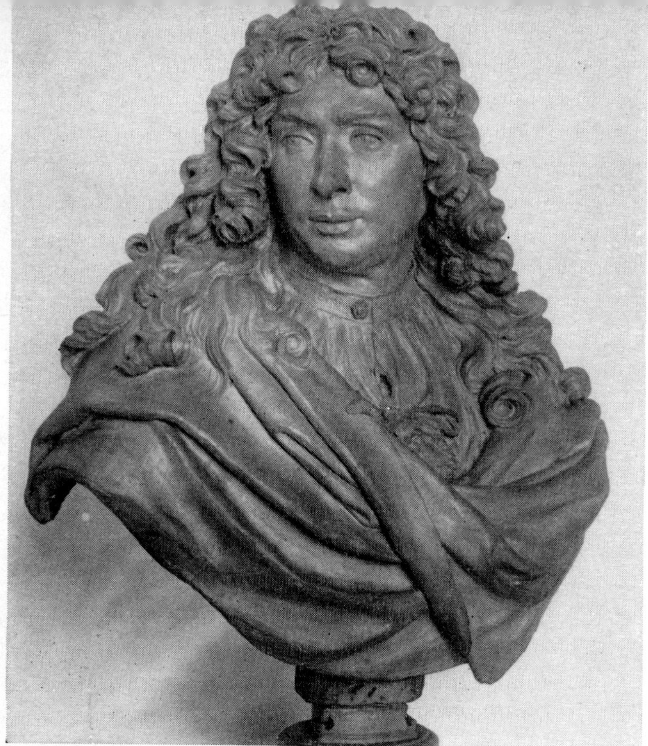

A. Coysevox *Charles Lebrun* 1676
Wallace Collection, London

As Michael Levey has pointed out, the rococo is the flimsiest of all the generic labels used by art historians, and does not at all imply a profound change from the baroque. Indeed the term 'rococo' in so far as it can be applied to sculpture should be understood as describing not a different style from the baroque, but merely a variation on the style brought to fruition by Bernini and his contemporaries. One may, however, talk about rococo qualities in a work of sculpture—informality, gaiety, a concern for matters of the heart and a self-conscious avoidance of seriousness.

The eighteenth century opened in France in a mood of reaction against the extreme formality of the court of Louis XIV, and the new spirit that was expressed by the victory of the 'Rubenistes' at the French Academy over the academic 'Poussinistes' can also be seen in the unforced naturalism of Coysevox's late busts. Yet

on pages **62** *and* **63**
E. Bouchardon *Fontaine c.* 1725
Rue de Grenelle, Paris

sculpture could boast no Watteau, for it was scarcely a medium adapted to express the subtleties of human behaviour.

Probably the most successful sculptor of the first half of the eighteenth century was Guillaume Coustou (1677–1746), Director of the French Academy from 1707, who continued the baroque trend of his uncle Coysevox. His principal works, *Les Chevaux de Marly*, 1740–45, which now stand on the Champs Elysées in Paris, were originally designed for the gardens of Marly, another

G. Coustou one of *Les Chevaux de Marly* 1740–45
Champs Elysées, Paris

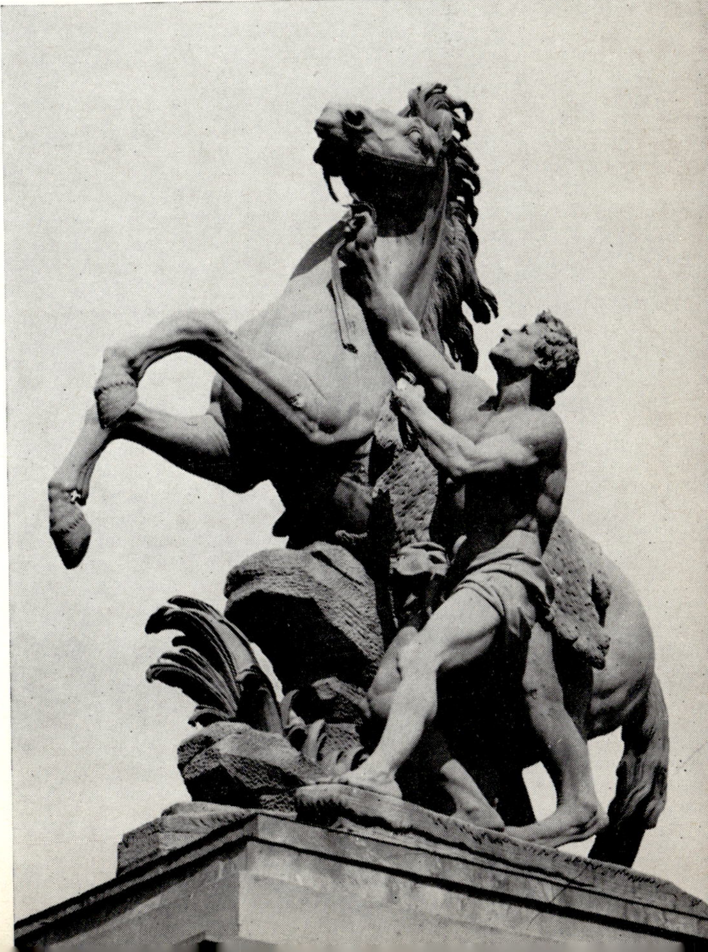

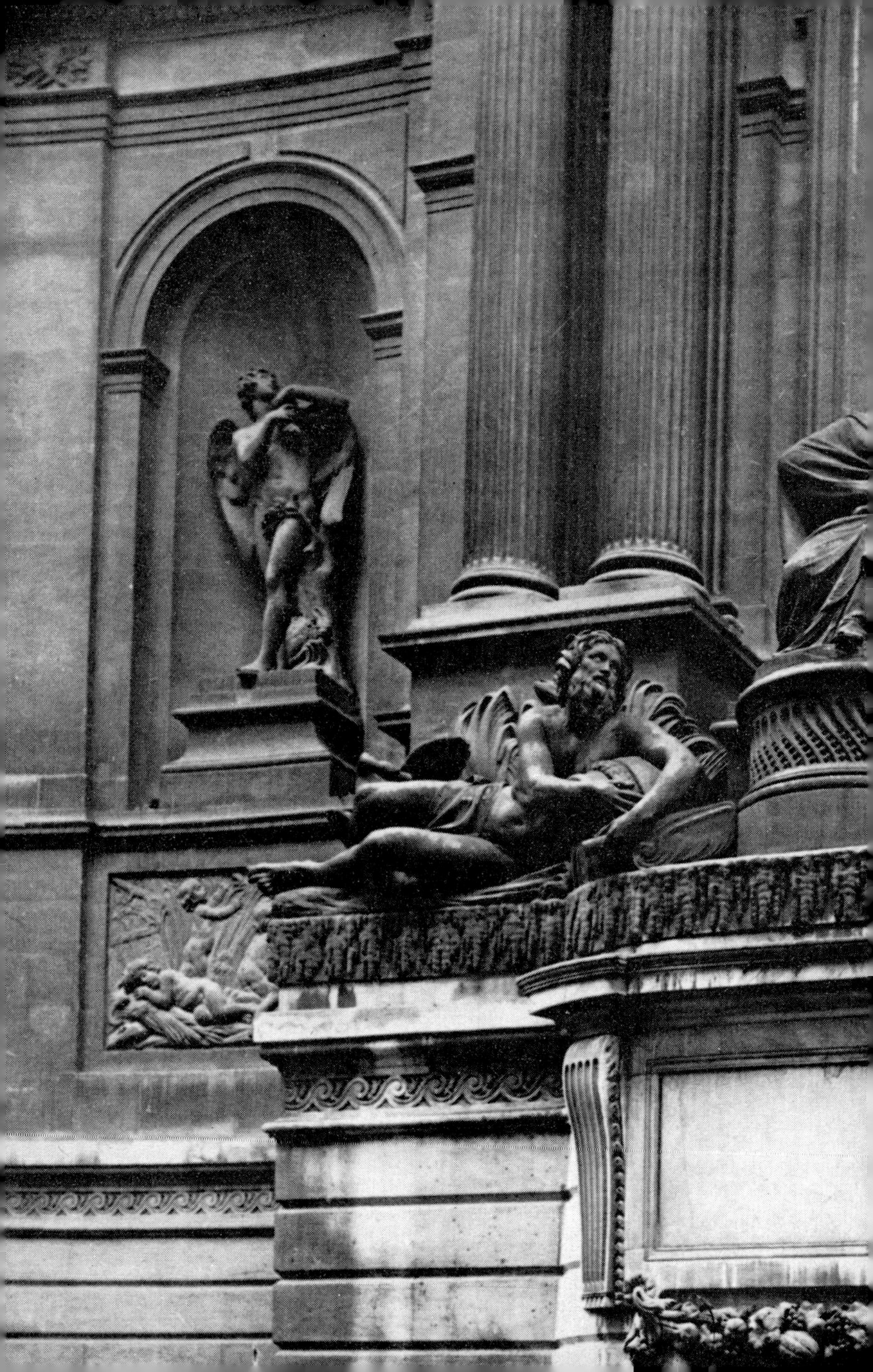

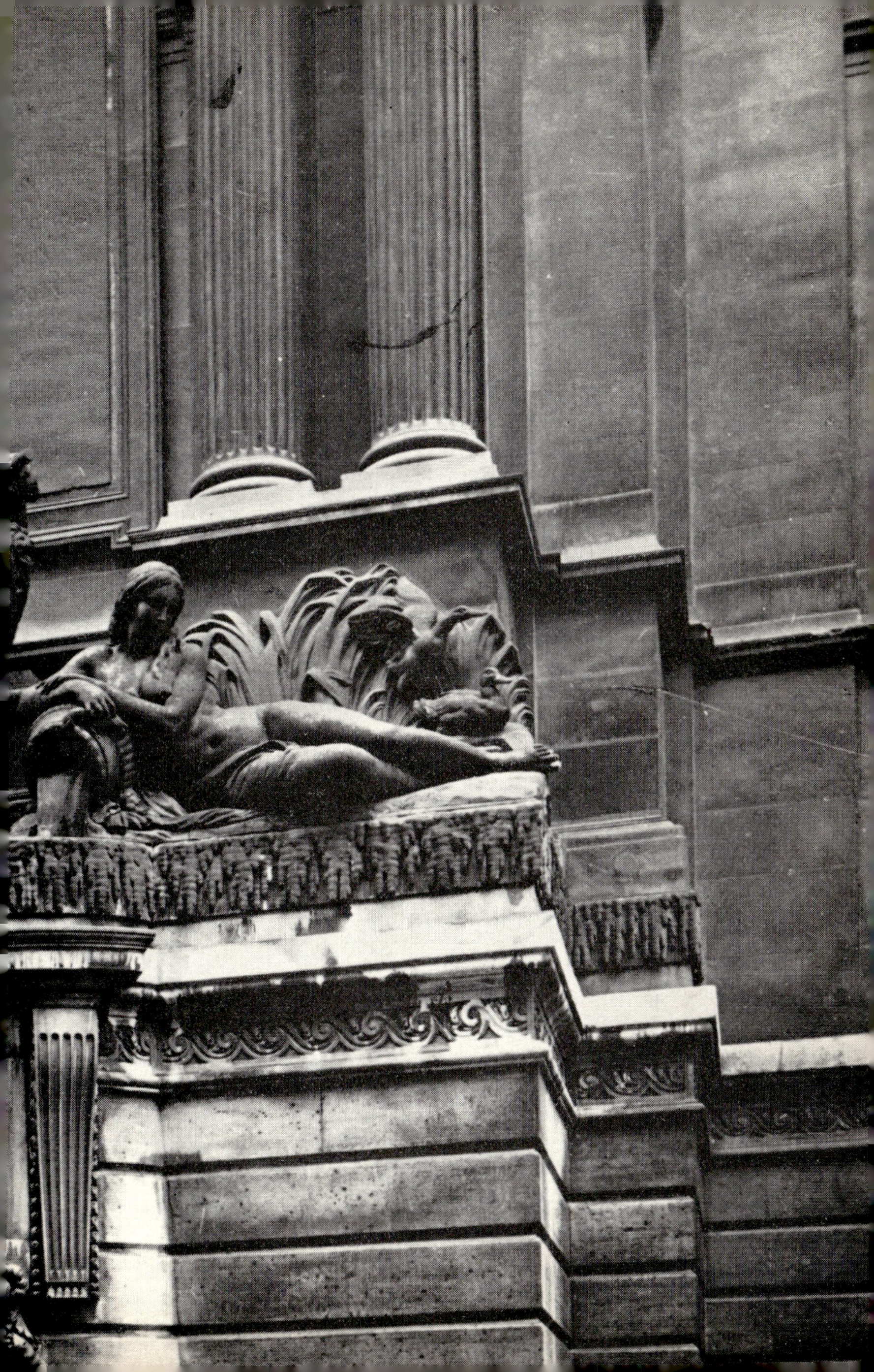

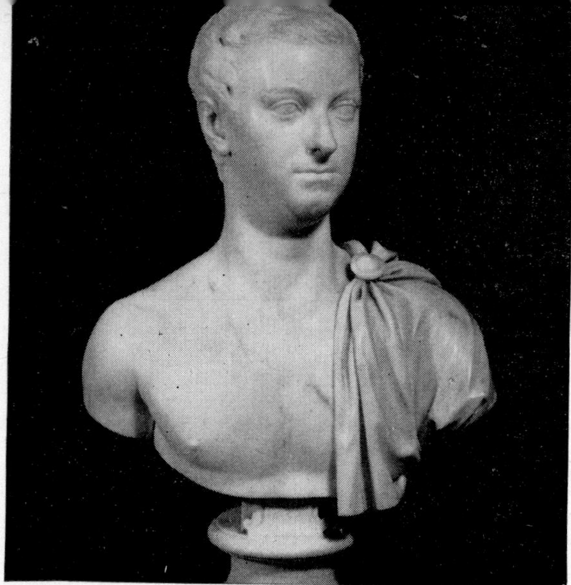

E. Bouchardon *John, Lord Hervey* 1729
Heim Gallery, London

of Louis XIV's residences. His pupil, Edme Bouchardon (1698–1762), is a more interesting figure, whose feeling for the antique led him to anticipate the later trend towards neoclassicism, as in his fountain of the Rue de Grenelle. His equestrian statue of Louis XV, destroyed in the Revolution, was more severe than Girardon's statue of Louis XIV, and it was criticized by Cochin as being too polished and finished, but, like the former, it was based on *Marcus Aurelius* in Rome, and despite the distance in time from Girardon it is not greatly dissimilar in style. Bouchardon also shows himself as a pioneer in his portrait of John, Lord Hervey, in which the torso is simplified in deliberate imitation of a Roman imperial bust.

Perhaps only one sculptural project really captured the nuances of amorous feeling that we associate with the circle of Madame de Pompadour, and that belongs to a period when there were already stirrings against the rococo. In 1750 Madame de Pompadour was rejected as a mistress by Louis XV, but intent on maintaining her position she set herself up as a friend and companion of the king rather than as a lover, and an allegorical sculpture of herself as

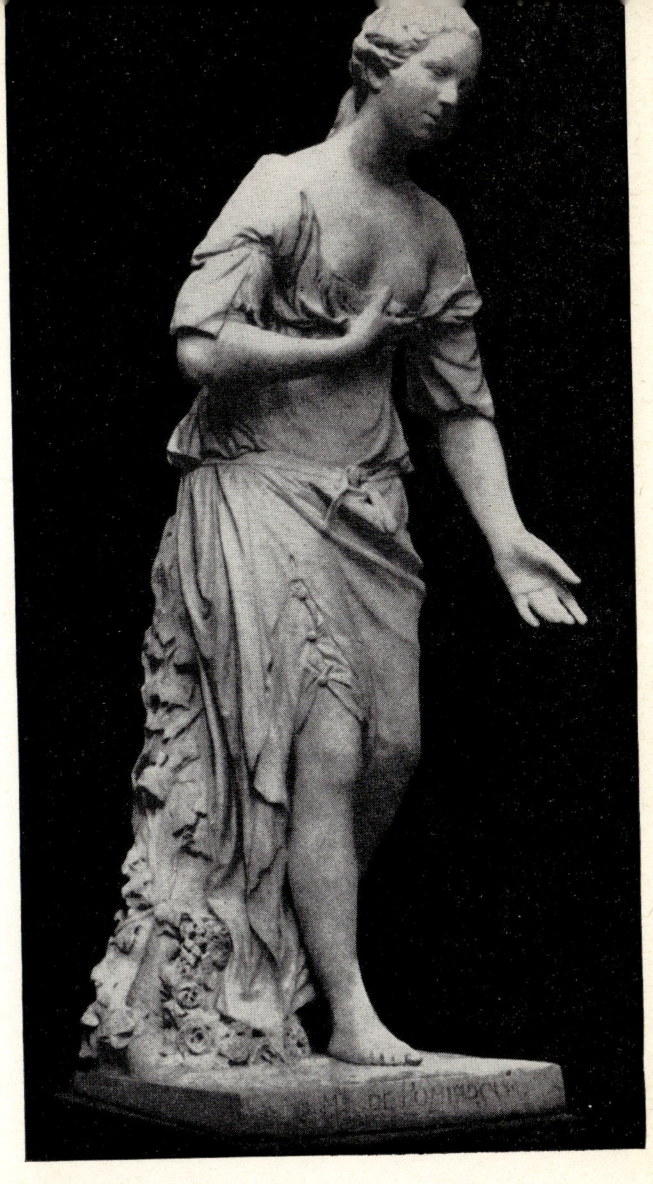

J. B. Pigalle *Madame de Pompadour as Amitié* 1750
Formerly Collection Baron Edmond de Rothschild

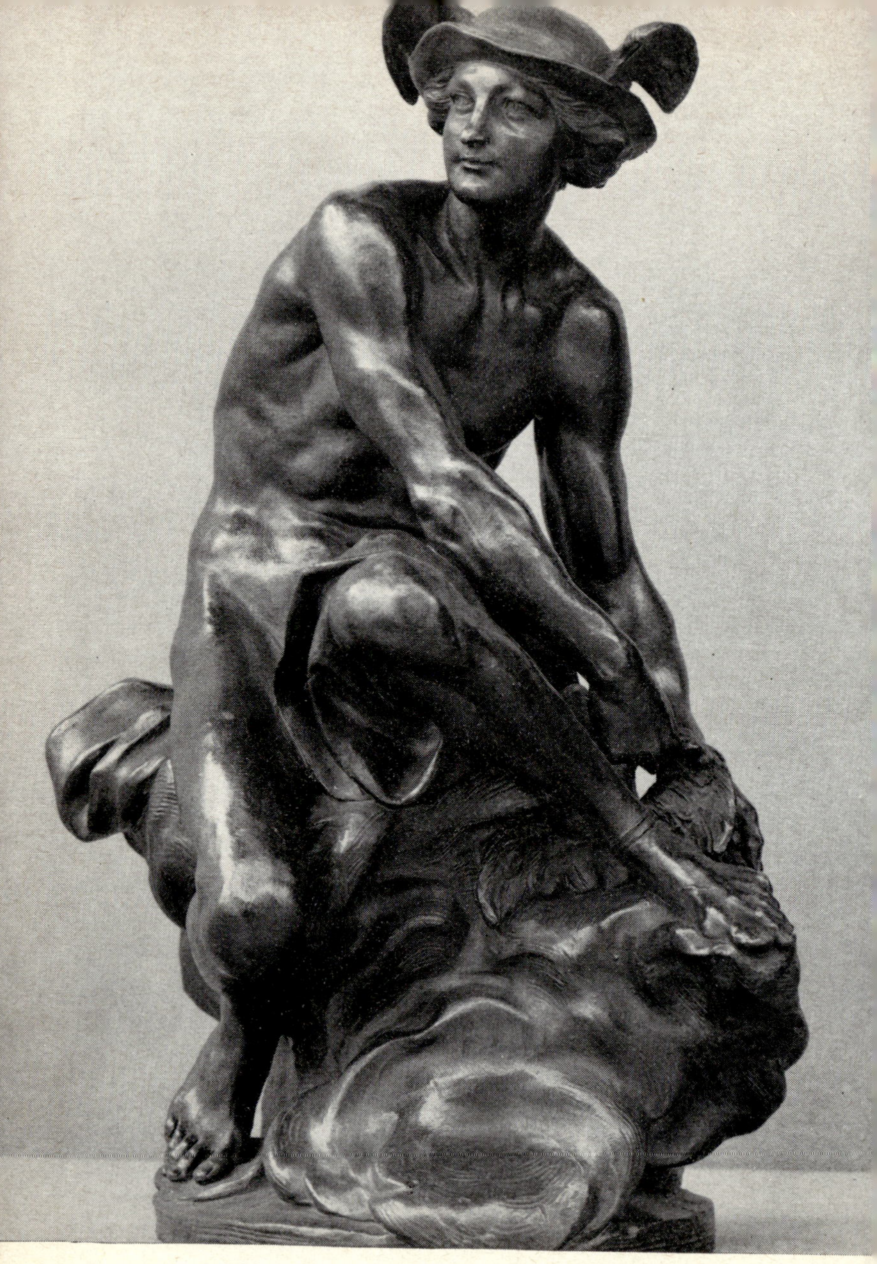

'L'Amitié' was made to symbolize her new relationship. The sculptor she chose was Jean-Baptiste Pigalle, a favourite of her brother the Marquis de Marigny, who was responsible for official commissions at the time.

Pigalle (1714–85) reflects with remarkable precision the shifts in taste and ideas of the Ancien Régime, and he was to cultivate also the friendship of the Philosophes and attempt to give some of their ideas a sculptural form. After studying with Slodtz and Bouchardon in Rome, he made his name with a figure of *Mercury*, exhibited at the Academy of 1744. This work was intended for Frederick the Great's garden at Sans Souci, and although of great elegance and lightness of feeling, it remains within the tradition of the garden sculpture at Versailles. His rise to fame was swift, and in 1752 he was made professor of the Academy. In 1755 through Marigny, he was given the commission for a monument to Louis XV to be placed in the Place Royal in Rheims. Pigalle's solution to the problem of the allegory of a royal statue illuminates the way in which the Enlightenment caused artists to reconsider their use of imagery. Pigalle, determined to be up-to-date, wrote to Voltaire to ask his advice on a suitable allegory to show the deeds of a benevolent ruler. Pigalle sought an alternative to the kind of monument condemned by Voltaire, which showed slaves in chains around the pedestal 'as if one can only commemorate the great by the wrongs they have done humanity'.

J. B. Pigalle *Mercury* 1744
Metropolitan Museum of Art, New York

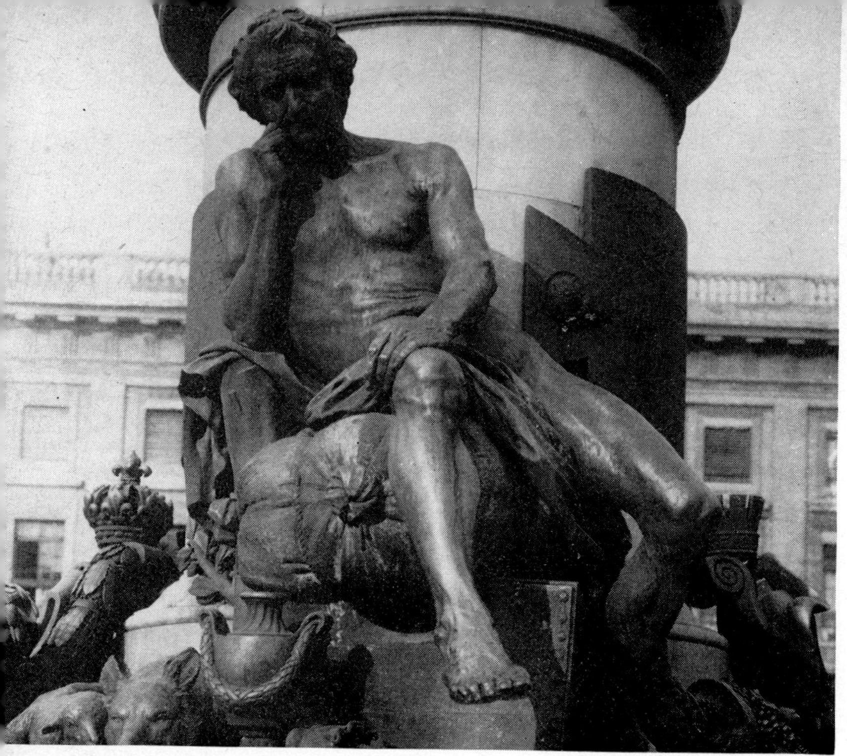

J. B. Pigalle *Louis XV Monument c.* 1755
Rheims

Pigalle's alternative scheme, which was carried out, although the
figure of the king was destroyed during the Revolution, shows
Louis XV as the model ruler of the Enlightenment, the protector
of the welfare and prosperity of his people. Pigalle in a letter to
Voltaire describes the pedestal as follows: 'On two sides of the
pedestal are two emblematic figures, one symbolizing Benign
Government [*Douceur du Government*] and the other Well-being
of Subjects [*Félicité des Peuples*]. *Douceur du Gouvernment* is
represented by a woman holding in one hand a rudder and
directing with the other an unchained lion to show that a Frenchman, despite his strength, submits willingly to a beneficial
government . . . *Félicité des Peuples* is rendered by a happy

68

citizen enjoying perfect calm in the middle of abundance, symbolized by corn which bears fruits, pearls and other riches. The olive branches grow around him; he sits on sacks of goods; he has his purse open to denote his security.'

Pigalle's chief rival was Etienne-Maurice Falconet (1716–91) who certainly leaned towards the rococo, specializing in erotic figures that have a tenuous derivation from Hellenistic originals. He was a writer on art as well as a sculptor, and he believed that the moderns had surpassed the ancients in the rendering of human flesh; an opinion that is borne out by the vibrant surface of his own figures that is lost in the many porcelain versions produced in the Sèvres factory of which he was director of sculpture.

Pigalle and Falconet regained for France the ascendency in European sculpture which it retained until the French Revolution and their works were exported widely, in particular to Prussia and Russia, whose rulers were influenced by the Enlightenment. England however remained apart, and sculpture in the early eighteenth century was dominated by two foreign artists, Michael Rysbrack (1694–1770) and Louis François Roubiliac (?1705–62). Before Rysbrack's arrival, in 1720, England was a provincial country, graced occasionally by foreign artists. The few English artists of talent, such as Cibber or Grinling Gibbons, had little opportunity to study abroad or receive worthy commissions. There was no proper training for artists in England and their social status was on a level with decorative craftsmen. The arrival of major Flemish artists at the beginning of the eighteenth century, combined with a surge of interest in the antique amongst writers like Addison, led to a realization that England was far behind the Continent in artistic achievement and that the first stage in rectifying this situation was to make available casts and copies of antique works and the best moderns. The members of the new Whig aristocracy which had come to power in the early years of the eighteenth century were secular and commercial in temperament, and the success of their mercantile endeavours led to an increasing self-confidence and a feeling that they were the new Romans, upholding liberty and stoic virtue. Portrait busts became fashionable largely because the Romans had used them and tombs were based on antique models. As the century wore on more patrons became aware of the achievements of Italy and had first-hand knowledge of antiquity.

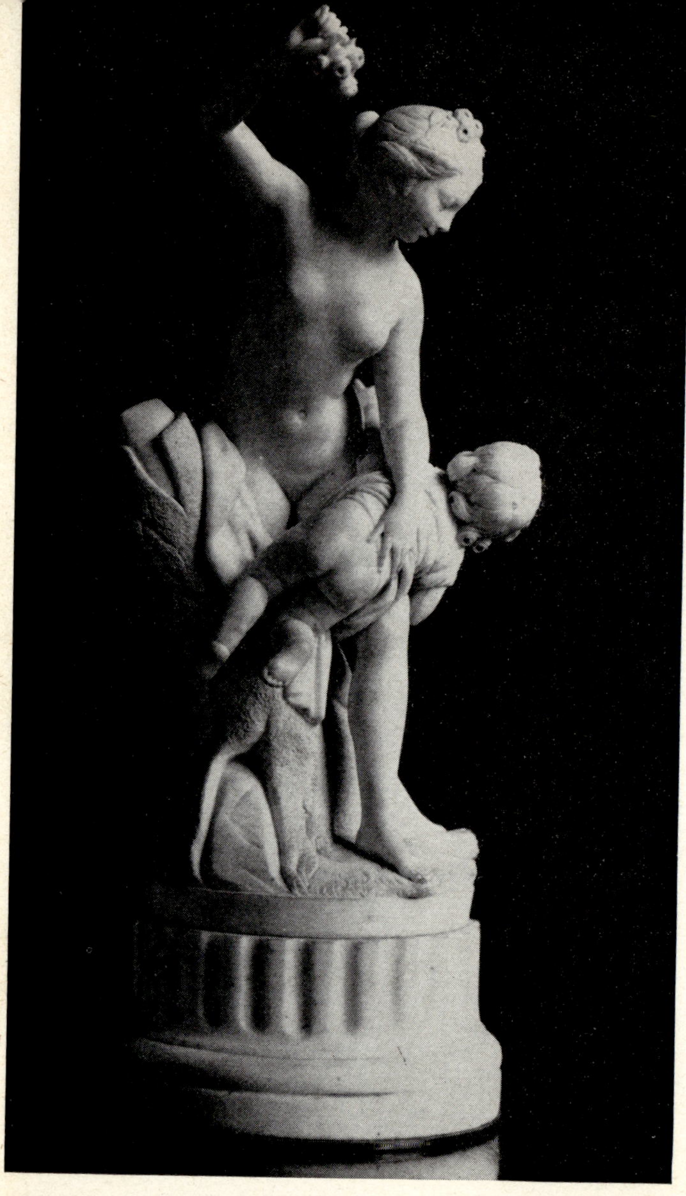

E. Falconet *Venus Chastising Cupid* and *opposite, Venus Nursing Cupid* 1750—65
Wallace Collection, London

70

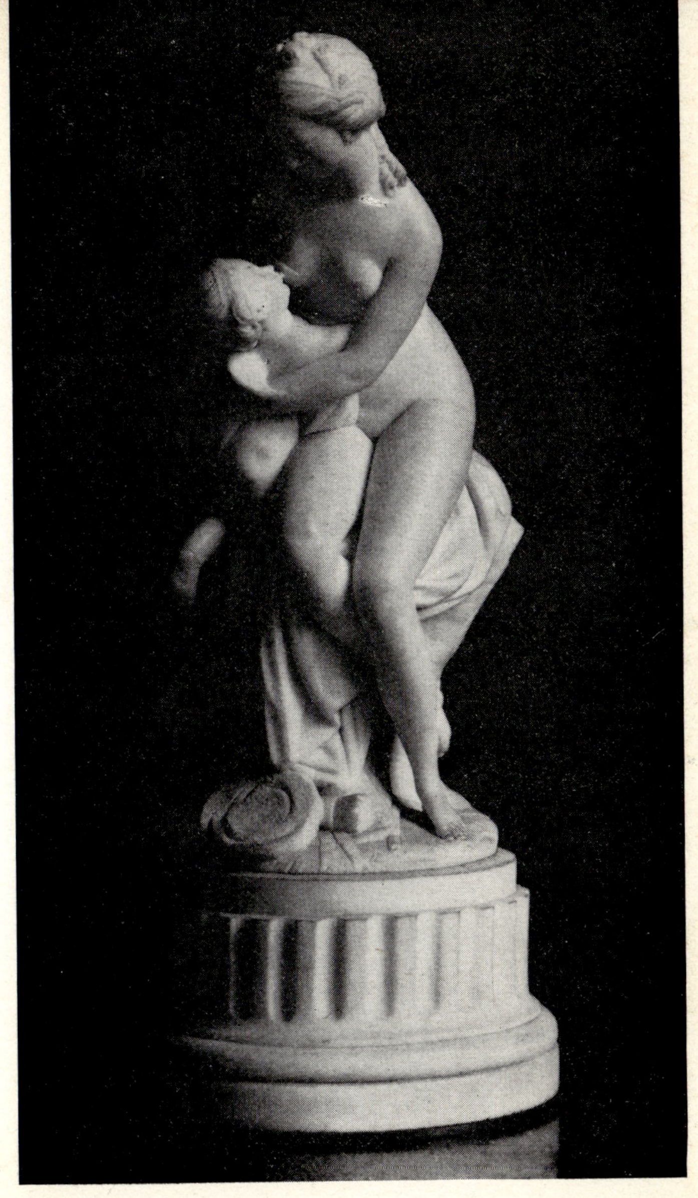

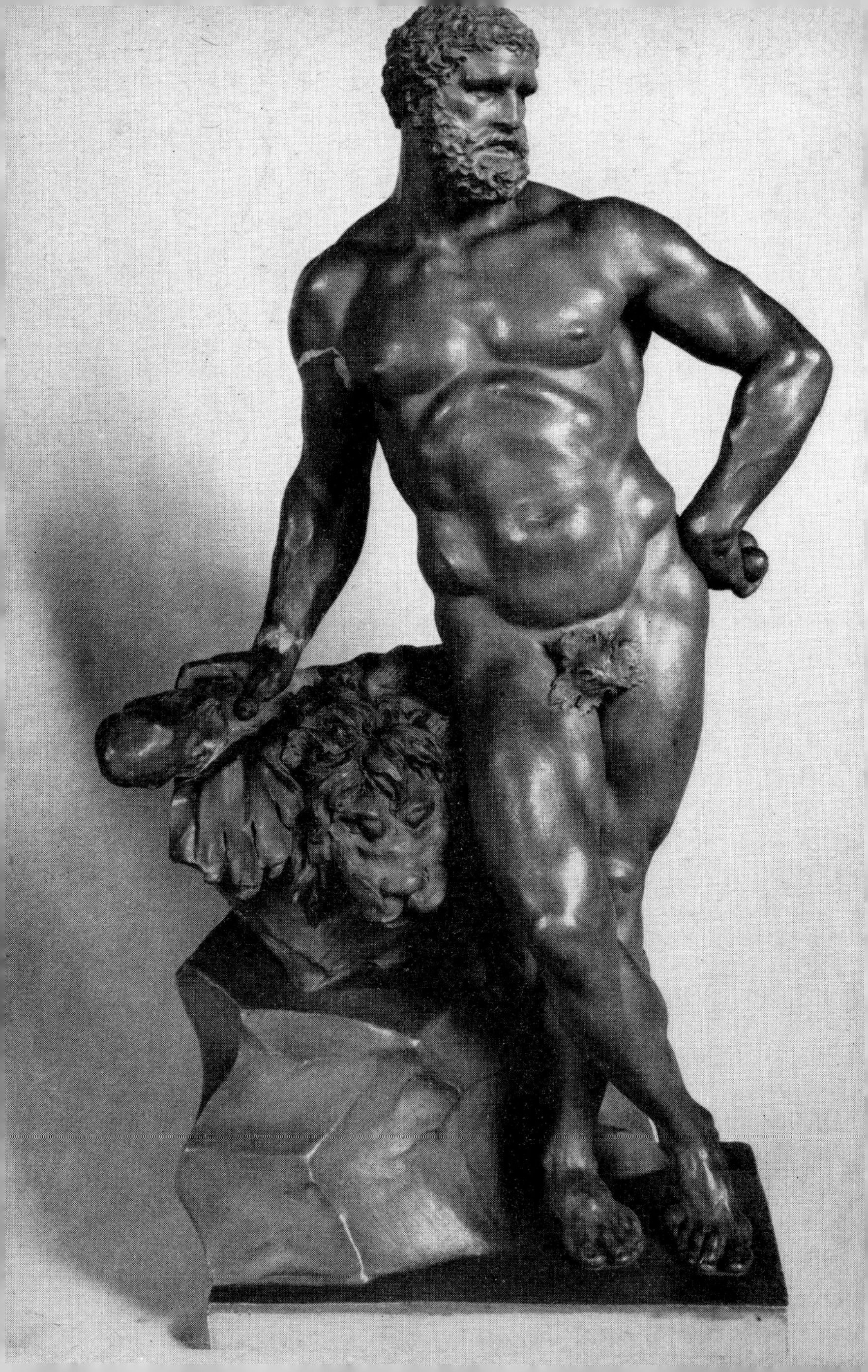

Thanks largely to the writings of the Earl of Shaftesbury, the contemplation of works of art was associated with virtuous conduct and became a part of the education of English gentlemen, whose peregrinations around Italy led to the growth of a whole industry of restorers, archaeologists and fakers to satisfy their demand for knowledge and acquisition.

Rysbrack was the ideal sculptor to cater to the demands of the new patrons, and his judicious mixture of conscious classicism and baroque vitality left him without a rival until his supremacy was challenged by the more graceful and naturalistic works of the Frenchman Roubiliac, who came over to England shortly after 1730. Rysbrack was a pupil of the classicizing Antwerp sculptor Vervoort, whose adherence to the tradition of Duquesnoy was handed on to his pupil. Roubiliac, however, studied in the French Academy, where he knew Nicholas Coustou, and also under the German baroque sculptor Permoser in Dresden; a background that is reflected in his leanings towards a more theatrical conception of the tomb and a more vivid naturalism in portraiture. In practice, the work of the two artists is sometimes extremely close, for both artists had the ability to accommodate themselves to the fashion of the day, and the requirements of connoisseurs. The Stourhead *Hercules* (1747), for example, is a deliberate attempt by Rysbrack to put conventional academic theory into practice by making an ideal figure of Hercules by combining parts from the strongest men available. According to Horace Walpole, 'This authentic statue for which he (Rysbrack) borrowed the head of the Farnesian god, was compiled from various parts and limbs of seven or eight of the strongest and best-made men in London, chiefly the bruisers and boxers of the then flourishing amphitheatre for boxing, the sculptor selecting the parts which were the most truly formed in each.'

J. M. Rysbrack *Hercules* 1747
Stourhead, Wiltshire

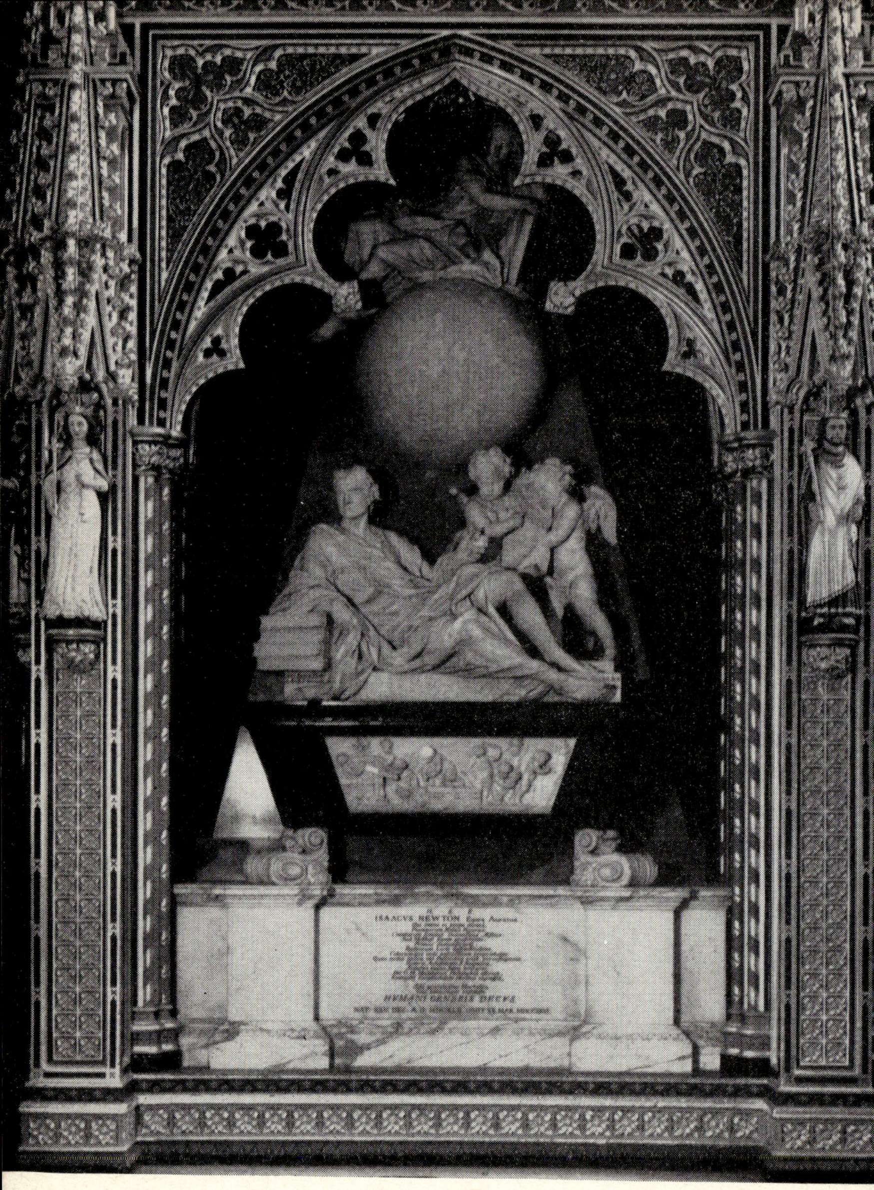

J. M. Rysbrack *Isaac Newton Monument* 1730–31
Westminster Abbey, London

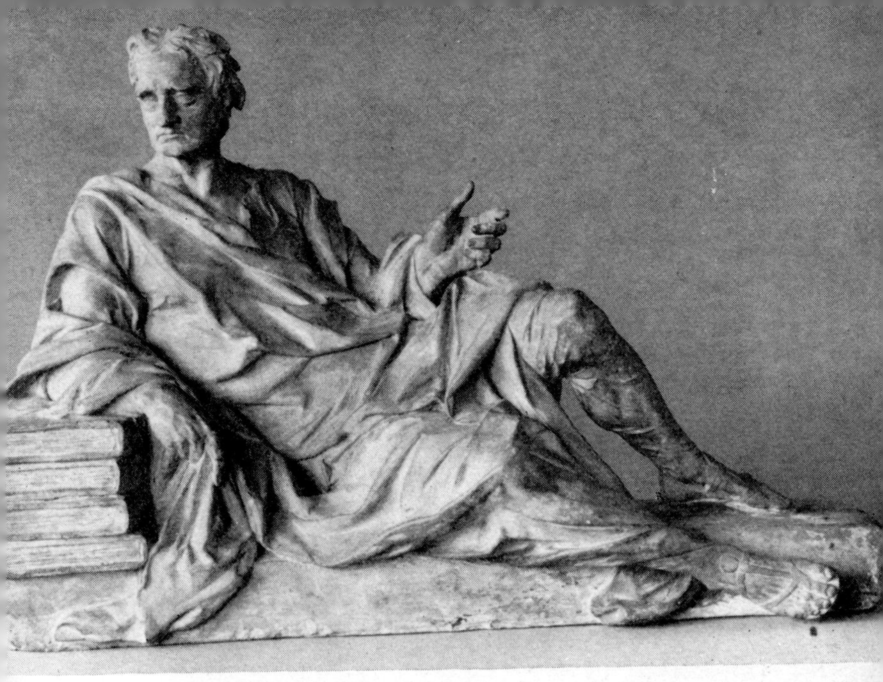

J. M. Rysbrack *Isaac Newton* 1730–31
Victoria and Albert Museum, London

The monumental tomb had been one of the principal sources of sculptural commissions in the seventeenth century and both Rysbrack and Roubiliac extended the current formulae by using their knowledge of tomb sculpture in other countries. Perhaps Rysbrack's most noble achievement is the monument to Sir Isaac Newton (1730–31) in Westminster Abbey, which combines a baroque handling with a classical dignity formerly considered appropriate only for politicians and rulers. The composition is now wrecked by gothic additions, but it shows Newton resting on his achievements, his elbow placed on four huge volumes. The allegory, in the form of two Duquesnoy-like weeping *putti* and the mourning figure of Astronomy seated on a globe, is secondary to the noble figure of Newton, whose body is draped with a grandly carved toga while the noble head is enlivened by the broken silhouette of the hair. Although Newton is pointing towards a scroll held by the *putti*, the action is kept to a minimum. Rysbrack's tomb is a repudiation of the theatrical qualities of the kind

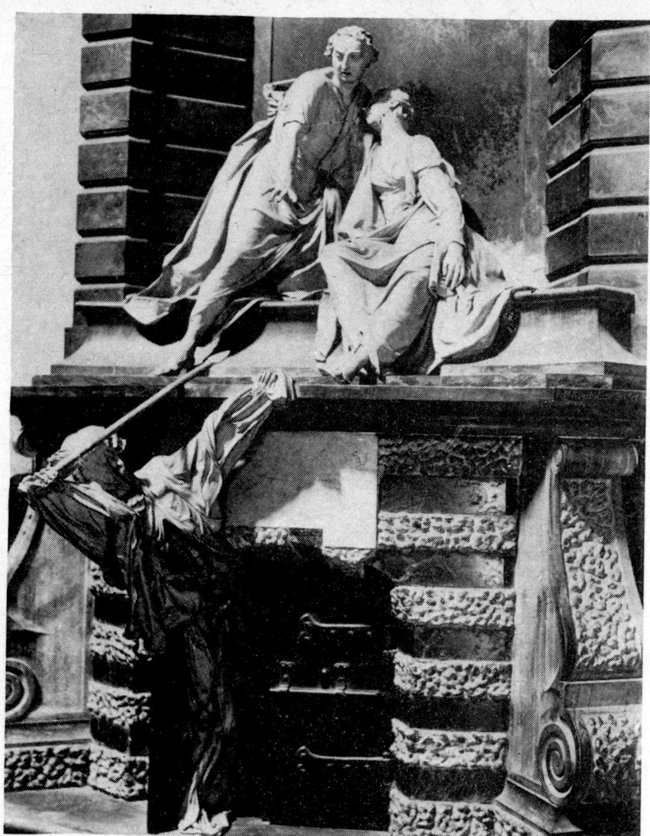

L. F. Roubiliac *Lady Elizabeth Nightingale Monument* 1761
Westminster Abbey, London

of baroque tomb pioneered by Bernini, but the rococo taste of
the next generation allowed occasional reversions to a full-
blooded pictorial conception. In Roubiliac's monument to Lady
Elizabeth Nightingale of 1761, the figure of Death, which is
obviously drawn from Bernini's Alexander VII tomb (see page 43),
is the only allegorical figure left in the composition, and the
husband, trying vainly to deflect the fatal dart, is depicted with
harrowing naturalism. Unlike Bernini's tomb, in which the pope's
composure suggests the triviality of death in the face of faith and
goodness, Roubiliac shows death as something that deprives the
world of a beautiful soul despite man's feeble efforts to forestall

76

him. The formal vocabulary of the tomb is derived from Bernini,
but in its more secular imagery it is closer to the later tomb of the
Comte d'Harcourt by Pigalle of 1771–7, which concentrates on
the human implications of death and resurrection, showing the
widow, 'la nouvelle Artemise', as she was called at the time, at
the moment of her reunion with her husband after death.

J. B. Pigalle *Comte d'Harcourt Monument* 1771–7
Notre Dame, Paris

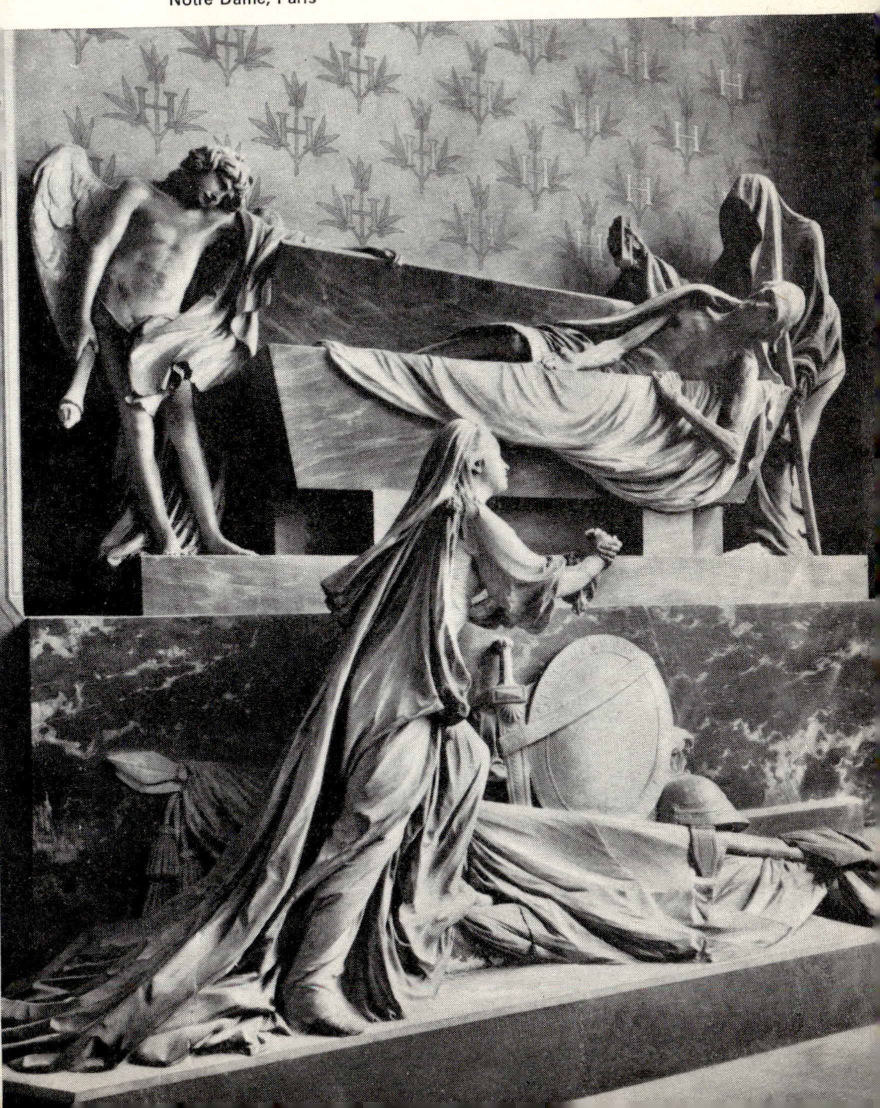

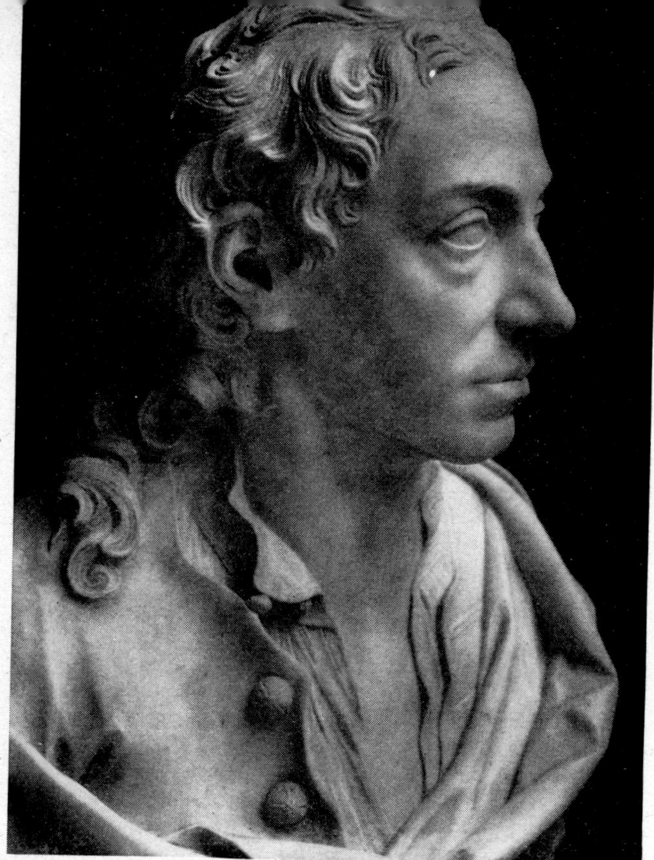

J. M. Rysbrack *Alexander Pope* 1730
Athenaeum, London

The contrast between Rysbrack and Roubiliac can be seen most clearly in their respective busts of Alexander Pope. Rysbrack shows the poet *en négligé*, his shirt unbuttoned in a manner derived from Coysevox's portrait of Matthew Prior, but the head is given an intellectual grandeur that gives no hint of Pope's ugliness and vulnerability. Roubiliac's image of the poet is more tragic, for

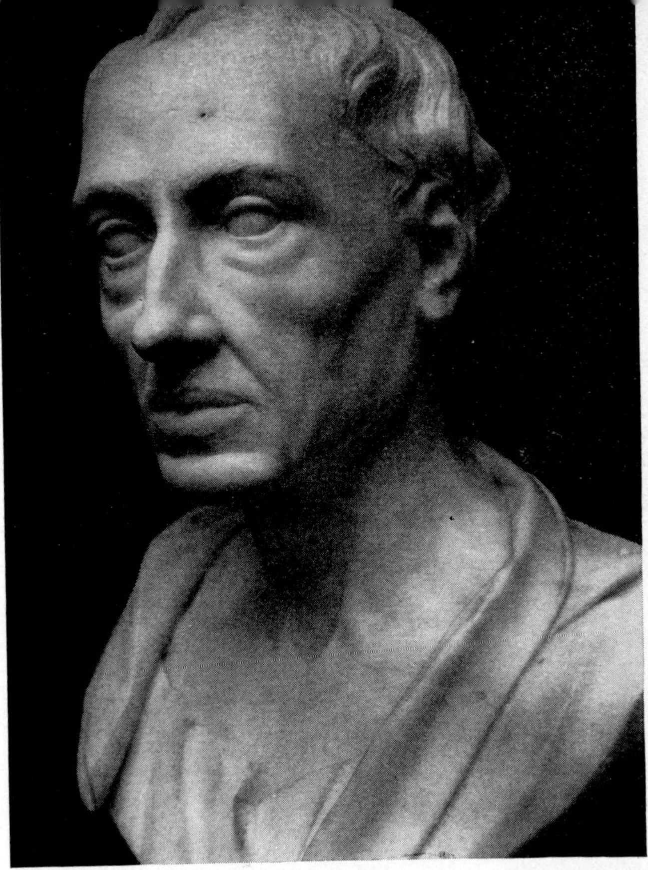

L. F. Roubiliac *Alexander Pope* 1741
Shipley Art Gallery, Gateshead

the carving is particularized, exploring the bone structure and wrinkles of that extraordinary head. Roubiliac has attempted a 'speaking likeness', though the cropped head and toga are, ironically, in conscious imitation of a Roman bust. Roubiliac's success in assimilating the more relaxed mood emanating from France in the 1730s can also be seen in the figure of Handel made for Vauxhall Gardens (1738). Handel is shown playing a heavenly lyre, while a cherub below records the promptings of the Muse, but the easy naturalness of the pose almost parodies the pomposity of the allegory.

L. F. Roubiliac *Handel* 1738
Victoria and Albert Museum, London. Detail *below*

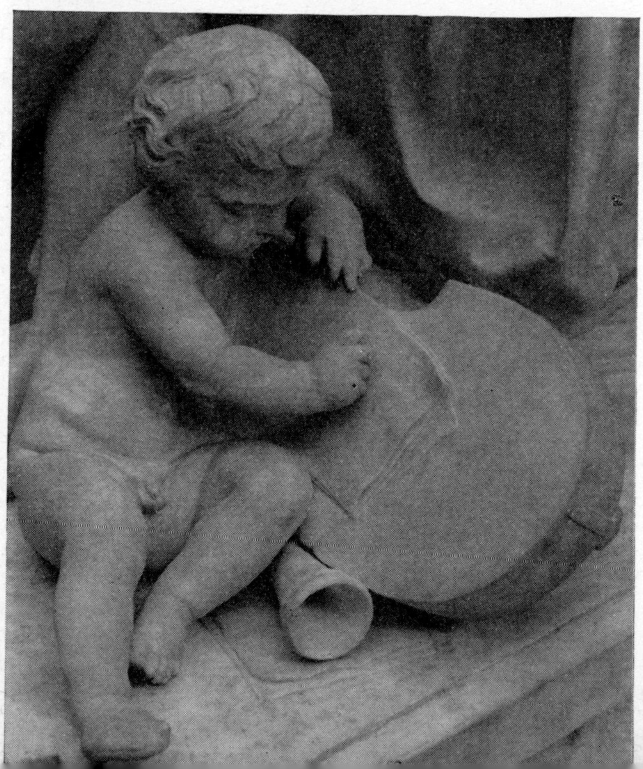

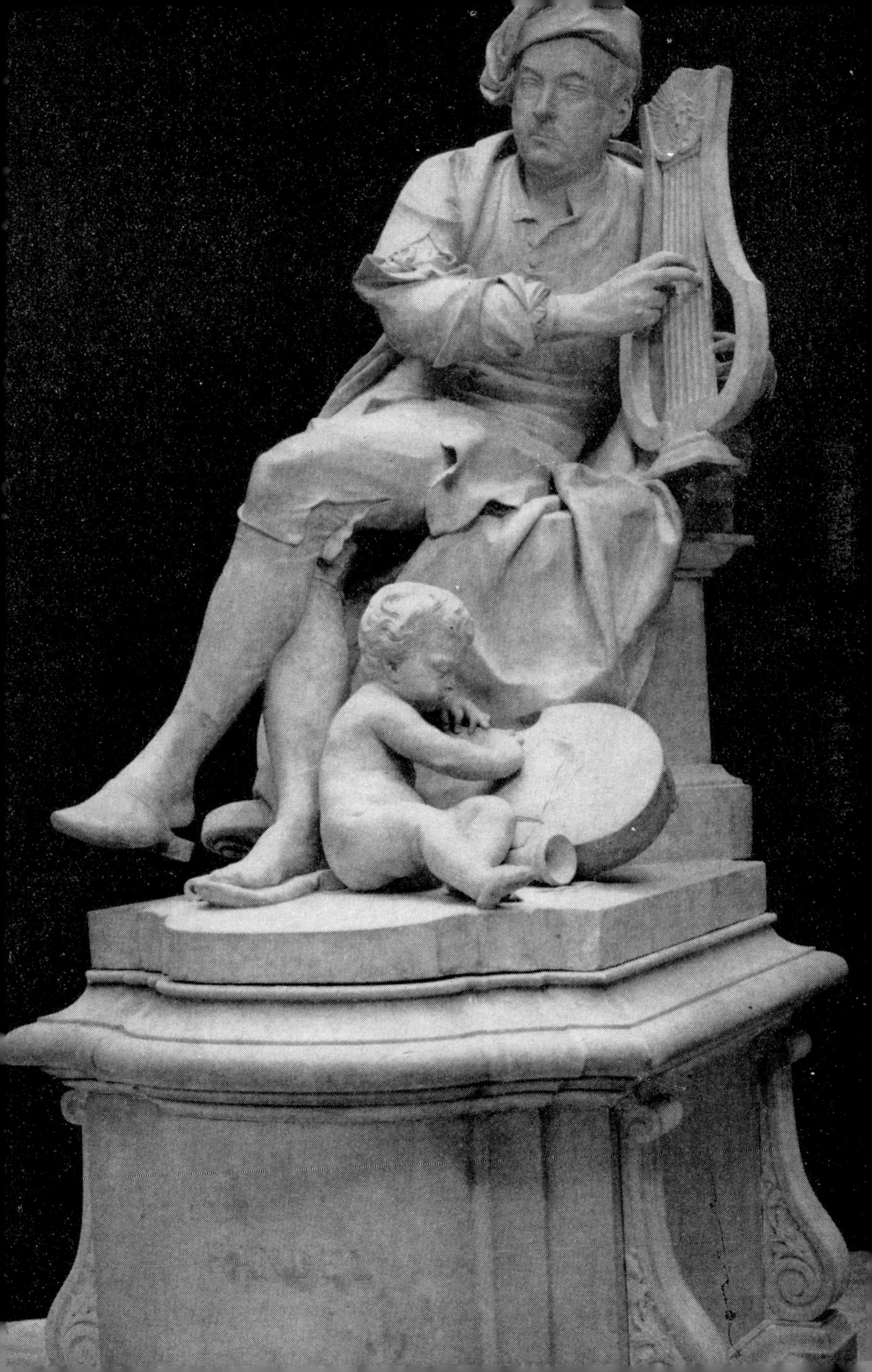

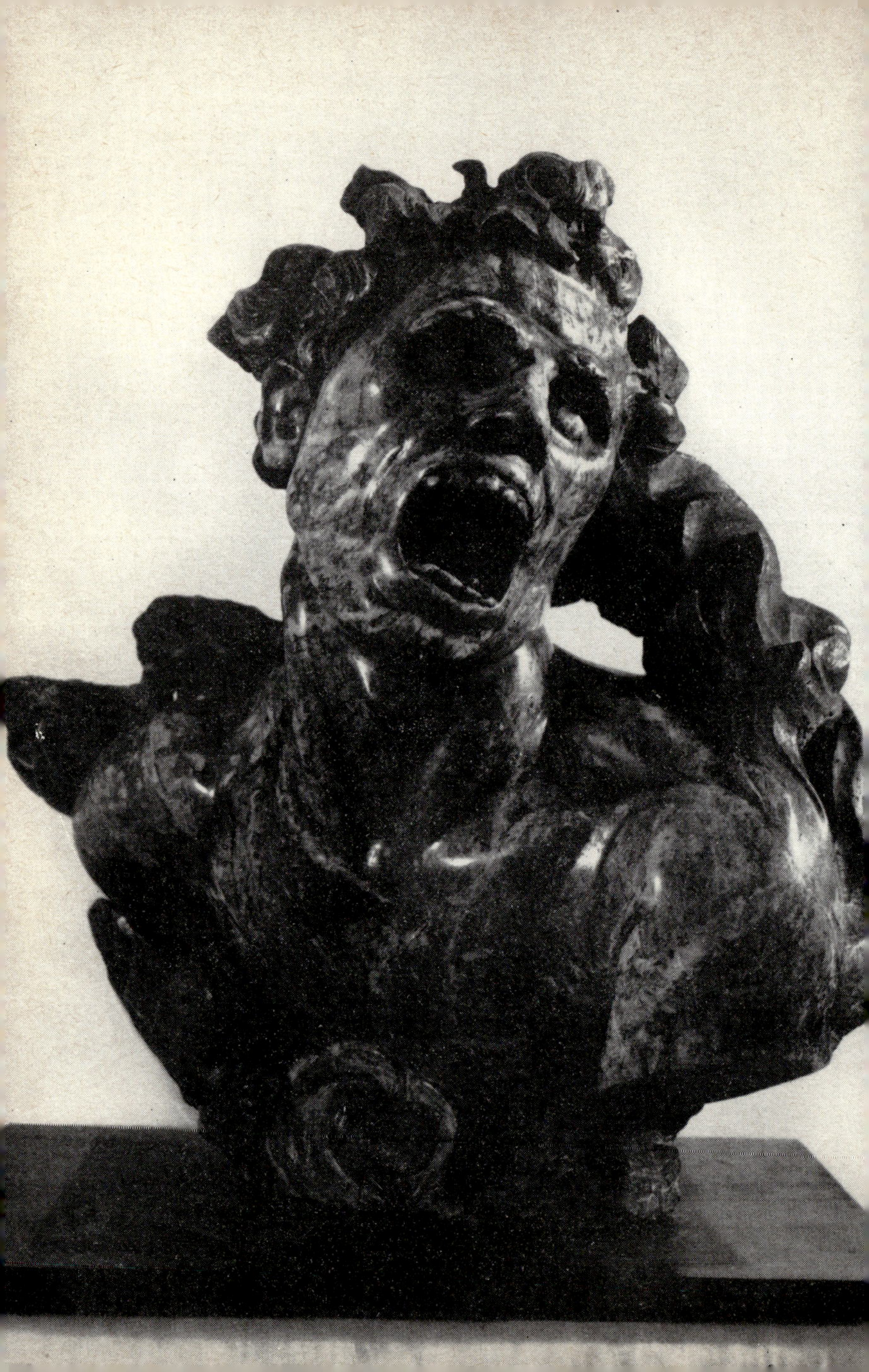

The most extreme manifestation of the rococo in sculpture is to be found in Germany, although it is usually of a less sophisticated character than the decorative art of Paris salons of the early eighteenth century. The sculpture produced in the German principalities in the eighteenth century is too diverse to permit generalization, but much of the best and most characteristic work of the period shows a remarkable continuation of the earlier spirit of the high baroque. Balthazar Permoser (1651–1732), the Dresden sculptor, had studied in Italy in the latter part of the seventeenth century, but his desire to bring pictorial qualities into sculpture was certainly derived from a study of Bernini's works, and he left as a personal testament a now-destroyed group of *Painting Embracing Sculpture*. None the less, the elegance of his figures is unmistakably a development of the late baroque, and nothing illustrates more clearly the ambiguity of the term 'rococo' as an art-historical style than these German works of the eighteenth century.

The only full-blooded successors to the *Gesamtkunstwerken* or total art works of Bernini, such as the *Cathedra Petri* (see page 32), are to be found in the Catholic churches of southern Germany, which are conceived with a total vision that once again breaks down the distinction between architecture, sculpture and painting. They were not, however, the product of a master-mind like Bernini, whose genius enabled him to cope with all the diverse skills required, but were created by small groups of craftsmen who would take on the problem of creating a church interior with all its fittings from start to finish, sometimes designing the church as well. The most successful group was formed by the brothers Asam, Egid Quirin (1692–1750) being a sculptor and Cosmas Damian

B. Permoser *Damned Soul c.* 1720–30
Museum der Bildenden Künste, Leipzig

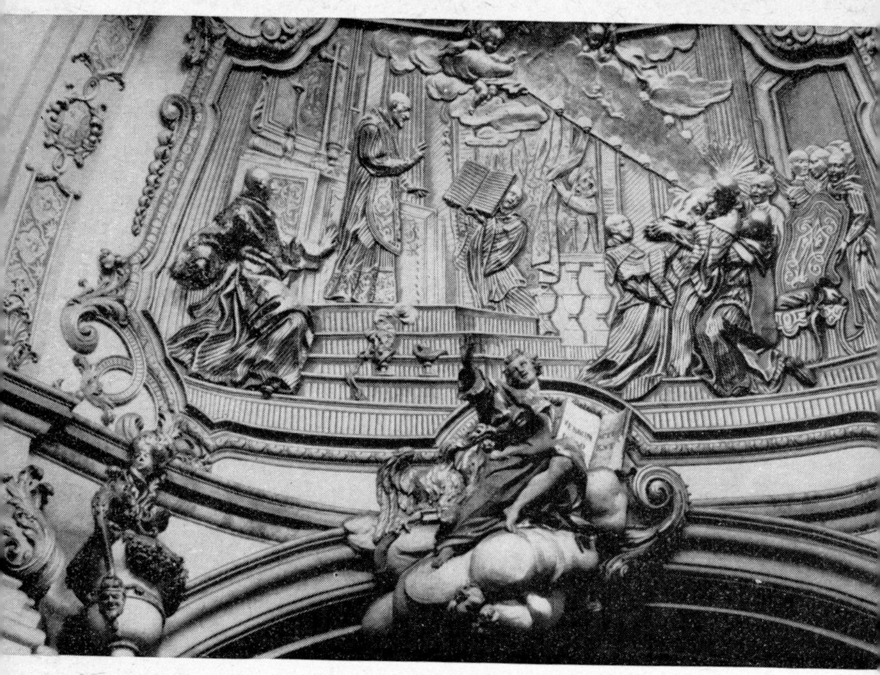

Asam Brothers *Weltenberg Monastery Church* 1721–30
Detail of cupola

Asam Brothers *Weltenburg Monastery Church* 1721–30

(1686–1739) a painter. Both had studied in Rome, and the former's absorption of Bernini's work in St Peter's is clearly revealed in their joint schemes. Although Egid Quirin Asam was a sculptor by profession, his sculptures can hardly be considered apart from their setting, but in the work of Ignaz Gunther (1725–75) there is a tendency for the sculpture to assert its independence within the framework of the *Gesamtkunstwerk*. Gunther's work shows a strong affinity to mannerist sculpture of the end of the sixteenth century, which he is known to have studied, with its extreme elongation and elegant outline, but at the same time, his figures have a hard surface realism and polychromed surface that remind one of mediaeval German woodcarving.

84

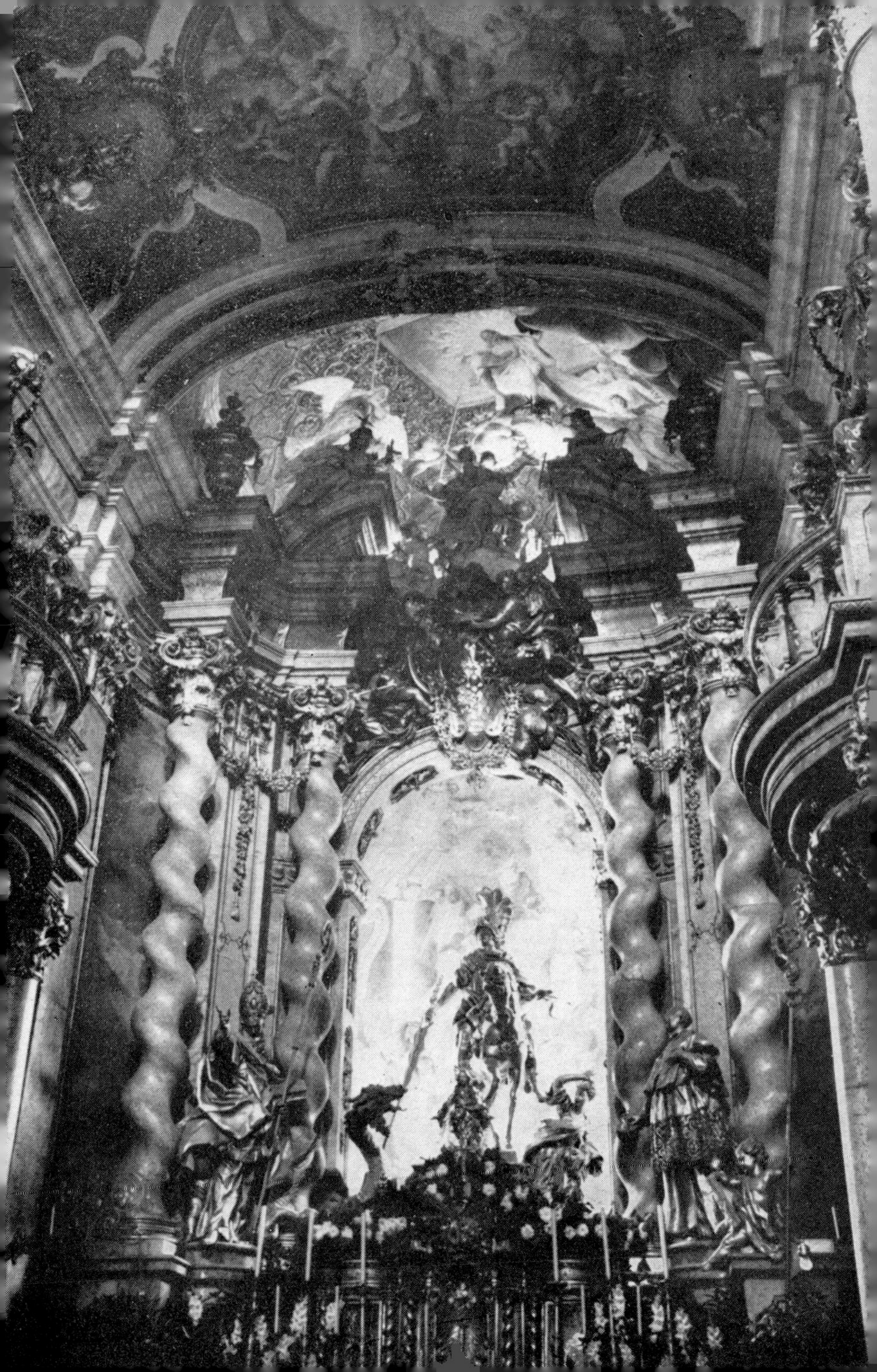

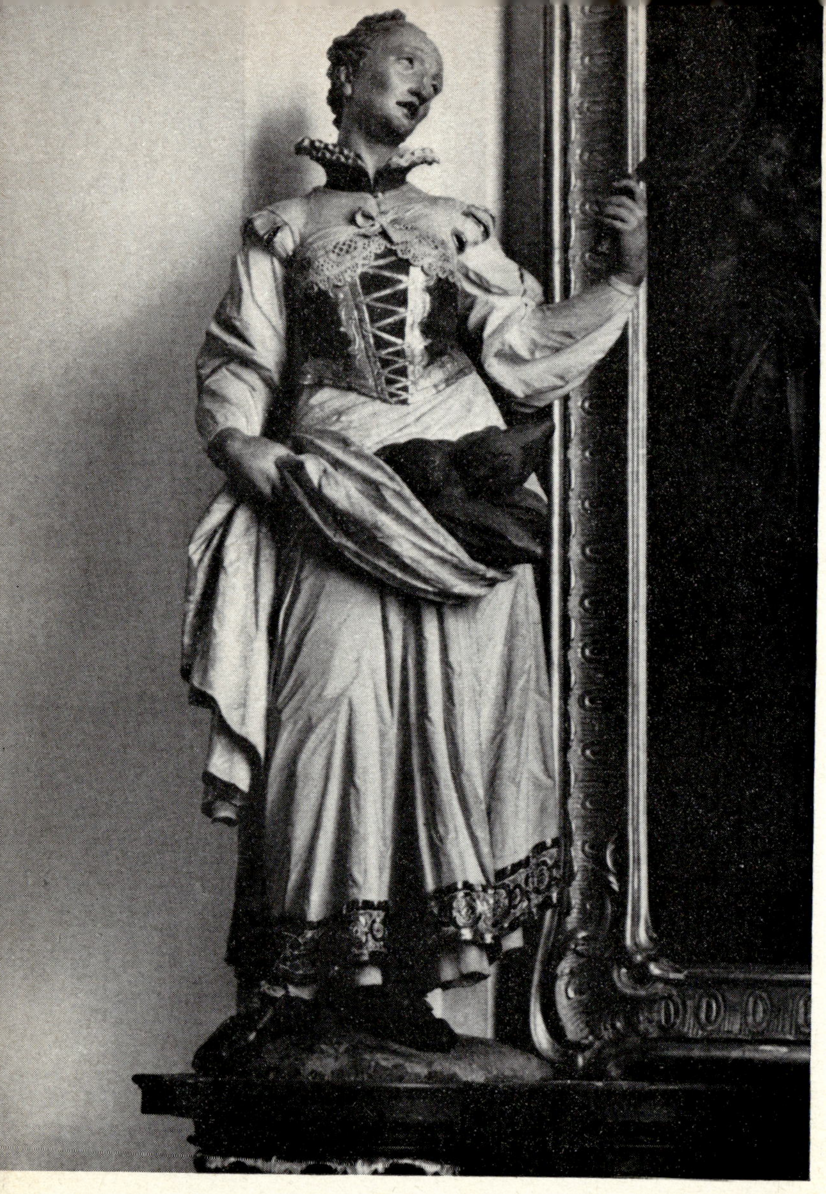

I. Gunther *St Notburga* 1763
Rott-am-Inn Monastery Church
Bavaria

The neoclassical reaction

In France, the tenuous ascendency of the rococo during the Régence period led to a reaction in favour of a nobler and more serious style in the 1740s which, as we have seen, was associated with a feeling of nostalgia for the reign of Louis XIV. The classicism of the 1740s and of Bouchardon in particular should not, however, be seen as a rejection of the baroque, but as a further development of baroque classicism that looks back to the style of the later seventeenth century rather than directly to antiquity. Only in Rome in the 1760s did the growing dissatisfaction with what Jacques-Louis David called 'la queue de Bernin' or the tail-end of the baroque, find expression in a coherent theory. The spokesman and driving force of the neoclassical movement was Johann Joachim Winckelmann (1717–68), an antiquarian, who produced a number of works on Greek art that for the first time attempted to organize Greek statues according to their stylistic development. Winckelmann saw the baroque as an unfortunate inheritance that had to be swept away if artists were to return to the purity and simplicity of Raphael and the Greeks. He rather unexpectedly chose the *Laocöon* (see page 23), as one of the principal examples of the 'edle Einfalt und stille Grosse'* of the best Greek works, but he saw these qualities in the restraint and nobility with which Laocöon suffers his terrible agony.

The quality of restraint had always been admired by classical theorists, but the novelty in Winckelmann's argument is that his ideal of simplicity is not just an admonition to avoid over-elaboration, but a call to artists to purge themselves of everything extraneous to the pure realization of the idea of their work. As a result a convincing appearance of reality was no longer a *sine qua non*, and naturalism for its own sake was condemned as imitation of nature.

The theory and the earlier development of neoclassicism was essentially the achievement of foreigners in Rome, but the greatest exponent was Antonio Canova (1757–1822), an Italian who studied in Venice. He became a sudden convert to the doctrine of neoclassicism, and we can follow the change in his work and the reaction of his contemporaries to it. Canova was born in Possagno, near Venice, and had achieved a great reputation in

* Noble simplicity and calm grandeur

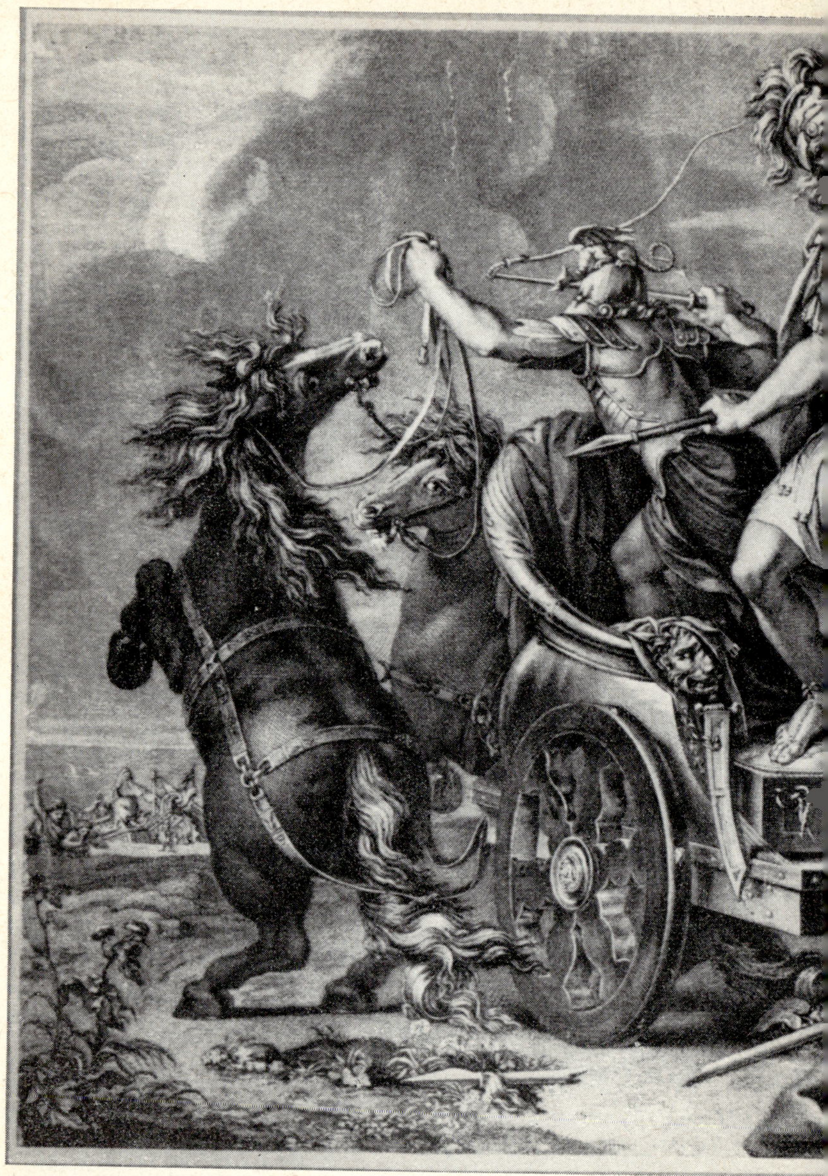

G. Hamilton *The Body of Hector* 1763
Engraving. National Gallery of Scotland

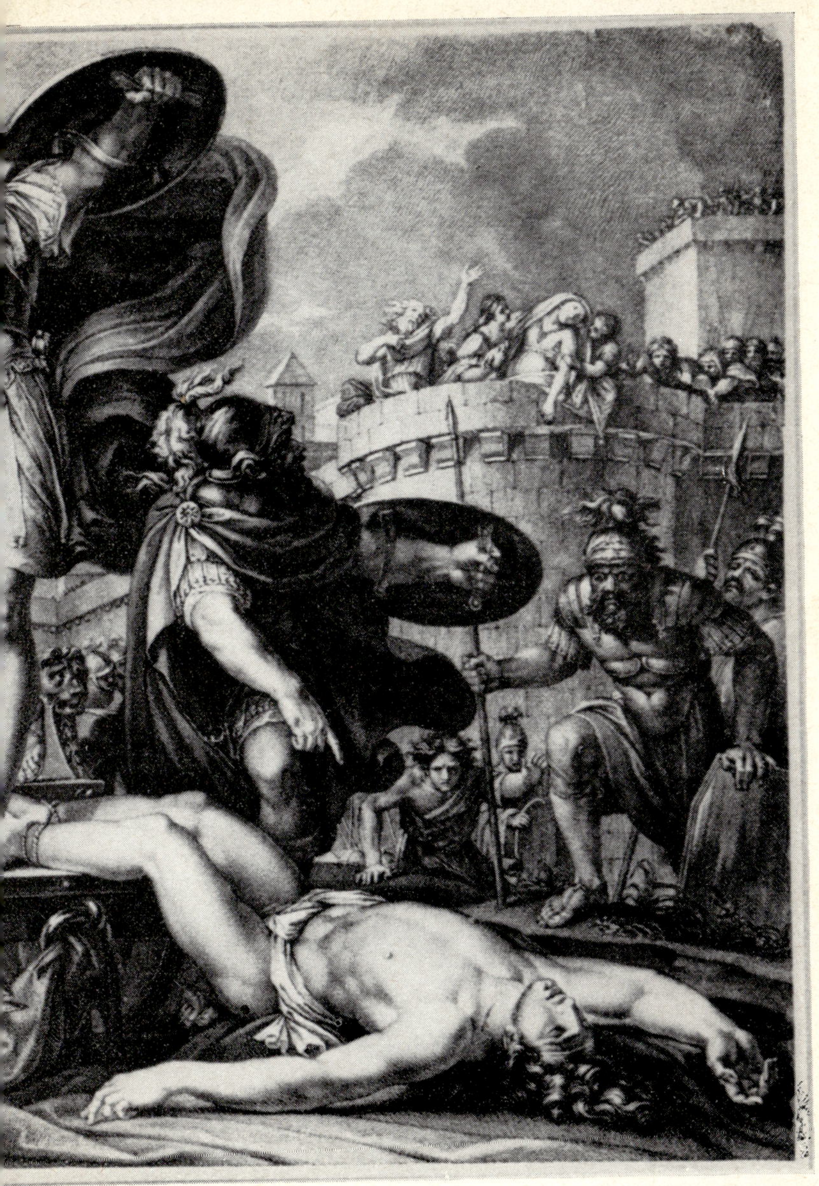

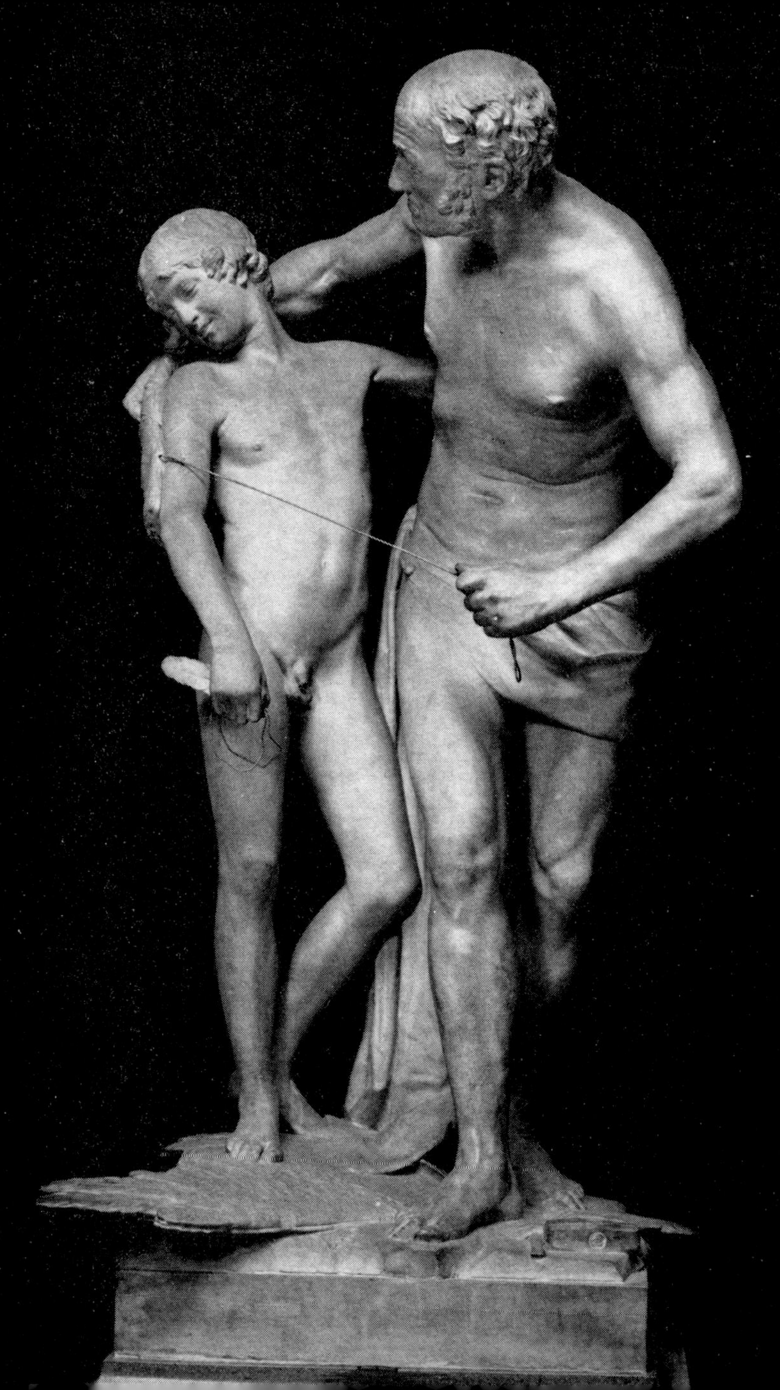

Venice, especially for the group of *Daedalus and Icarus* (1779). This work is still in an unmistakably late baroque idiom; the surface of the figures is minutely depicted and their relationship graceful and conversational. He brought a version of it to Rome in 1779 where he became friendly with the Scottish painter Gavin Hamilton, who had become the arbiter of neoclassical taste after the death of Winckelmann in 1768. In 1781 Canova was

A. Canova *Daedalus and Icarus* 1779
Museo Correr, Venice

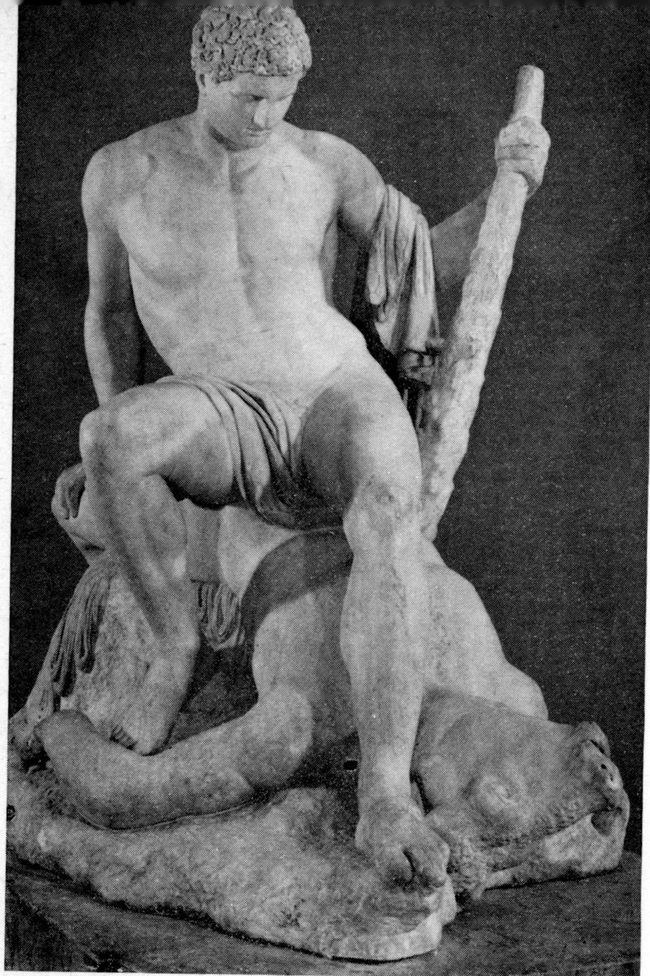

A. Canova *Theseus and the Minotaur* 1781–2
Victoria and Albert Museum

given a block of marble by the Venetian ambassador for a group
of *Theseus and the Minotaur* and, apparently on Hamilton's
advice, he decided to show the moment of triumph after the battle
instead of the battle itself. The work is revolutionary in its un-
compromising severity. It marks the end of the baroque era in
sculpture and henceforward the new Grecian style gradually
took over as the official style for all monuments and large-scale
sculptural projects. His success with the *Theseus* led to the
92

commission for the tomb of Pope Clement XIV (1784–7) in Ss. Apostoli in Rome. This project invited direct comparison with Bernini, and Canova's final realization can be seen as deliberate purification of Bernini's concept of the papal tomb (see pages 41, 43); the dazzling polychromy has been replaced by unsullied Carrara marble, and the curvilinear forms and strong diagonals have yielded to a rigid system of horizontals and verticals, while the figures are spaced out and separated from each other.

A. Canova *Clement XIV Monument* 1784–7
Ss. Apostoli, Rome

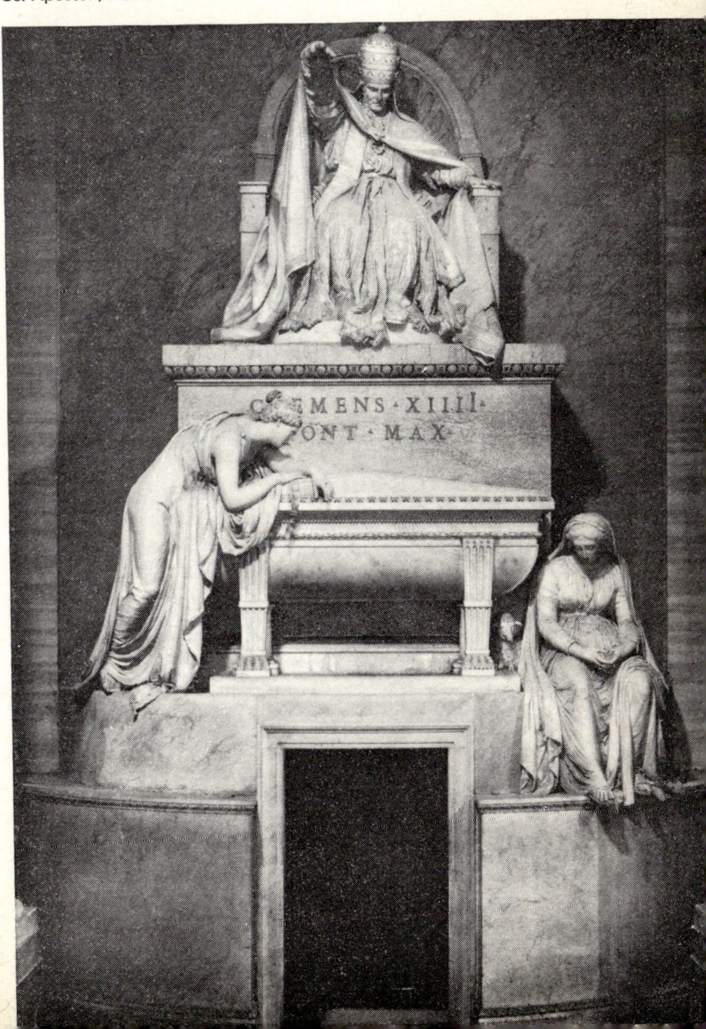

Canova's zeal in removing the excrescences from Bernini's conception has also removed much of the artistic vitality. His less ambitious works where a little rococo *esprit* remains are now much more acceptable than his grander tombs, but his contemporaries took a more high-minded view of his achievements. Milizia, a contemporary and supporter of Canova, praised the tomb of Clement XIV for its Grecian qualities, 'I feel assured, however, that if in Greece, and during the happiest ages of Grecian art, it had been required to sculpture a Pope, the subject would not have been treated in a manner different from the present', while spectators who saw the *Theseus* for the first time were convinced that it was a copy of a Greek original and were astonished to be proved wrong. Yet Canova always abhorred the practice of copying Greek works, for to him and to Winckelmann imitation meant the return to the original spirit of the Greeks, whose masterpieces were the natural outgrowth of a Golden Age when artists and philosophers were united in the contemplation of the perfection of the human body. The opposition to Canova, which was bitter in his early days, is summed up in the remark of the director of the French Academy, who on seeing the *Theseus*, asked Canova, 'Tell me, why have you changed your style; who persuaded you to abandon the pursuit of Nature?'

The disgust of the Enlightenment at the frivolity of the rococo contributed to the growing classicism of the French sculpture in the eighteenth century, but it is ironical that the country of Poussin produced no neoclassical sculptor to compare with Canova. That French sculptors were never able to throw off a residual baroque naturalism or rococo gaiety is demonstrated by the nude statue of *Voltaire* by Pigalle, which was conceived in a self-consciously classical spirit. The project was first suggested in 1770 at a dinner party given by Madame Necker for, amongst others, Diderot, Grimm, d'Alembert and Helvetius. The intention was to commemorate Voltaire as an example to posterity, for, in the words of Diderot, 'Posterity is for the philosopher what the other world is to the devout'. The original model submitted by Pigalle showed Voltaire draped, but under the influence of Diderot, applying the fashionable tag from Pliny, 'Graeca res est nihil velare', Pigalle decided to show Voltaire naked, and took the body from a war veteran of the same advanced age as

J. B. Pigalle *Voltaire* 1770–76
L'Institut, Paris

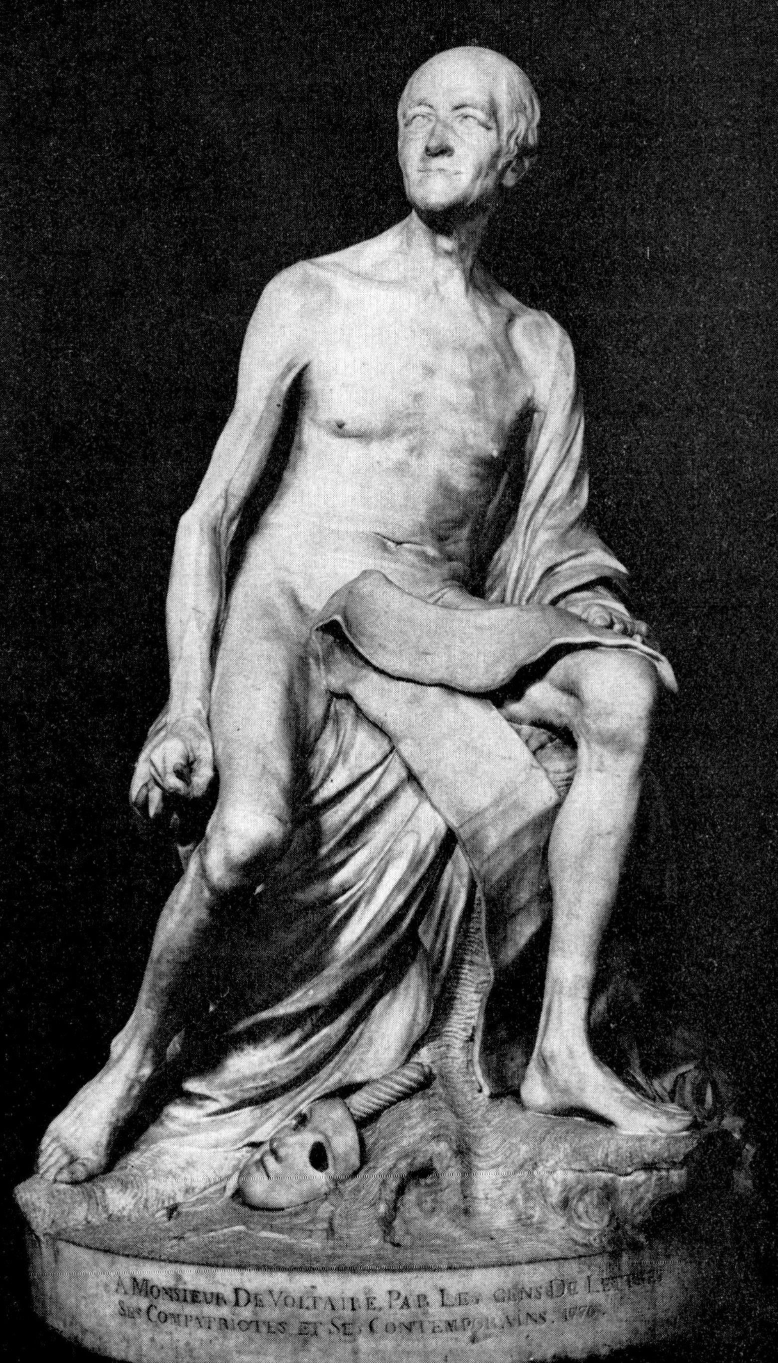

A MONSIEUR DE VOLTAIRE PAR LES GENS DE LETTRES
SES COMPATRIOTES ET SES CONTEMPORAINS. 1776.

Voltaire. This embarrassed most of the original group and Voltaire himself, who feared ridicule, but he eventually resigned himself to it and wrote: 'I can only admire the antique in the work of M. Pigalle; nude or clothed it does not matter as I will not inspire lascivious ideas in women, however I am presented to them.'

The statue is modelled on an antique statue of *Seneca Cutting his Veins* and it was regarded by the next generation as a landmark in the development of neoclassicism, but it was condemned by Quartremère de Quincy, the high priest of the Ideal in France, as too literal and anatomical, and by a biographer of Canova because 'propriety has been sacrificed to an appearance of science'. Both these criticisms hit upon the essential difference between Pigalle and Canova, for however much the former may protest his Graecism he has depicted the body of Voltaire with a naturalistic precision that differentiates it from the generality of Canova's modelling. A comparison can be made with Canova's heroic *Napoleon*, where the sculptor makes no concessions to the reality of Napoleon's appearance, but shows him with a god-like physique, following the Roman practice of deifying their emperors.

A far-reaching attempt to solve the problem of the 'contemporary nude' can be seen in Canova's reclining figure of Napoleon's sister, Pauline Borghese. She was a woman notoriously lacking in

A. Canova *Pauline Borghese* 1807
Borghese Gallery, Rome

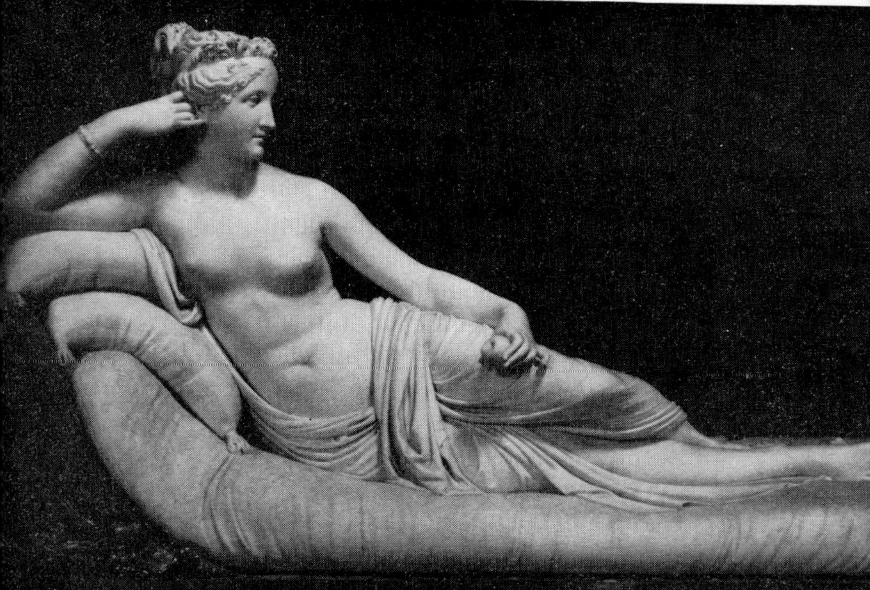

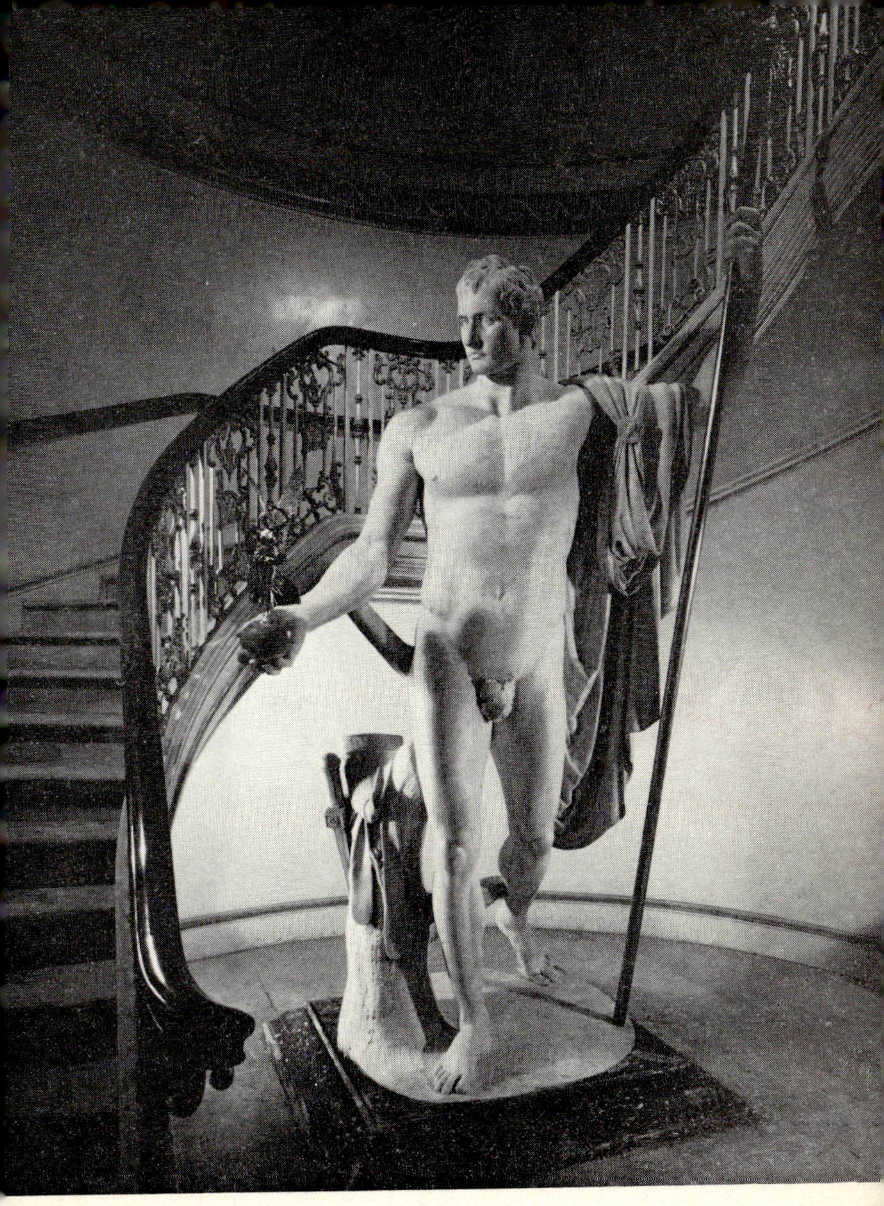

A. Canova *Napoleon* 1806–8
Wellington Museum, London

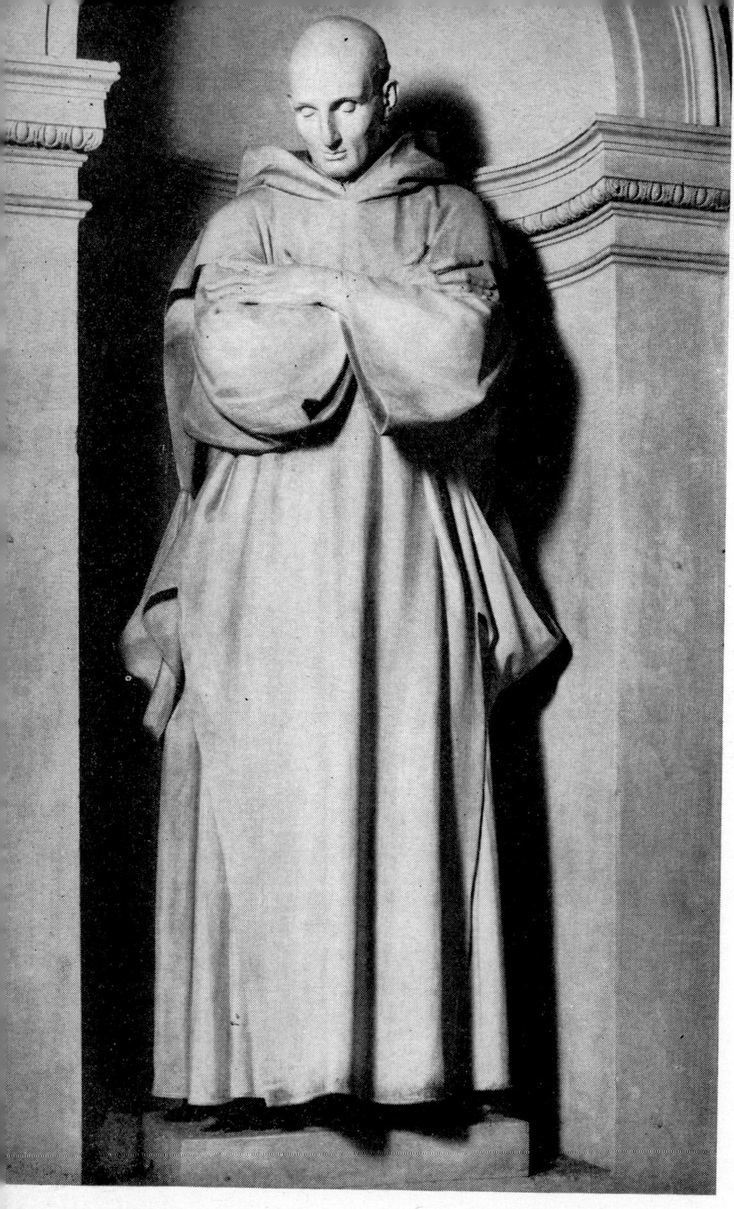

J. A. Houdon *St Bruno* 1766
S. Maria degli Angeli, Rome

98

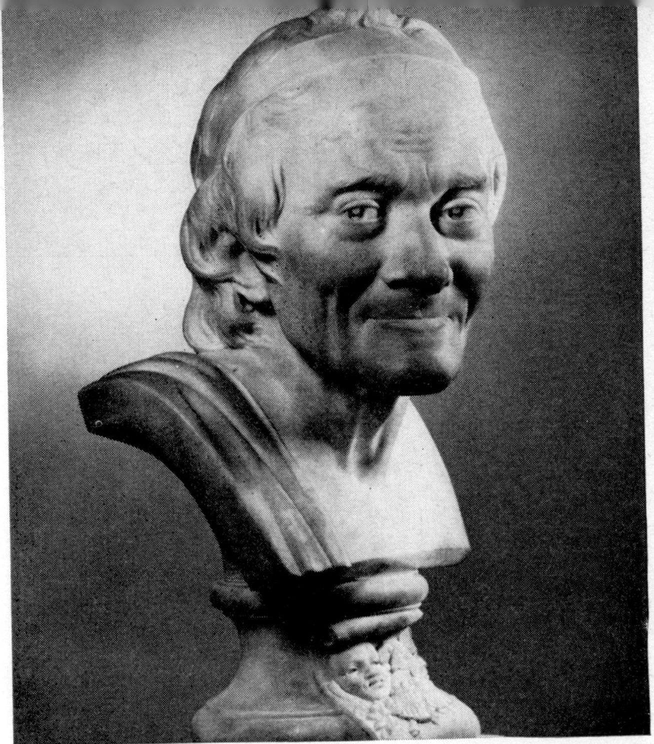

J. A. Houdon *Voltaire* 1781
Victoria and Albert Museum, London

antique virtue, but Canova elevates her coquettish personality to its Ideal form, showing her as *Venus Victorious*, with an apple in her hand to bestow on whomever she wished. It is, therefore, an accurate account of her personality, but at the same time true to the antique practice of associating the great with their most appropriate divinity.

Jean-Antoine Houdon (1741–1828) had also been influenced by the neoclassical climate of Rome in the 1760s, and his *St Bruno* (1766) for S. Maria degli Angeli in Rome is a notably lucid and contemplative rendering of an essentially baroque subject. He took a more pragmatic approach to the problem of portraiture on his return to France, choosing a style appropriate to the occasion. His bust of Voltaire, of which he made many versions, is a masterpiece of searching naturalism, in which the

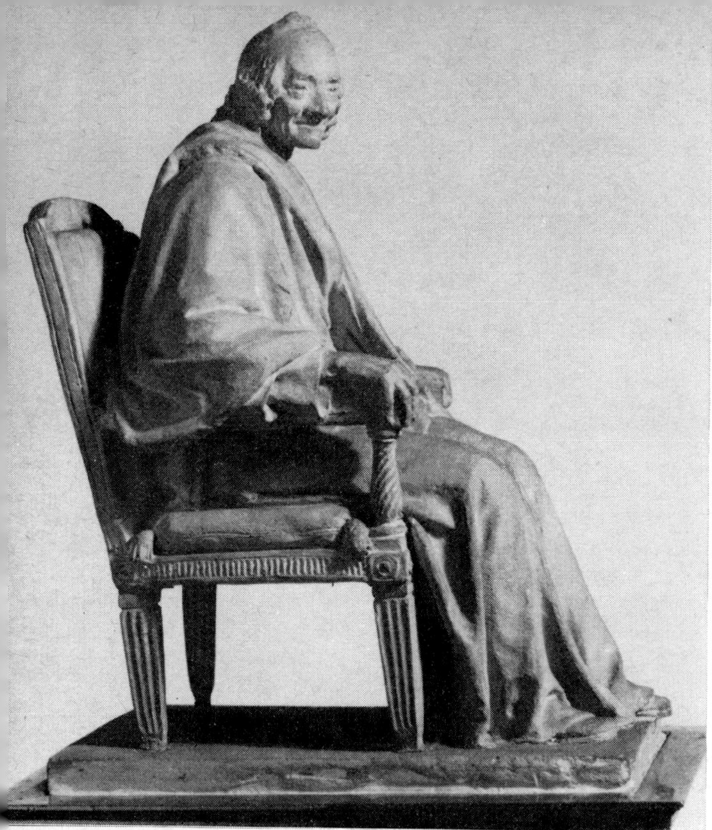

J. A. Houdon *Voltaire* 1781
Terracotta model for marble version in L'Institut, Paris
Fitzwilliam Museum, Cambridge

philosopher's extraordinary head is seen at the moment of greatest animation, revealing his sardonic wit. These busts were made to be mementos of Voltaire for his friends, but the full-length seated statue of 1781, for the Institut, was intended as a public commemoration and so the head is elevated to an image of commanding dignity, that, like Rodin's *Balzac*, is distilled from the writer's physiognomy.

Claude Michel called Clodion (1738–1814) is another example of an artist whose work tends to fluctuate between one style and another according to demand. He is best known for his small terracotta groups, like the *Cupid and Psyche*, which are in the

100

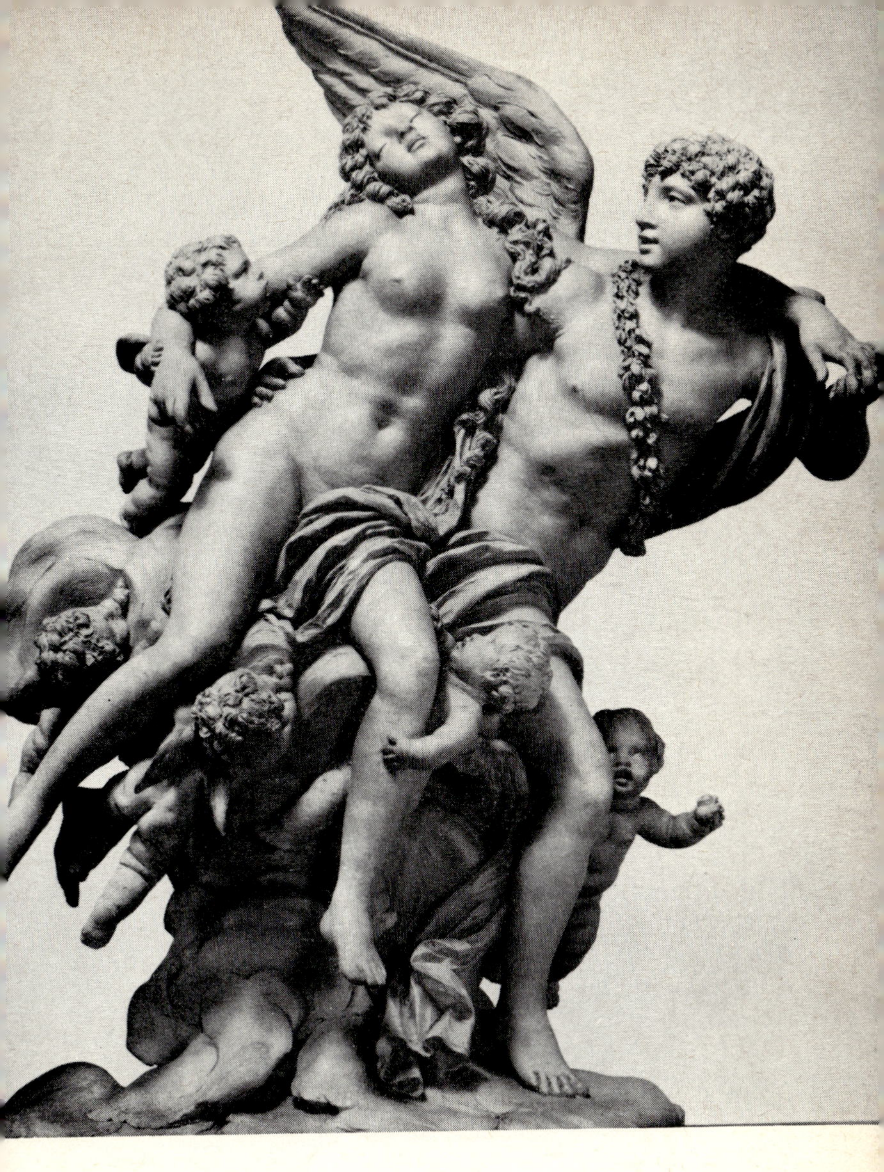

Claude Michel called **Clodion** *Cupid and Psyche* late 18th century
Victoria and Albert Museum, London

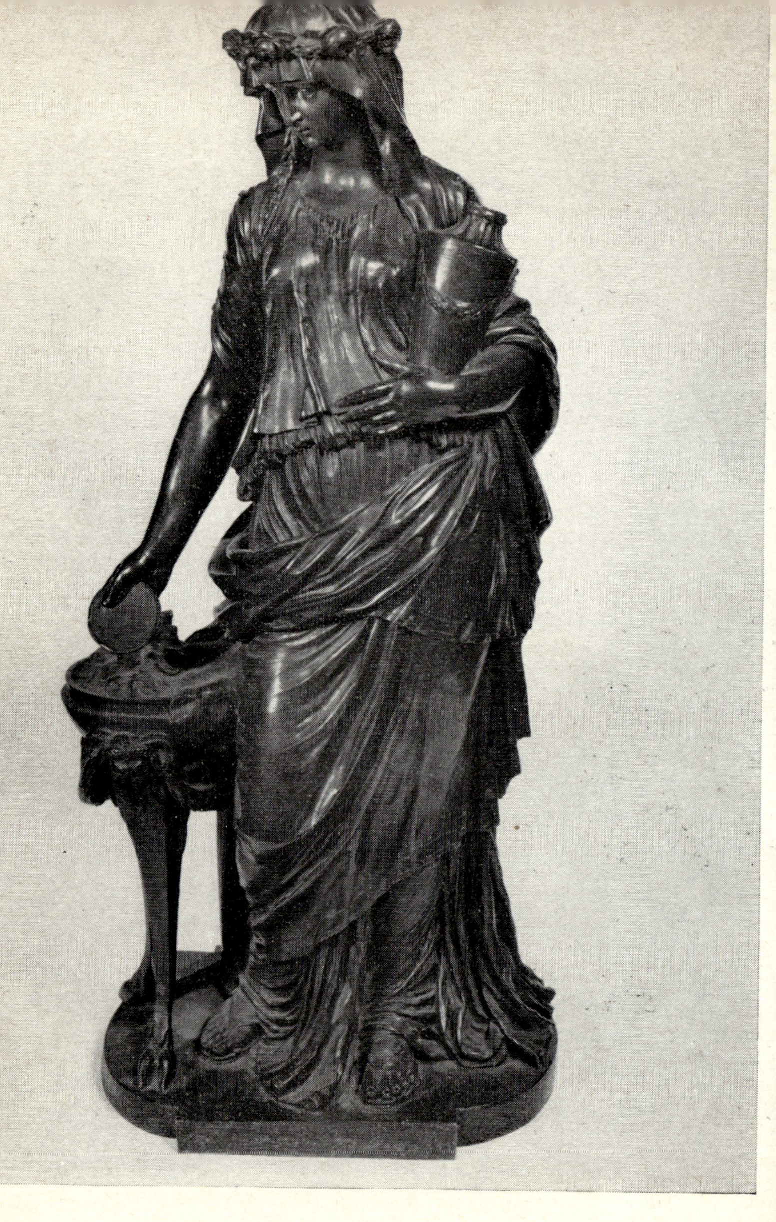

Claude Michel called **Clodion** *Vestal* late 18th century
Heim Gallery, London

purest rococo taste, but in his later years he was obliged to come to terms with the Grecian taste, and so adapted his style to incorporate Greek motifs. He was successful enough in this to obtain work on the Arc du Carrousel under Napoleon, but the archaeological pedantry of his *Vestal* is very far removed from the seriousness of Canova.

English sculptors were amongst the earliest to take up Winckelmann's theories in Rome, and it is likely that Canova learned much from their conversation and example. Many of them had been established there in restoring and copying antique marbles for English patrons as a way of supporting themselves. Joseph Nollekens's (1737–1823) copy of the antique *Castor and Pollux* was made for Lord Anson in 1768, and although Nollekens was probably not very interested in Winckelmann's theories, it is an accurate and sensitive copy. His real gift was for portraiture, and on his return to England in 1770 he set up a flourishing practice,

J. Nollekens *Castor and Pollux* 1768
Victoria and Albert Museum, London

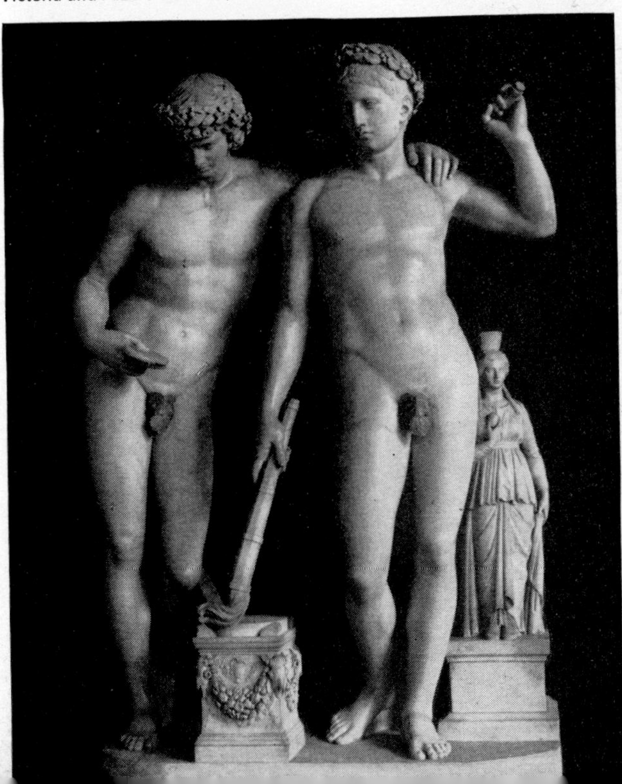

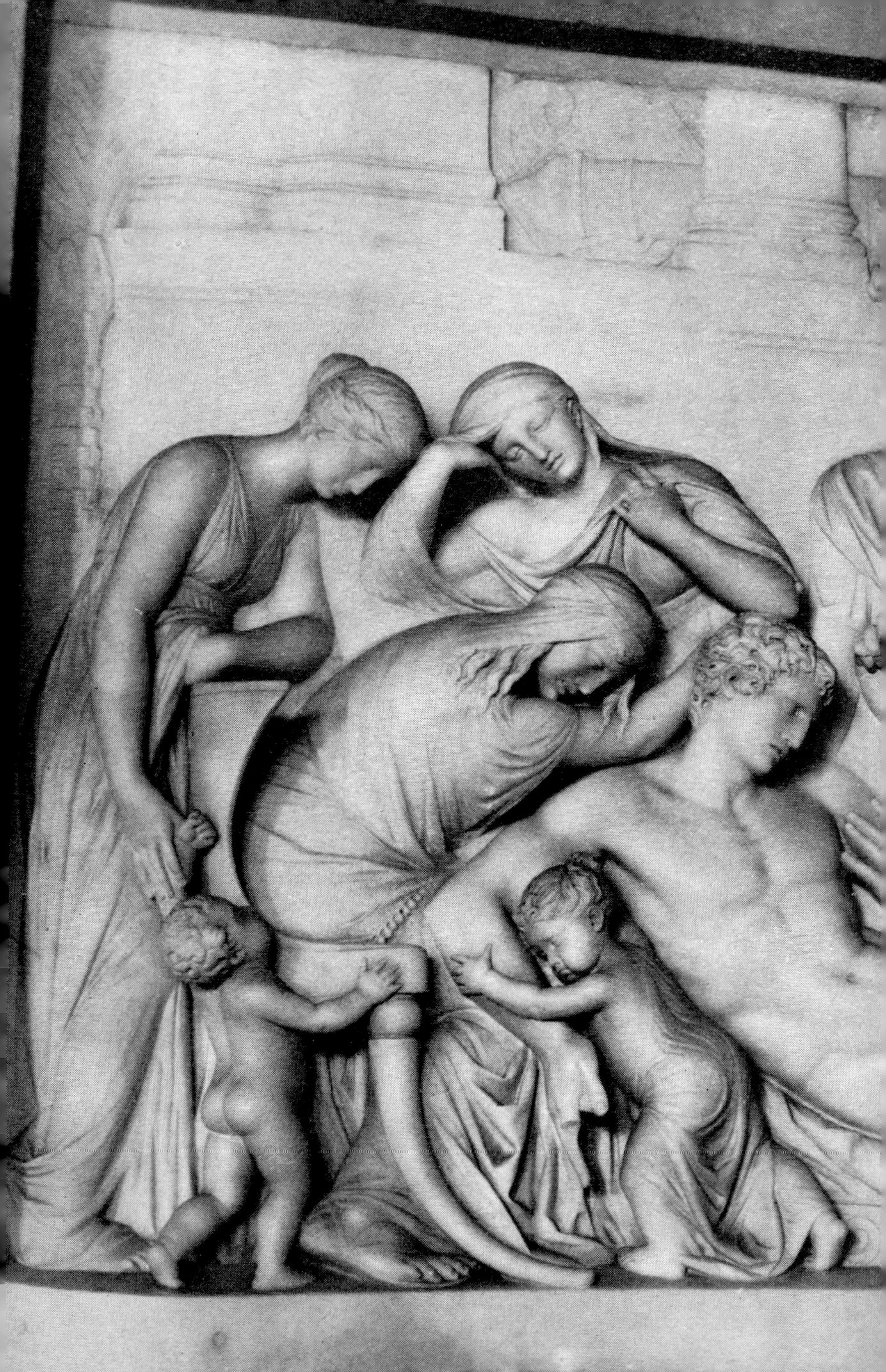

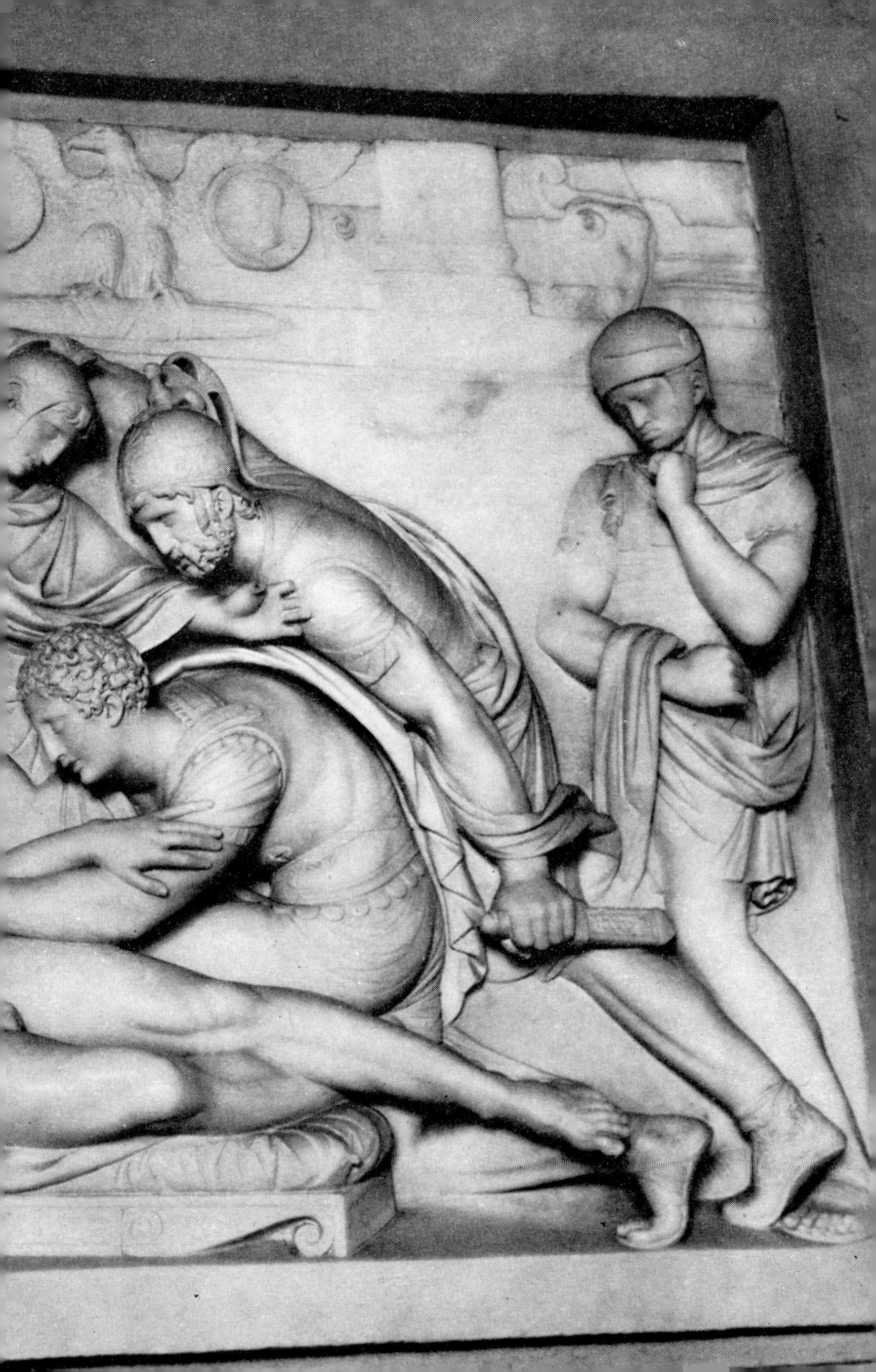

on pages 104 and 105
T. Banks *Death of Germanicus* 1774
Holkham Hall, Norfolk

making also a number of rococo designs for garden sculpture. Like Houdon, his inclinations were towards the baroque, but later in life he produced portraits in a severe Roman manner.

Thomas Banks (1735–1805) was the first English sculptor to imbibe the spirit of Winckelmann, and produce neoclassical works of real conviction. His earliest work in the new manner is the *Death of Germanicus* of 1774, which reveals a debt to the circle of Gavin Hamilton in its stoic theme and the way in which the action of the relief is kept parallel to the front plane, in the manner of a Roman bas-relief. The elongation of the figures and their impassioned gestures betray the influence of his friend the Swiss painter Henry Fuseli, and the combination of clear outline and agitated movement remind one of William Blake. The importance of Banks's work has been overshadowed by the reputation of Flaxman, but his contemporaries had no doubts of his greatness, even though he had little gift for the monumental.

John Flaxman (1755–1826) was equally unimpressive in works on a large scale, but he made more use of mechanical methods of reproduction, and his engraved outline designs for Dante and Homer made him celebrated and influential in Europe. As a young man he was a friend of William Blake at the Royal Academy, where they were both attracted to the literary mediaevalism of the 1770s and '80s, but Flaxman was much less imaginative than Blake. After making designs for the Wedgwood factory in 1787 he paid a belated visit to Rome, where he studied not only antiquities but also early Renaissance sculpture. He was taken up by Canova who obtained for him the important commission for the *Fury of Athemas* (1791–2) from the eccentric Englishman the Earl of Bristol and Bishop of Derry. Flaxman's group is a rather academic reworking of Canova's own idea for *Hercules and Lichas* (completed 1796), but it was greatly admired by his contemporaries. He was occasionally asked to work in this 'correct' style again by rich connoisseurs like Lord Egremont, but on his return to England in 1792 he found, like previous prodigies arriving from Rome, that there were too few collectors of sculpture in England to provide a living and that he would be judged as a carver of monuments. Fortunately for him, and for other

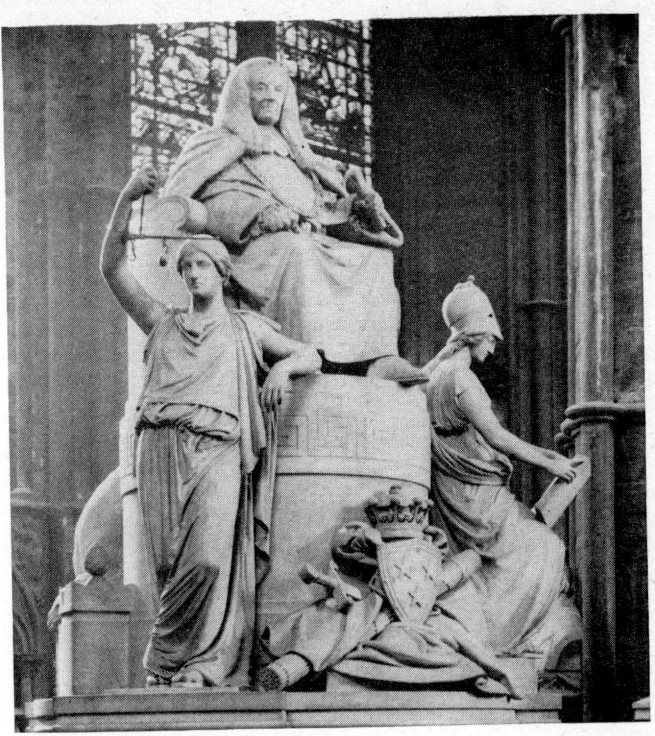

J. Flaxman *Mansfield Monument* 1795
Westminster Abbey, London

sculptors, the French wars had created a boom in the demand for heroic monuments to fallen officers, and his rather vapid classicism was considered to be entirely appropriate to commemorate their patriotic valour.

The Mansfield Monument (1795) shows fairly clearly the strengths and weaknesses of Flaxman as a maker of monumental sculpture. The structure of the monument, which is free-standing,

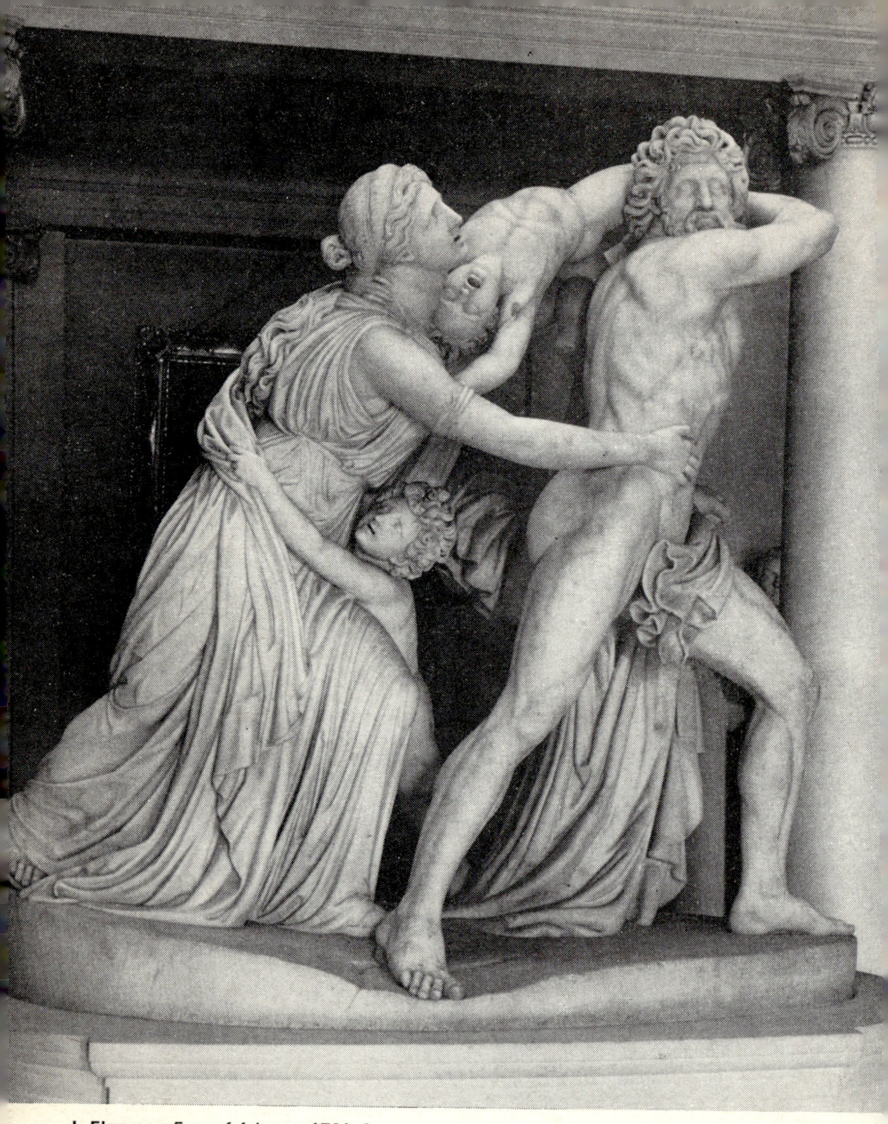

J. Flaxman *Fury of Athemas* 1791–2
Ickworth, Suffolk

A. Canova *Hercules and Lichas* 1796
Galleria d'Arte Moderna, Rome

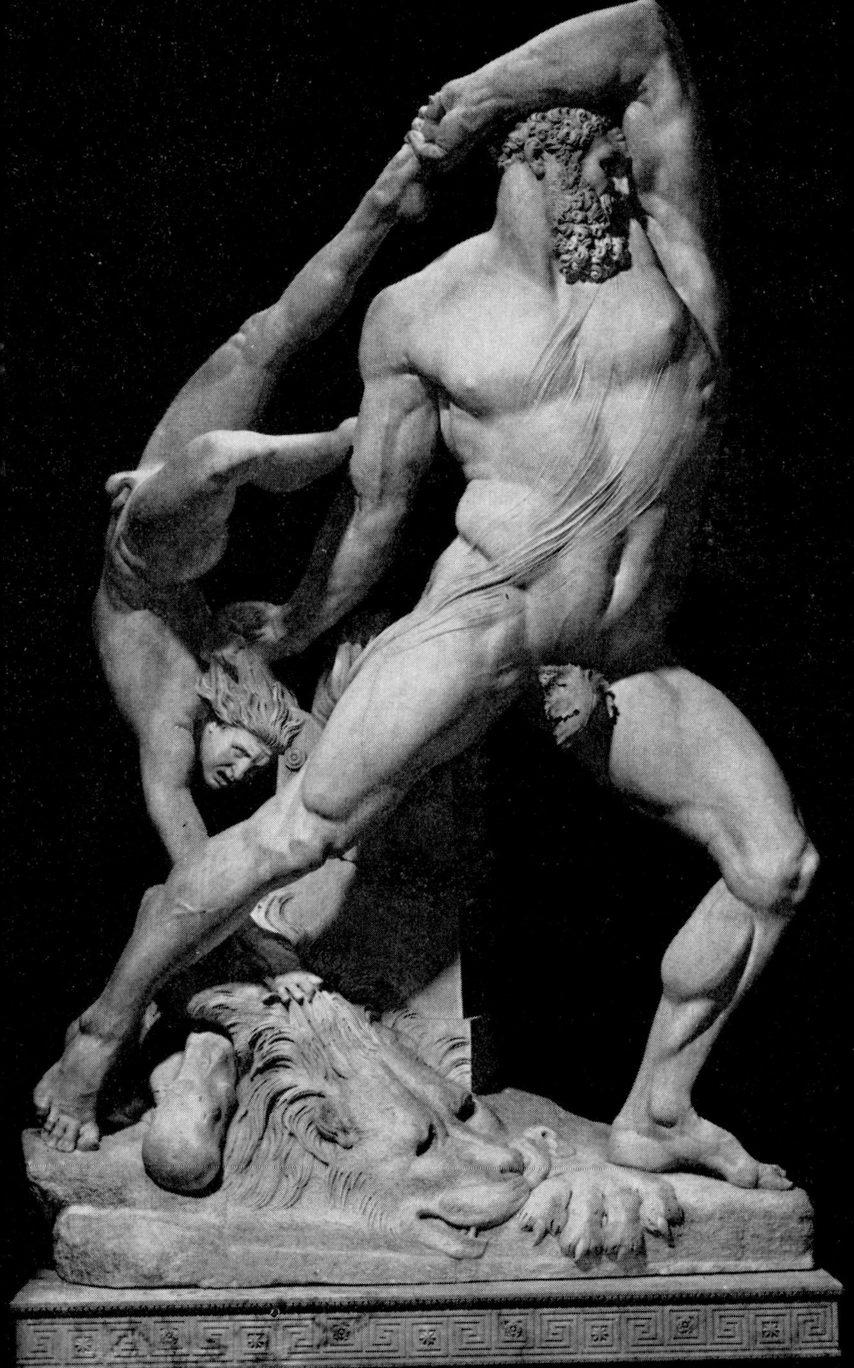

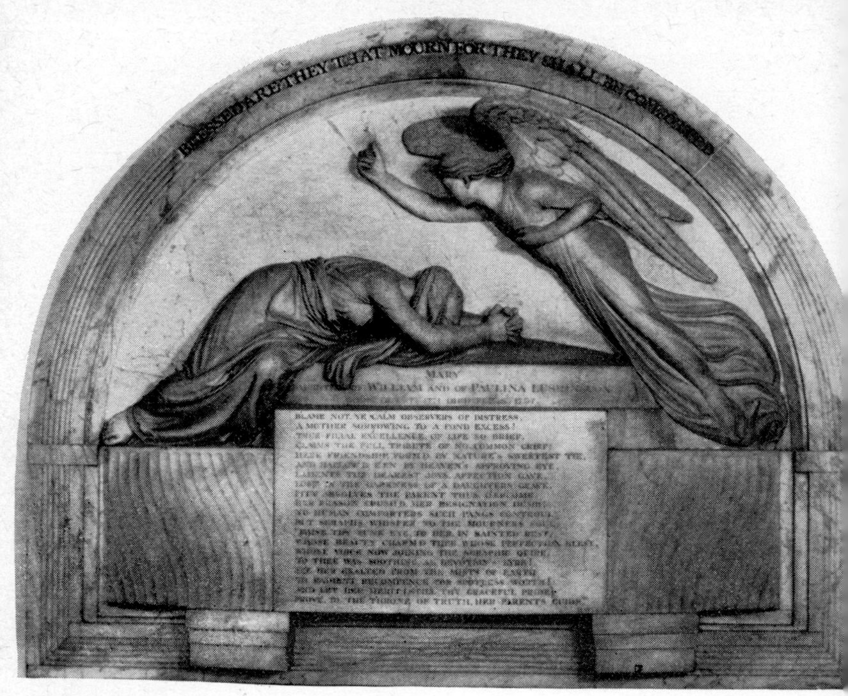

J. Flaxman *Mary Lushington Monument* 1799
Lewisham St Mary's

with the Earl of Mansfield supported by Justice and Wisdom, is derived from Bernini's papal tombs (see pages 41, 43), but the naturalistic rendering of Mansfield contrasts unhappily with the insipid allegorical figures.

Flaxman's real gift was for outline and so it is not surprising that he was very successful at the monumental relief, and in the Lushington Monument he was able to employ a gentle poetic

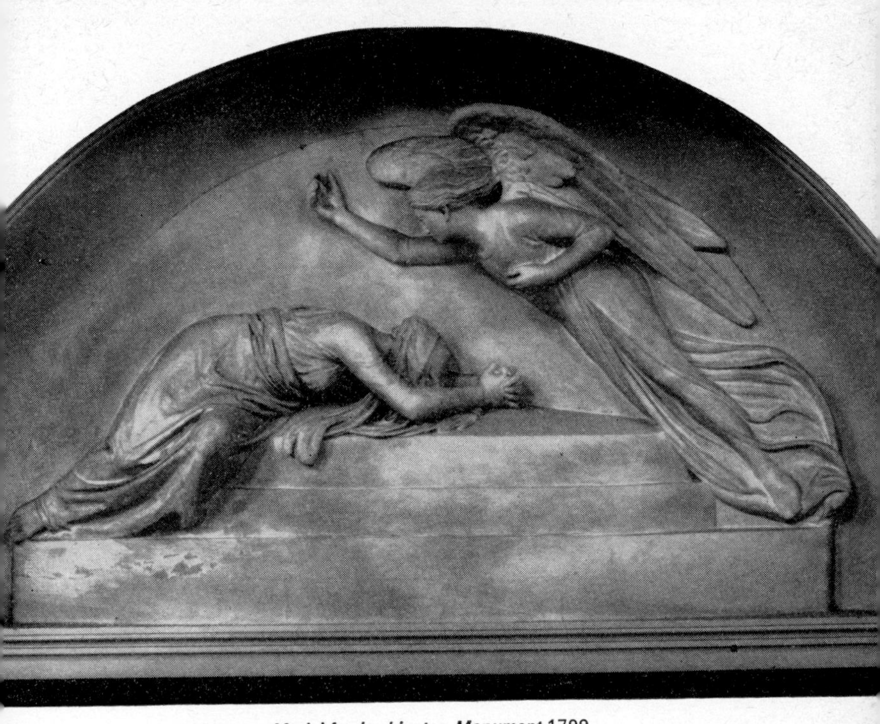

J. **Flaxman** Model for *Lushington Monument* 1799
University College, London

piety derived from his study of trecento Italian sculpture and the
ethereal simplicity of the angel, particularly in the sketch model,
recalls the work of Blake. Flaxman's simple piety and his interest
in children often led him into a mawkishness that provided a
disastrous example for his successors, but his preliminary sketches,
which are now largely preserved in University College, London,
show an inventive mind and a wide range of influences.

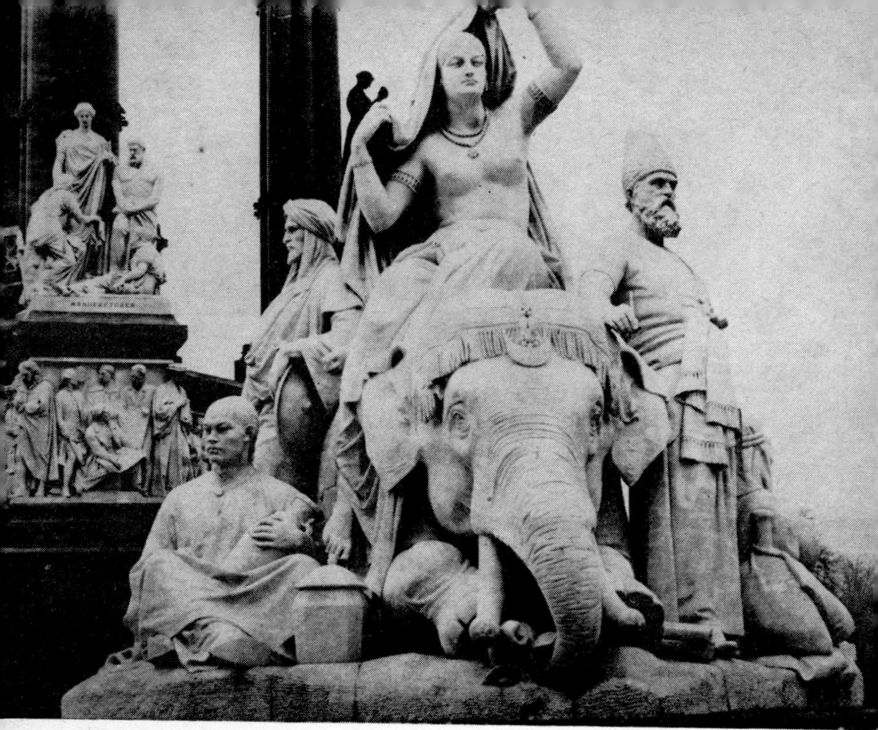

Albert Memorial 1864–76
Kensington Gardens, London

Flaxman is in many senses a transitional figure, and in his work we can see the beginning of a specifically nineteenth-century approach to sculpture. Neoclassicism had opened the way towards an appreciation of other 'primitive' periods apart from the Grecian, in particular the Gothic period. This led to the use of the history of art as a kind of dictionary, that could be plundered for styles and motifs, and to the idea that a style from the past could be arbitrarily applied to a particular task. Flaxman heralded this development, in one case offering a client a choice of either a classical or a gothic design for a monumental tomb; and in general his attempt to reconcile a 'stripped neoclassical' style with a 'gothic' piety foreshadowed the loss of stylistic autonomy that was to prove

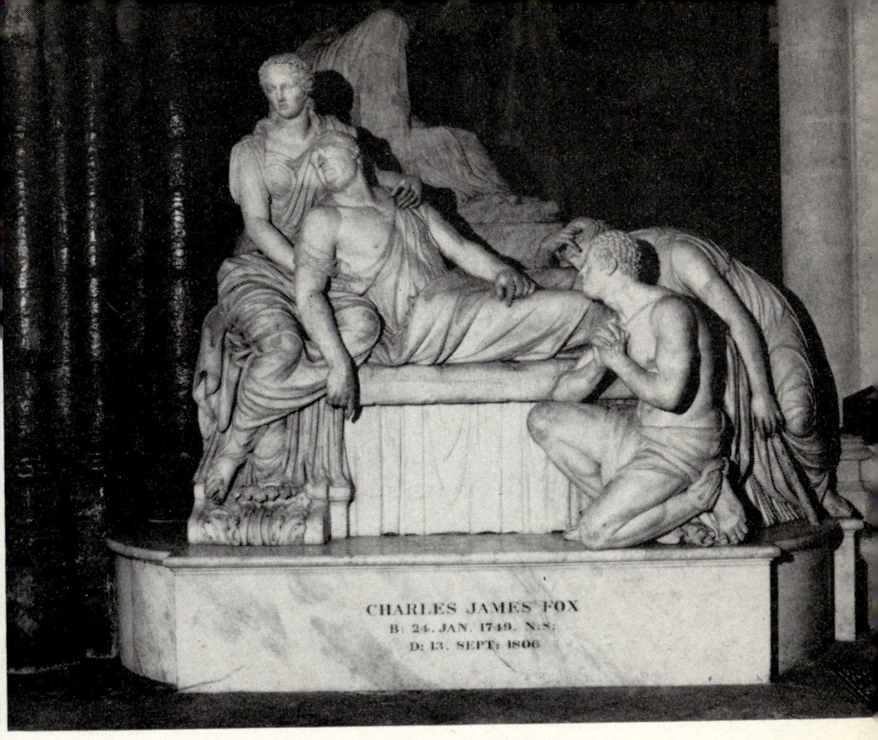

R. Westmacott *C. J. Fox Monument* 1810–23
Westminster Abbey, London

so dangerous in the nineteenth century. Equally his production of numbers of largely identical monuments for different patrons led to a carelessness about the final finish of the work that was to prove only too tempting to his followers, whose aridity reached an apotheosis in the Albert Memorial.

Flaxman's chief rival, Sir Richard Westmacott (1775–1856), was a pupil of Canova, and on rare occasions was able to equal the grandeur of his master. The monument to Charles James Fox (1810–23) is the best English monumental group of the period, and Canova thought that the figure of the Negro was as fine as anything produced in its time. But he was also a victim of mass-production, and the temptations of a style that renounced surface

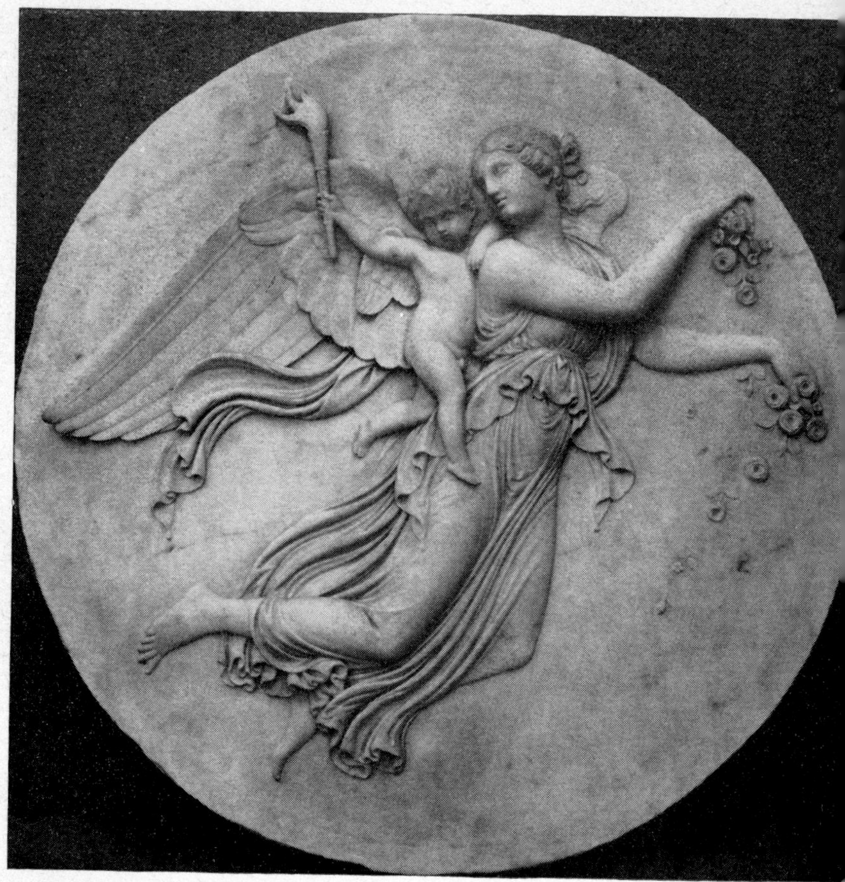

B. Thorwaldsen *Day c.* 1815
Victoria and Albert Museum, London

texture in favour of a smoothness that could be convincingly achieved by untalented assistants.

The successor to Canova's European reputation was the Danish sculptor Bertel Thorwaldsen (1770–1844), who approached the

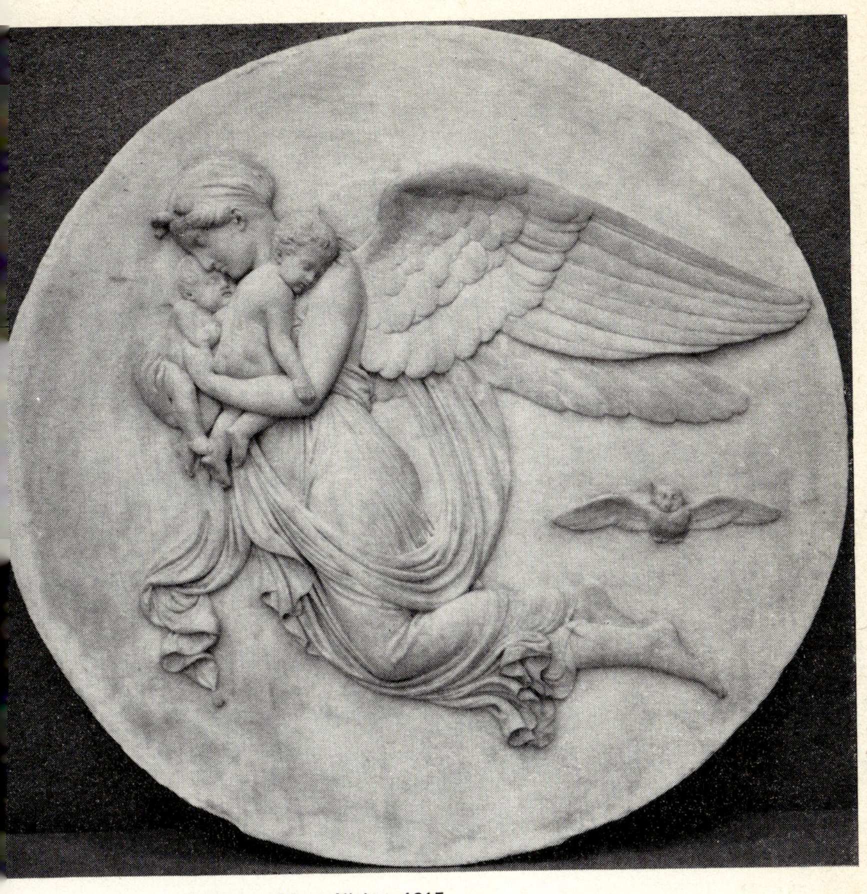

B. Thorwaldsen *Night c.* 1815
Victoria and Albert Museum, London

antique with a comparable high-mindedness but with less originality, and like Flaxman he attempted in later years to adapt his style to the demands of religious imagery.

The nineteenth century

The nineteenth century was an age of perpetual crisis in which a growing conflict of interest between the best artists and the public led to a sense of deep frustration on both sides. Never before had sculptors to endure such hostility or have their talents deployed so insensitively. This was largely the consequence of the growing alienation of the artist from society that was both a cause and consequence of the romantic movement, but sculptors were more vulnerable than other artists. One reason for this is obvious; the materials for sculpture cost more. No sculptor could erect a large monument without a commission, and they were there more than ever at the mercy of public opinion in the form of town councils and committees, who, by and large, had little patience with artistic subtleties. While painters could often find a small group of sympathetic patrons to keep them going, sculptors were obliged to come to terms with public taste, with the consequence that many of them were forced to work in two different styles: an academic style for public commissions and a freer, more spontaneous expression in their studios.

According to Reynolds sculpture could only aspire to the most elevated category of art, the art of idealization, because the imitation of the transitory effects of nature violated the essential character of marble and bronze. Sculptors were, therefore, denied the opportunity to work on the problems of the depiction of vision and nature that were so fruitful to romantic painters, and were obliged to confront the problem of public allegory, which had been made even more complicated by the French Revolution. The Enlightenment had already called into question the use by sculptors of personifications that show men as divine beings, and after the French Revolution Christian symbols were discredited as 'vestiges of feudalism and superstition'. Only appeals to patriotism, liberty and posterity were acceptable in allegorical terms; a helmeted or laurel-leafed Minerva figure may be La France, Liberty or even Fame; and in England, either Britannia or Victory. The change can be seen in the fate of the pediment of the Pantheon in Paris. As the Church of La Madeleine the pediment was adorned by a baroque frieze of *Angels Carrying a Cross* by Coustou, but after its secularization following the Revolution it was replaced by a patriotic subject carved by Moitte in 1791.

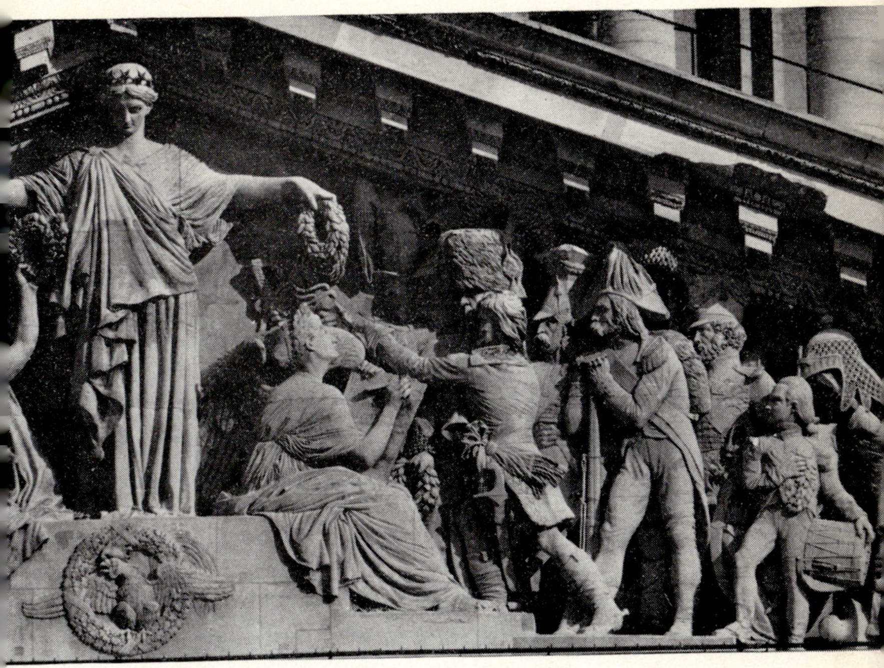

David d'Angers *Pediment of the Pantheon* 1830
Paris

Finally, this was replaced in 1830 by the frieze by David d'Angers
of *La Patrie distribuant des Couronnes au Génie*.

The power of the jury of the Salon, whom the sculptor Préault
called 'les reptiles de l'Institut', was a dominant factor in the
situation throughout the nineteenth century in France. Despite
changes in régime the jury remained unwavering in its academic
taste, but rather than imposing on the Salon a classical severity
it encouraged a harmless timidity of approach that was calculated
to appeal to the 'juste-milieu'. The most successful practitioner
of the Salon style in the first half of the century was James
Pradier (1790–1852), whose style manages to be rococo, classical
and *réaliste* simultaneously to the point of total stylelessness. His
success was to Baudelaire indicative of the feebleness of contemporary sculpture. 'An excellent proof of the pitiable state of

sculpture today is the fact that M. Pradier is its king. His talent
is cold and academic. He has spent his life fattening up a small
stock of antique torsos and equipping them with the coiffures of
kept women.'

Baudelaire was bitter about the way the art of sculpture had
been debased by mass-production for trivial purposes. 'They are
as learned as academicians—or as vaudevillistes; they make free
with all periods and all genres; they have plumbed the depth of
all the schools. They would be happy to convert even the tombs
of St Denis into cigar- or shawl-boxes, and every Florentine

J. Pradier *Chloris* c. 1830–50
Toulouse Museum

A. Préault *Tuerie* 1834
Chartres Museum

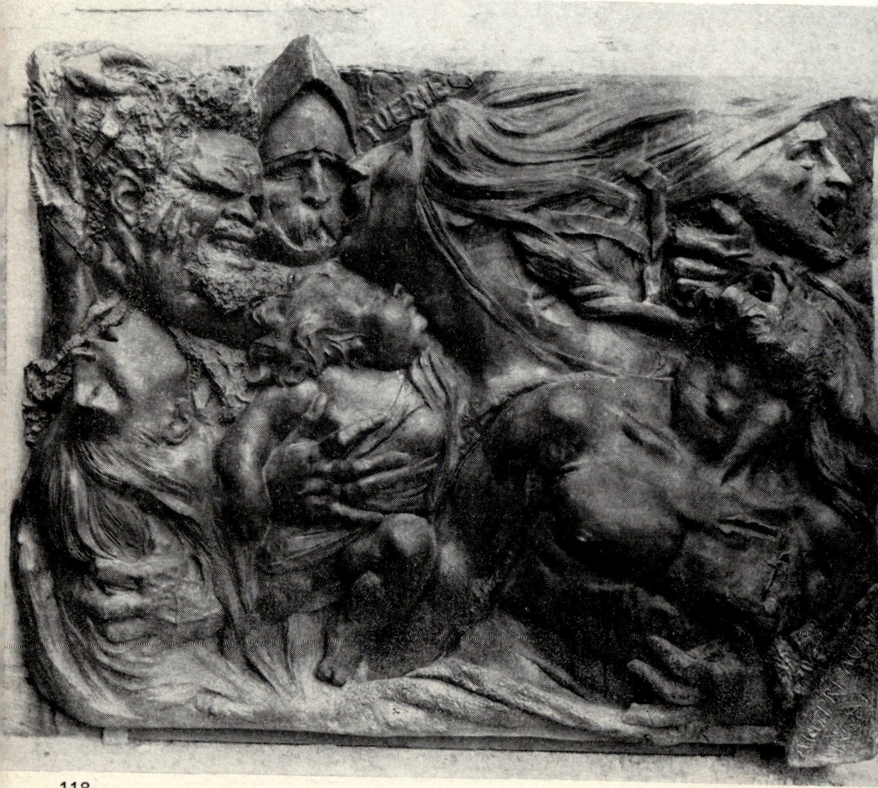

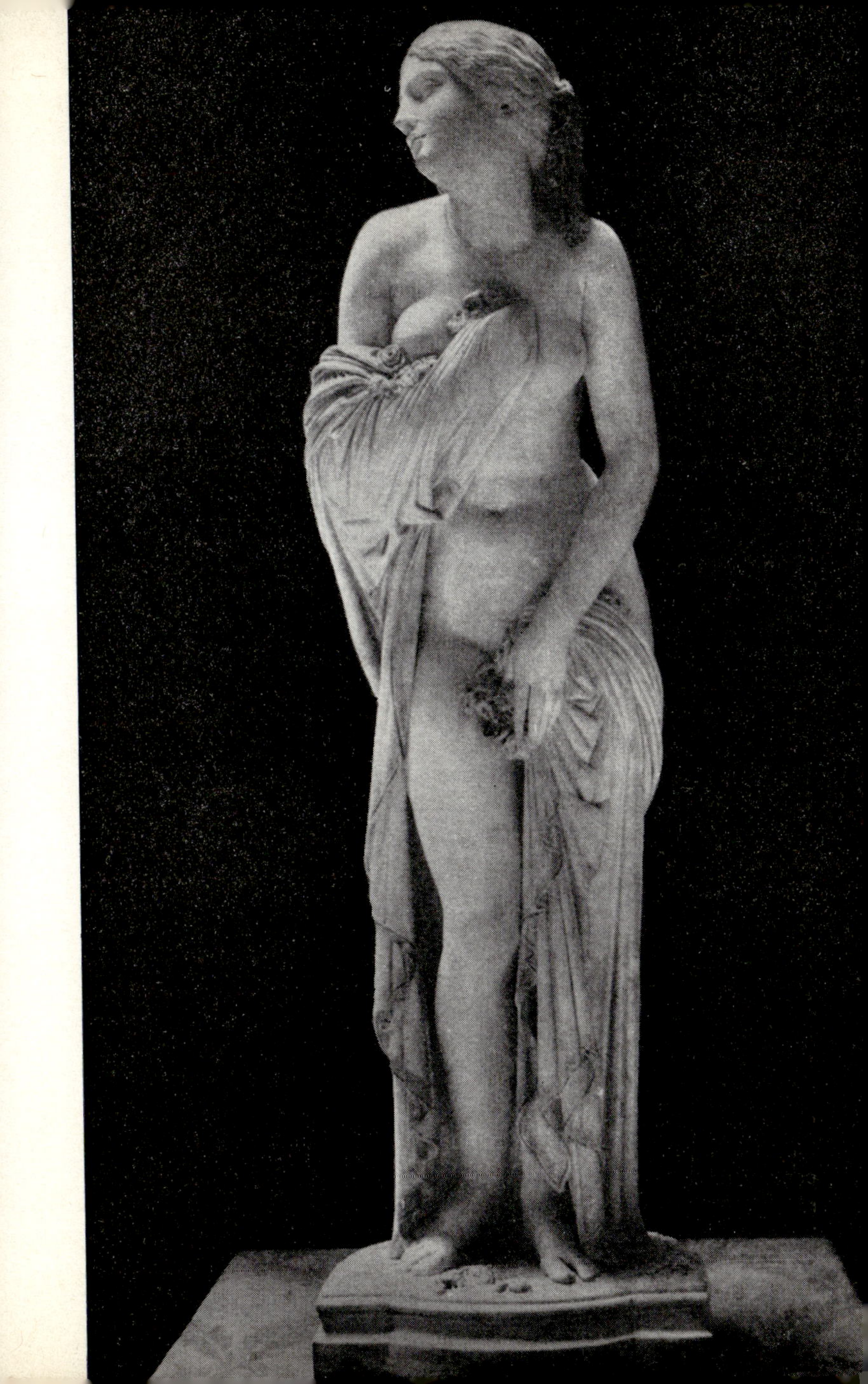

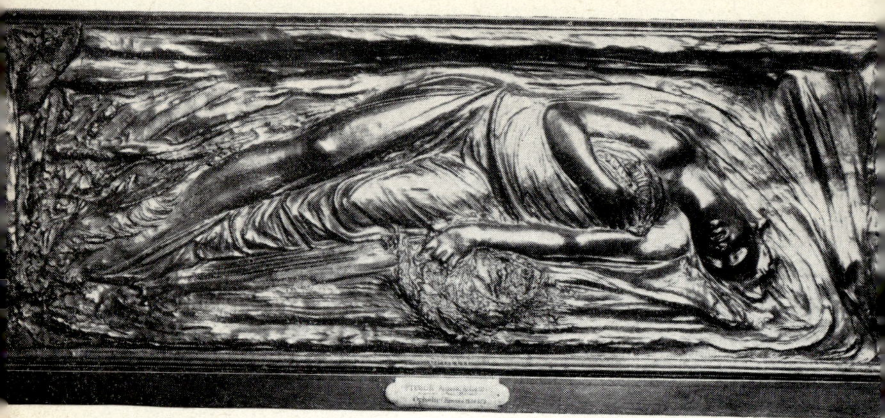

A. Préault *Ophelia* 1843
Marseilles Museum

bronze into a threepenny bit.' Sculptors raided the history of art
for picturesque forms and mawkish effects. The official condemna-
tion of romantic sculptors in the Restoration period in France
meant that only those prepared to work under a double standard
were given major commissions.

Augustin Préault (1810–79) was exceptional in taking an un-
compromisingly romantic view of his work. He emerges from the
occasional references in writings of the time as a complete
bohemian: a man of sharp wit whom Baudelaire recognized as
the only fellow spirit working with a chisel, and as contemptuous
of the 'Caribs' and the 'sculpturizers' as himself. Baudelaire
quotes him as saying, 'I am a connoisseur of Michelangelo, of
Jean Goujon, of Germain Pilon; but of *sculpture* I am a complete
ignoramus.' Writers of the time felt that sculpture was the art
least fitted for the expression of romanticism, for as Madame de
Stael said, 'Elle semble avoir reçu de l'Antiquité sa forme défini-
tive,' but Préault seems to have set out deliberately to challenge
this view by attempting the expression of intense personal emotion
within the framework of relief sculpture. *Tuerie* (1834) lacks a
clearly defined subject, and was conceived as a fragment, but
the anguish of the victims finds no parallel in the visual arts of the
century until Rodin's *Burghers of Calais* (see page 151). The
relief of *Ophelia* (1843), is equally astonishing, for if one did not
know that it was originally conceived in 1843 one might well
mistake it for an art nouveau production of the turn of this
120

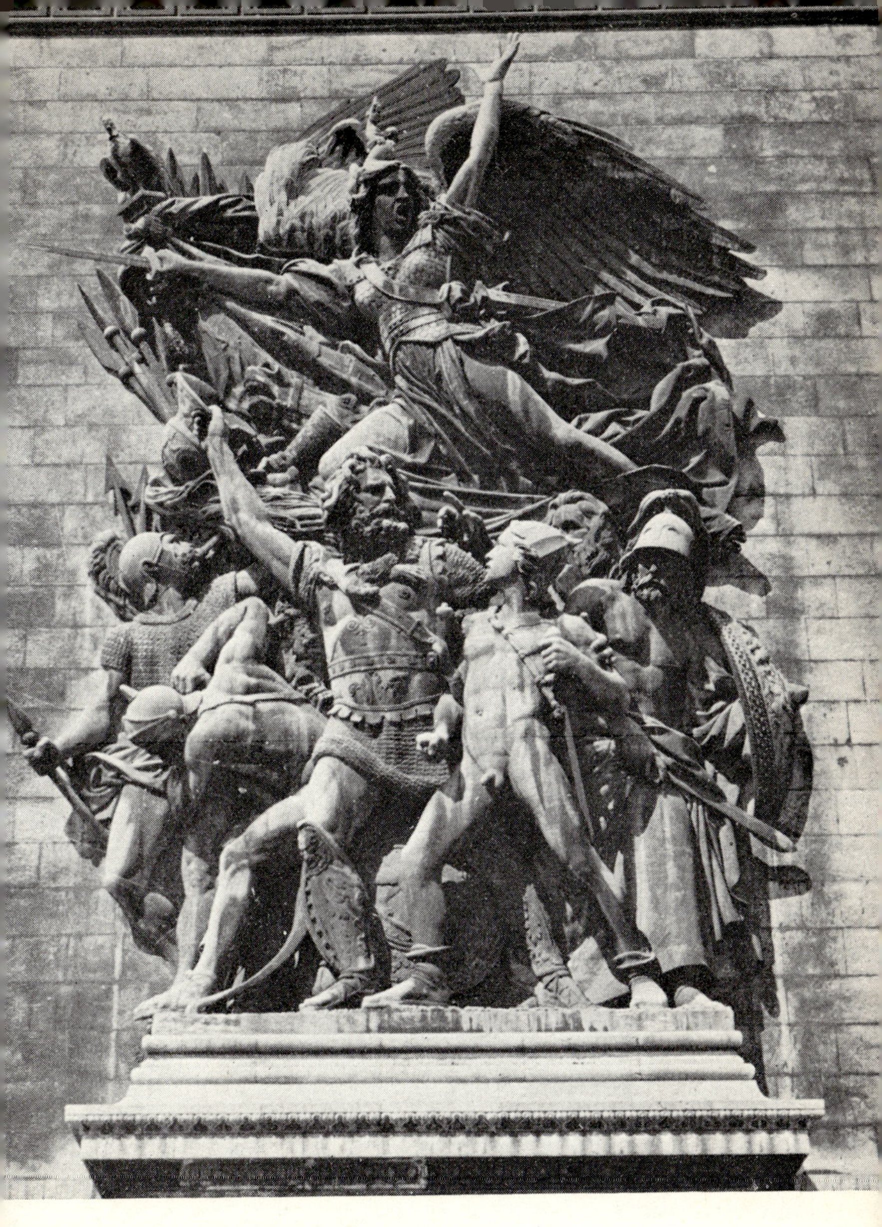

F. Rude *La Marseillaise* 1833–6
Arc de Triomphe, Paris

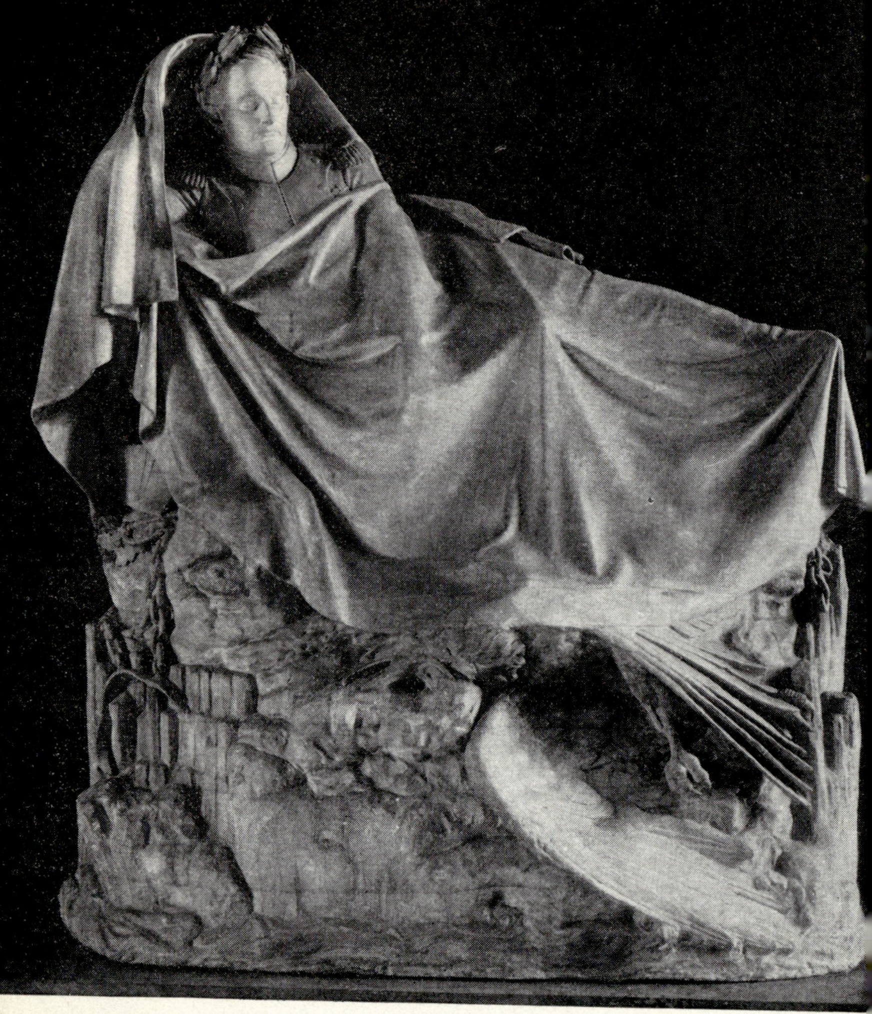

F. Rude *Napoleon Awakening to Immortality* 1845
Louvre, Paris

century. One can find echoes of the sculpture of the French sixteenth-century artist Jean Goujon, but almost nothing of the great classical tradition that nourished his contemporaries.

Préault was born in 1810, and studied in the studio of David d'Angers. He made his Salon début in 1833 with a bas-relief of the *Death of the Poet Gilbert*, from *Stello* by Alfred de Vigny, and *La Misère* which shows a girl dying in her mother's arms, but his

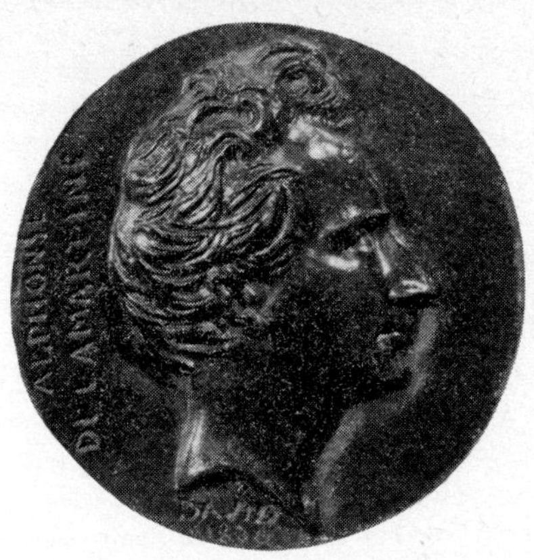

David d'Angers *Lamartine* early 19th century
Heim Gallery, London

works were continually refused by the Salon until 1848, although they were much admired by romantic writers.

Although called romantics, other sculptors of the time compromised with traditional modes. François Rude's (1784–1855) *Marseillaise* (1833–6) is an example of the difficulty of isolating the romantic elements in a composition that owes something to a variety of styles. The movement of the figures along a single plane and the sequence of the action are traditional in conception, but the cry and gesture of La Patrie have a theatricality that is startling within the context of a patriotic monument. The figure of La Patrie was too histrionic for contemporary taste, but its unrestrained passion enlivens the academic clarity of the main group. The heroism of the soldiers expresses a nostalgia for the post-Revolutionary period as one of patriotism and civic virtue, while Rude's tomb of *Napoleon Awakening to Immortality* (1845) shows a purer romantic feeling that replaces the classical form with a visionary conception, making the contrast of light and shade important for the sculptural expression.

David d'Angers (1788–1856) was considered in his day to be the essential romantic sculptor but his public performances, like the pediment of the Pantheon, are dull and academic. His work shows more clearly than other artists, the hiatus between private and public work, and he was never able to carry the spontaneity of his terracotta sketches through into his monumental work. He commemorated the great men of Europe in a series of portrait medals which are sharply characterized but monotonous in technique.

123

The romanticism of Antoine-Louis Barye (1796–1875) parallels the paintings of Delacroix which celebrate the strength and power of exotic animals. He is best known as the first of the *animaliers*, who produced bronzes by the thousand through the cheap and coarse sand-casting process, but he himself preferred to work in the more costly and painstaking *cire-perdu* method, for the sake of preserving his original handling of the surface. Unfortunately his craftsman-like fastidiousness was against the trend of the time, which called for ever cheaper reproductions, and the very quality of his work on a small scale led to a great number of casts of indifferent calibre being made from his bronzes without his consent. Barye also made a notable contribution to what may be called historical romanticism. For his official commissions he adopted an archaic Grecian style based on pre-classical marbles, in which a sense of impetuous movement is reconciled with an hieratic use of gesture, as in the example illustrated of *Theseus Fighting the Centaur Bienor*. This interest in 'primitive' forms of art can be

A. L. Barye *Panther and Stag c.* 1850
Heim Gallery, London

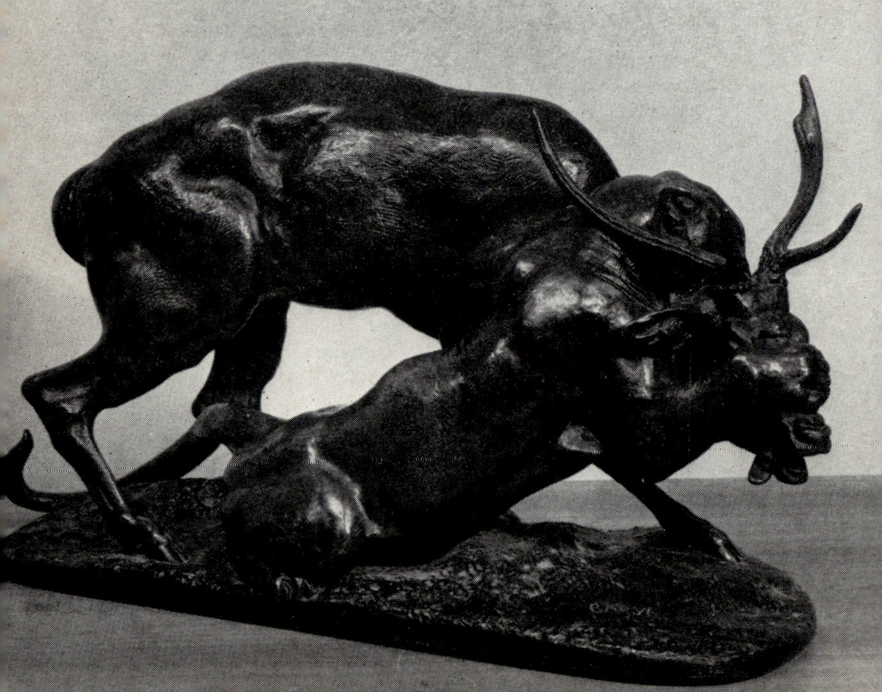

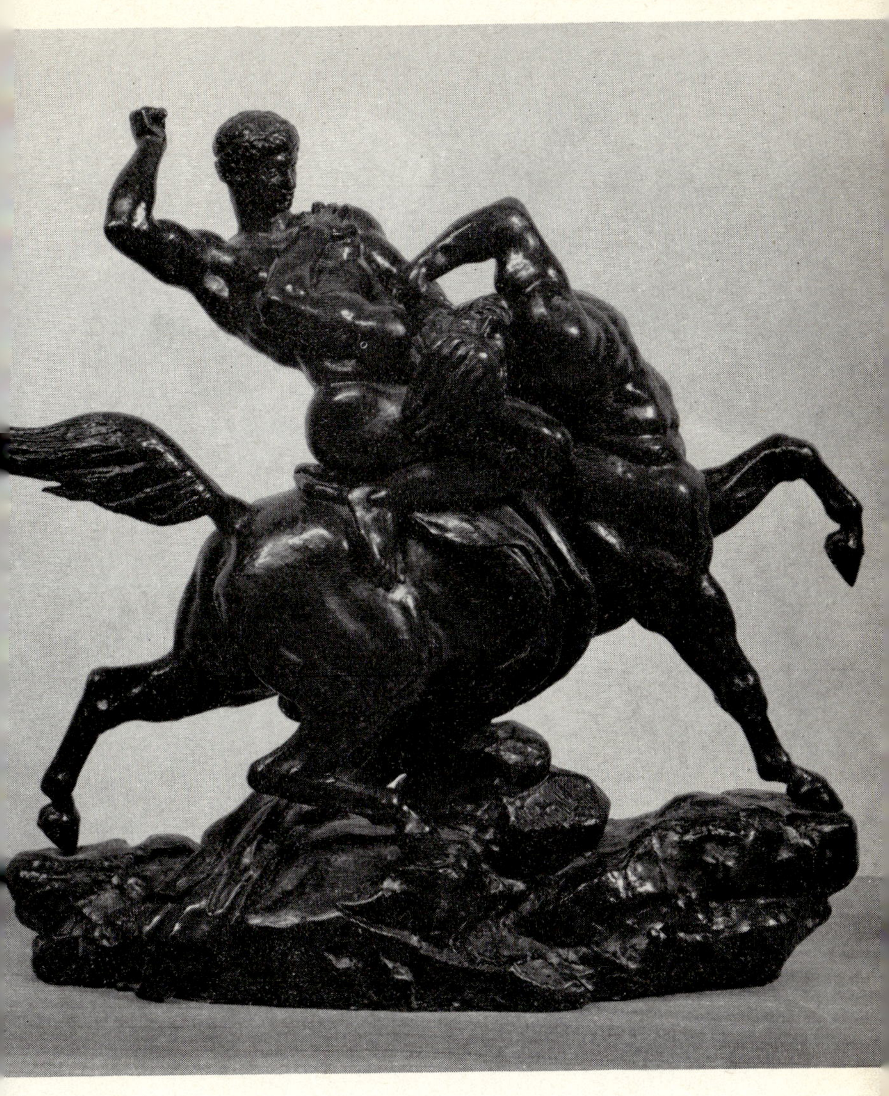

A. L. Barye *Theseus Fighting the Centaur Bienor c.* 1850
Heim Gallery, London

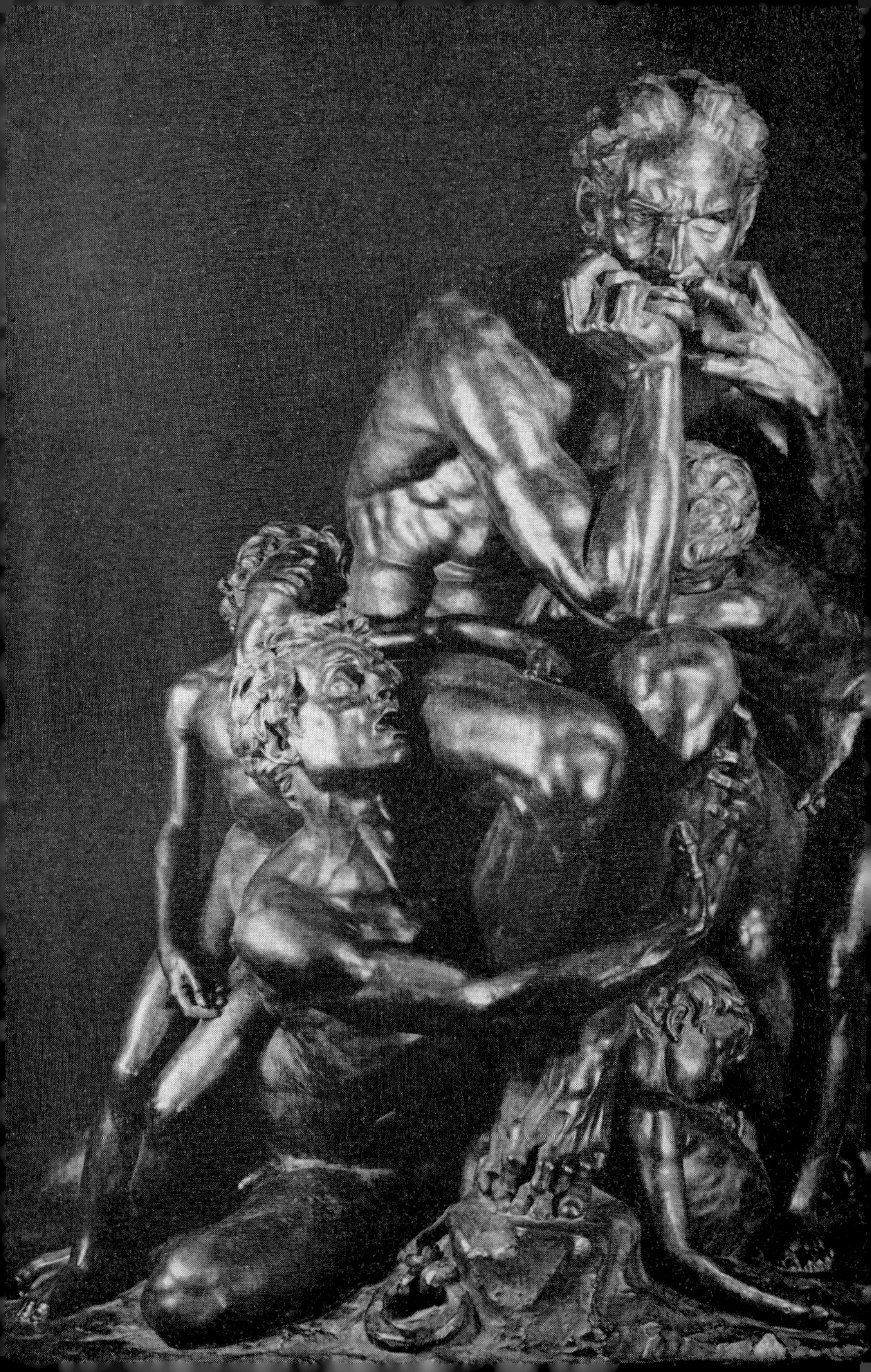

paralleled in the activities of the 'Florentines' led by Felicie de St Fauveau (1799–1886), who based her style on the Florentine trecento, and whose principal work is an elaborate monument to Dante. The activity of these artists, who sought to replace the traditional models by works of periods that had recently returned to favour, led Quatremère de Quincy to remark that 'Florence and Athens were places of perdition'.

Romantic sculptors had explored a variety of alternatives to academic orthodoxy, but in the first half of the nineteenth century the baroque remained unacceptable, being regarded still as a facile and meretricious style. In the second half of the century with the Second Empire, there was a growing nostalgia for the light-heartedness of the eighteenth-century court style and the work of Jean-Baptiste Carpeaux (1827–75) was to find favour despite the continuing intransigence of the Salon. In Carpeaux's sculpture a freshness of response and handling came together with a bacchanalian feeling that had its closest precedents in seventeenth-century painting. Carpeaux began as a pupil of Rude and in 1853 he went to Rome where he remained for a number of years. He completed there a group of *Ugolino and his Children* in 1860 that was highly praised in Rome but coldly received by the Institut in Paris. It is the most complete expression of nineteenth-century eclecticism. The subject, which is taken from Dante, was popular with English romantic painters of the late eighteenth century but was considered as too harrowing by later artists. Carpeaux's treatment of the subject is naturalistic, but the composition and surface handling reveal a wide range of influences. The composition immediately reminds one of the *Laocöon*, but the powerful sense of inner anguish recalls the tradition of Michelangelo and Puget and looks forward to Rodin. It is unashamedly academic in the sense that it shows great learning and impeccable technique, but its high seriousness was not attempted again by Carpeaux.

J. B. Carpeaux *Ugolino and his Children* 1860
Louvre, Paris

After his return to Paris his work no longer sought the sublime but explored the possibilities of light and shade and rhythmical movement that culminates in his masterpiece, *La Danse* of 1868–9, for the façade of the Opéra. Carpeaux was able to sidestep the disapproval of the academics because of the favour of Napoleon III and his family, but this did not protect him from abuse and *La Danse* became a *cause célèbre* in its public position. To Rodin and his fellow students at the time its freshness of approach was a revelation, but its detractors saw it as an attempt to create a monument to eroticism. It brought the freedom of handling that had formerly been associated with the small terracottas of Clodion and Marin into a public work, and it repudiated the patriotic and civic content of Rude's *Marseillaise* (see page 121). It stands as a work of art in its own right and its quality lies in the exultant movement of the figures and the complexity of the spatial relations, while the sense of transient movement had scarcely been attempted since the baroque. Like the baroque it laid itself open to the charge of frivolity, and even Rodin, who had learnt a great deal from Carpeaux, felt that Rude's *Marseillaise* was the more profound work.

J. B. Carpeaux *La Danse* 1868–9
Terracotta version of marble on the Opéra, Paris
Louvre, Paris

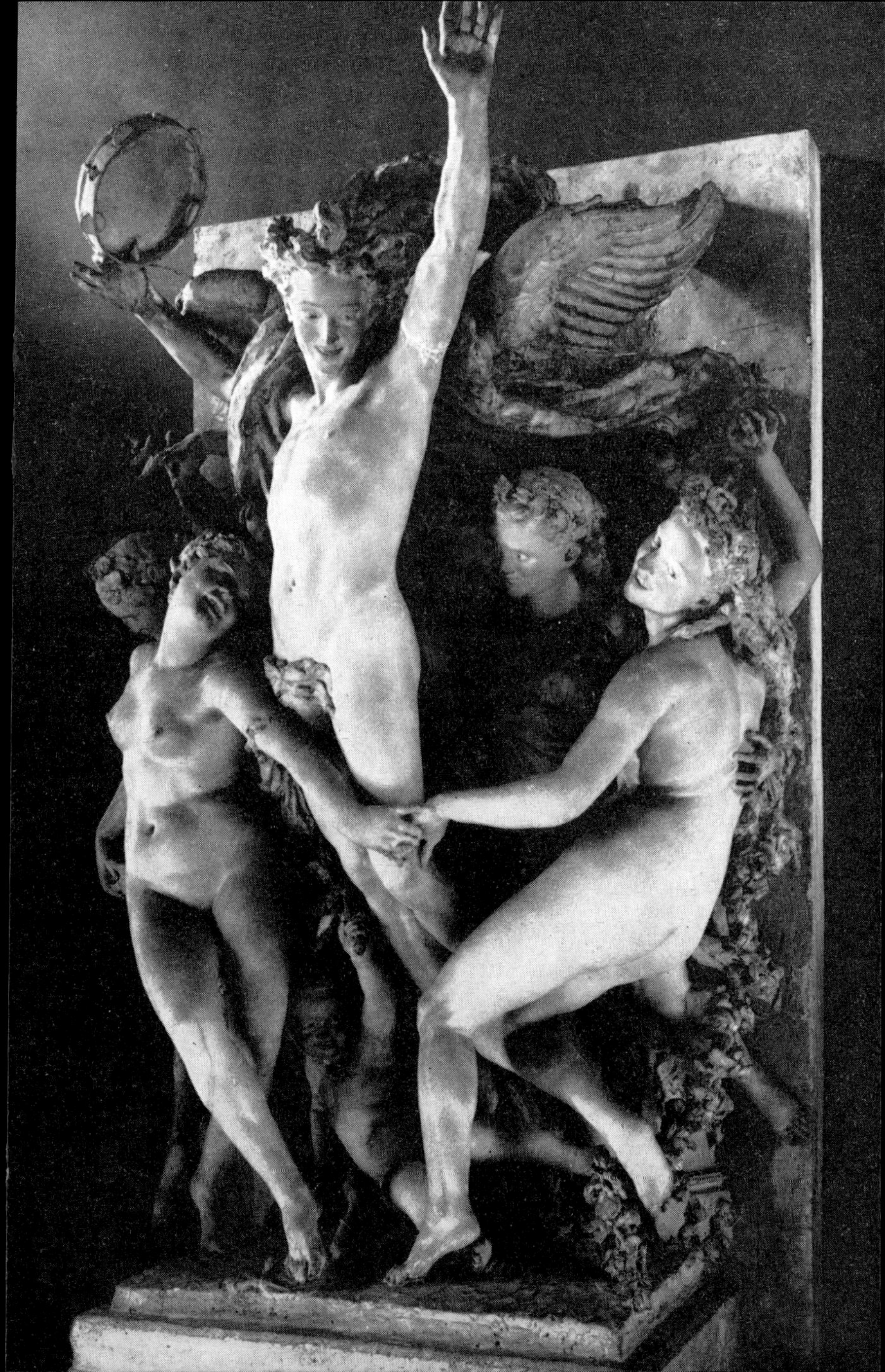

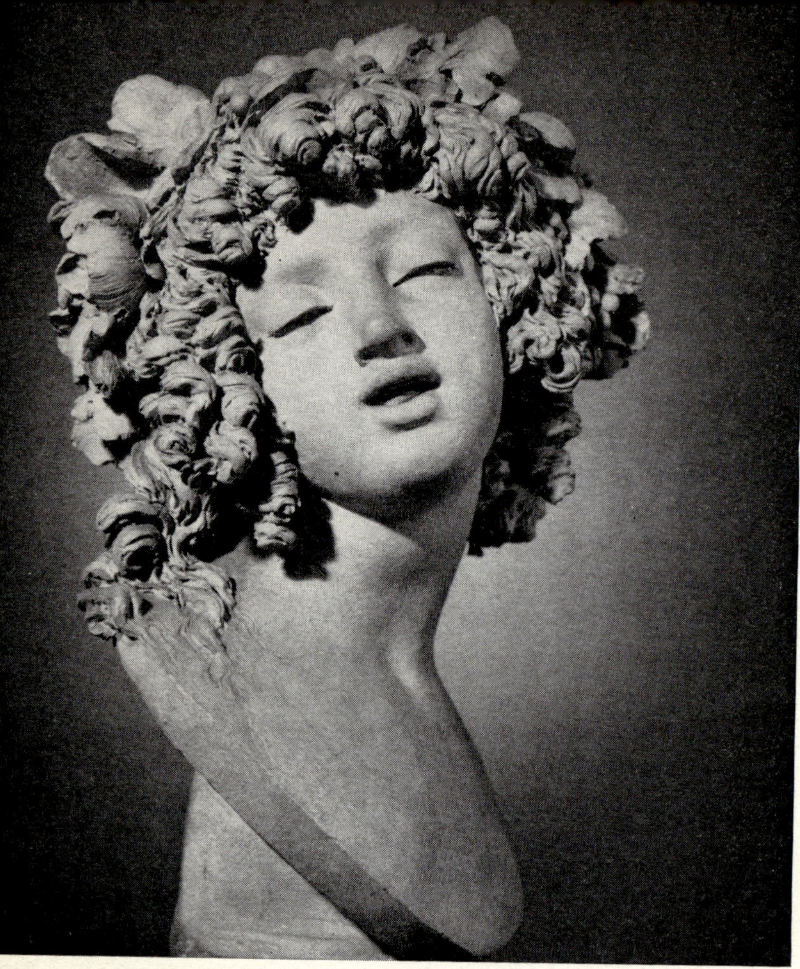

J. C. Marin *Bacchante* late 18th or early 19th century
Victoria and Albert Museum, London

His more intimate studies and sketches show a greater exploration of the broken surface and silhouette. In the portrait of Dr Flaubert, the freedom of the modelling creates a sense of animation that reminds one of Bernini's portrait of Scipione Borghese (see page 17). While academic sculptors of the time

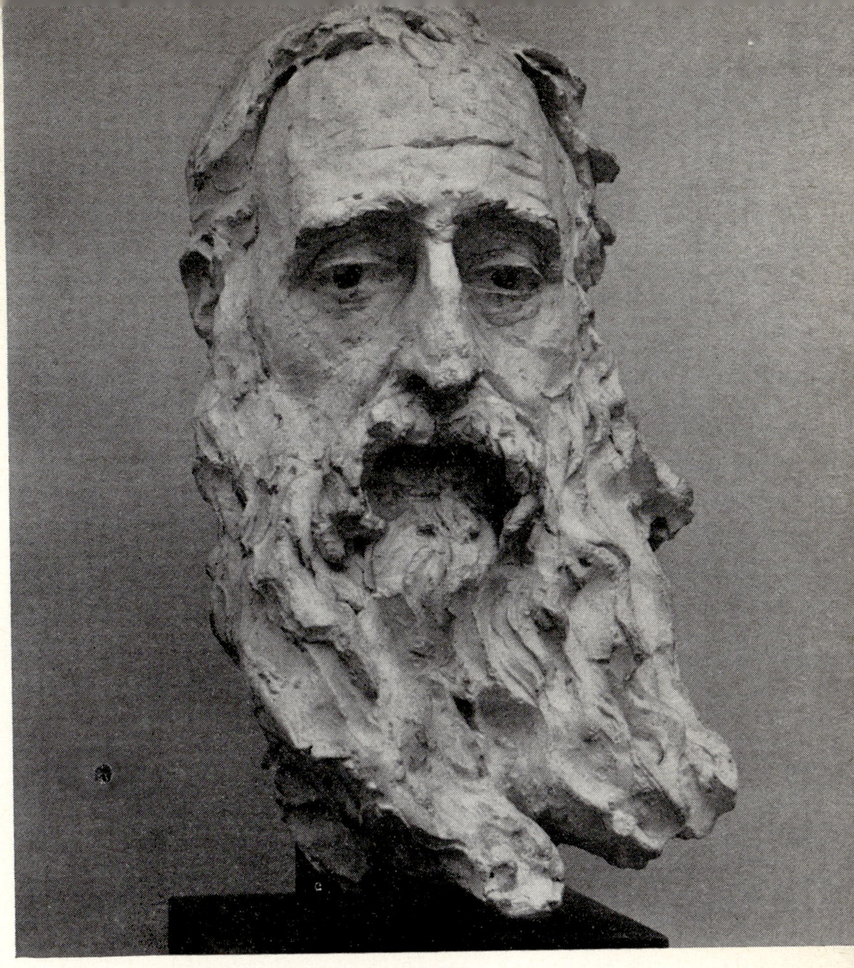

J. B. Carpeaux *Dr Flaubert* 1860–75
Valenciennes Museum

still used a polished surface, Carpeaux liberated the expressive possibilities of the surface almost to the point of abstraction, but not at the expense of three-dimensional structure. This deliberate lack of finish, a revolutionary development in sculpture, led to the gradual breaking down of the barrier between sketch and finished work.

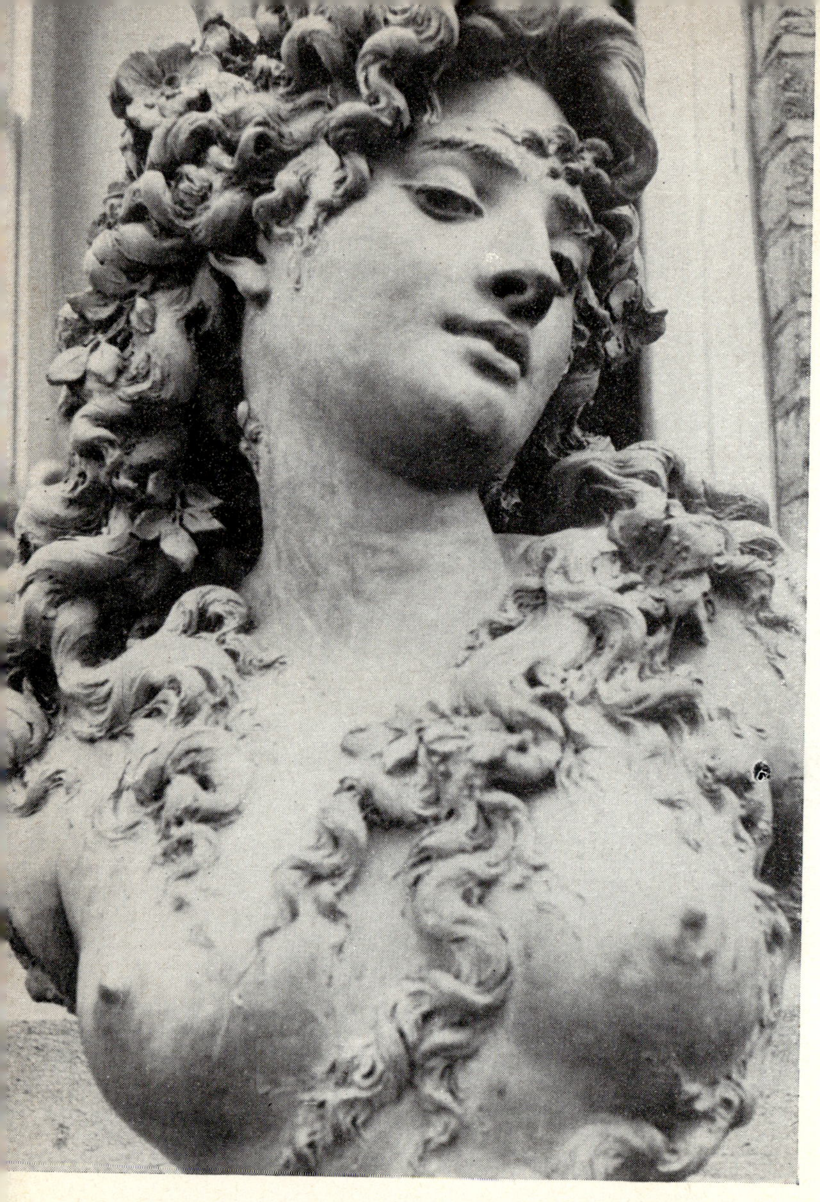

E. **Carrier-Belleuse** *Bacchante* 1860–70
Private Collection

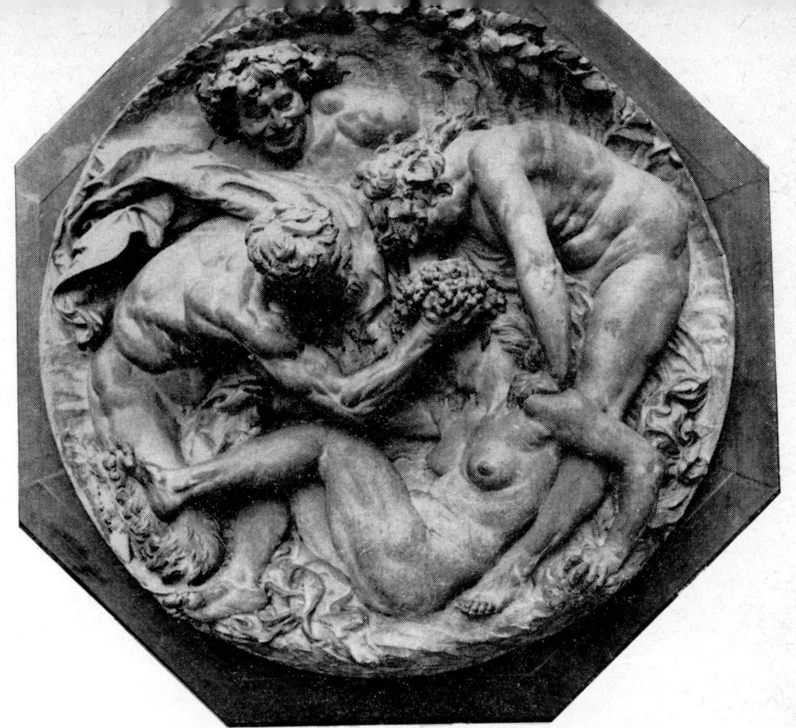

J. **Dalou** *Bacchanale* 1860–70
Victoria and Albert Museum, London

Carpeaux's sensuality was adapted to the demands of decorative sculptors of the 1860s by Ernest Carrier-Belleuse (1824–87) who had the largest workshop devoted to the production of bronze busts and ornaments. He was described by Edmond Goncourt as the Clodion of his time, and his work undoubtedly owes a lot to small terracottas of that master, but he worked on a much larger scale and his handling has something of the freedom of Carpeaux, particularly in the hair of the *Bacchante* illustrated. His real importance, however, lies in the fact that Rodin was employed by him in his workshop, and gained great facility by turning out a large number of terracotta models for his master.

Jules Dalou (1838–1902) also came under the influence of Carpeaux (he was called 'un Carpeaux gras'), but his best work is more contemplative and serious. Dalou lacked Carpeaux's breadth of vision and command of grouping, but his realism was more

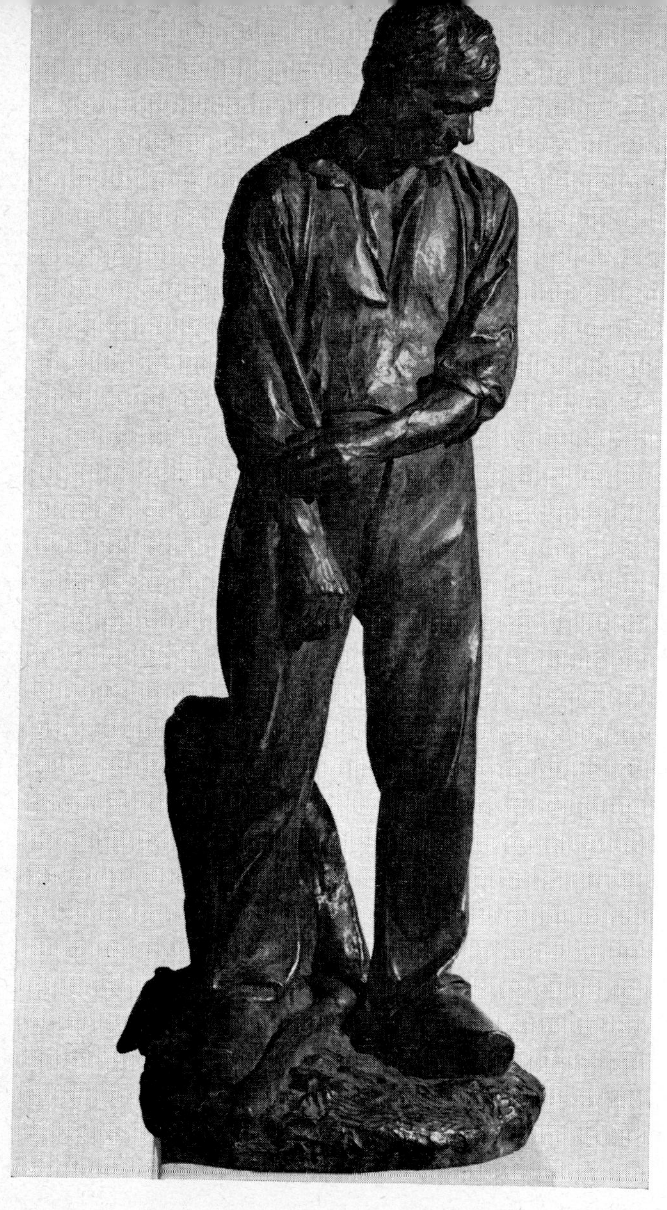

J. **Dalou** *Le Travail* 1880–95
Tate Gallery, London

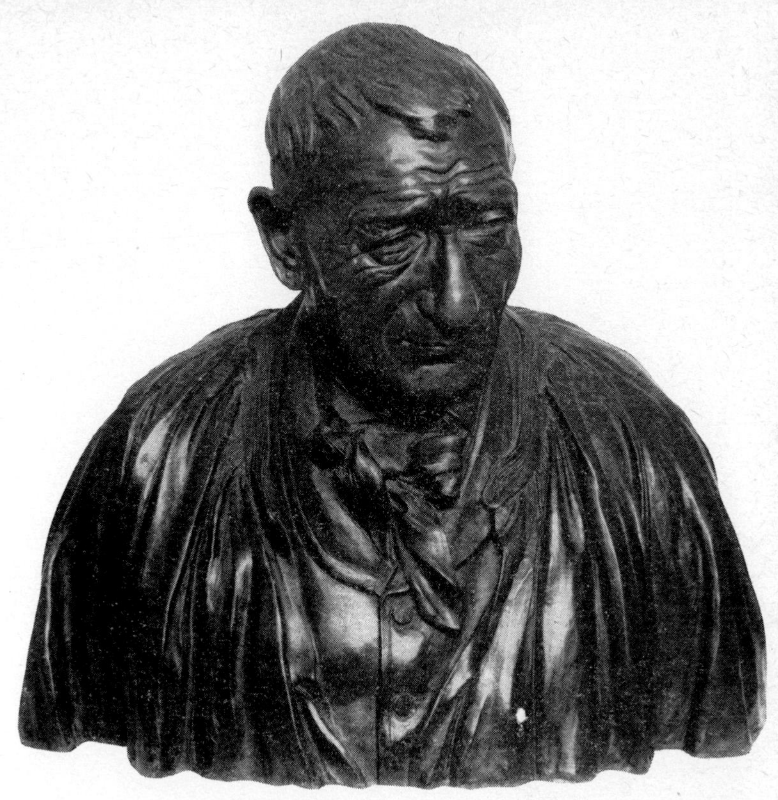

J. Dalou *Paysan à la Blouse* 1880–95
Heim Gallery, London

searching and his studies of workers, made in the intense socialist spirit of Millet's paintings, also have something of the intimacy of Degas's private studies. Like Van Gogh he absorbed his interest in working-class themes from a study of English Victorian artists, but he was unable to reconcile this realism with his desire for the monumental, and his *Triumph of the Republic* (1899) in the Place de la Nation in Paris is unimpressive except in its parts. His scheme for a monument to work, to show all human activities and work, got no further than the preparatory studies. It was conceived in the form of a huge tower and provided a precedent for Rodin's even more abortive monument to work begun in 1894.

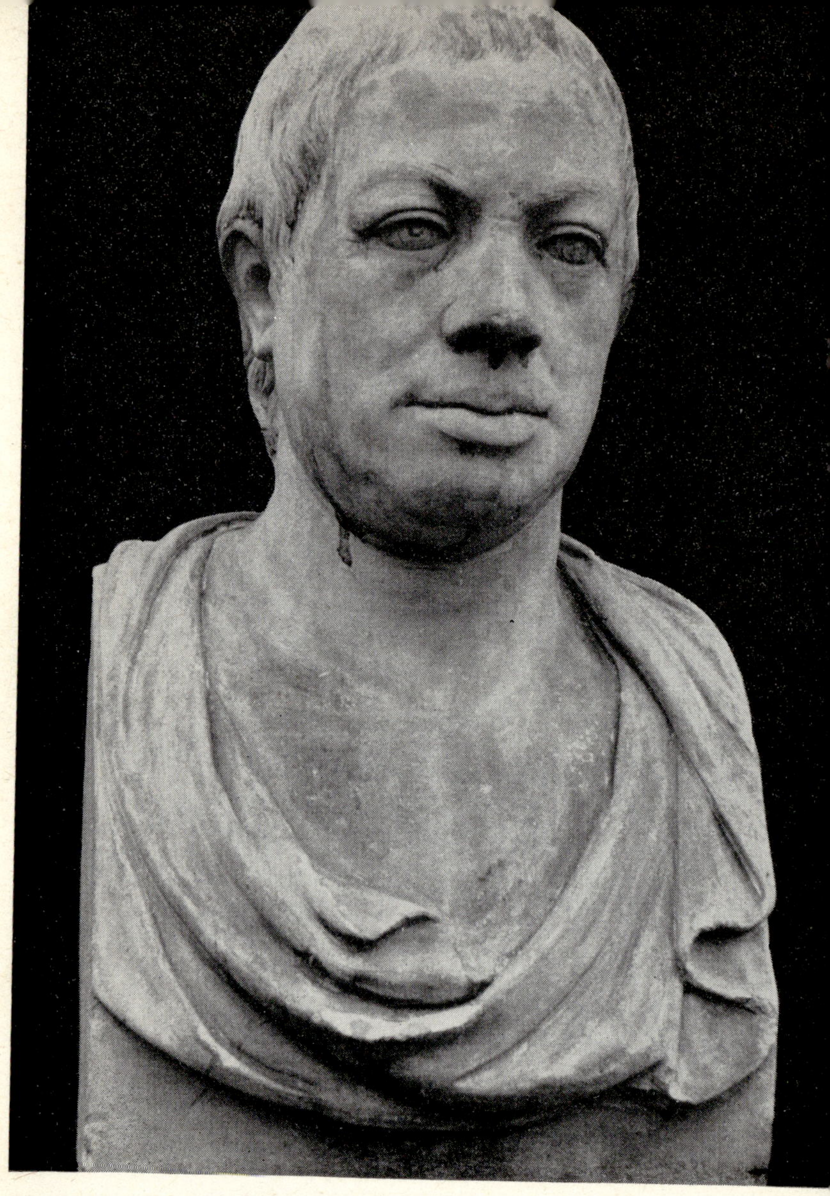

Coade Factory *Bust of a Man* 1818
Private collection

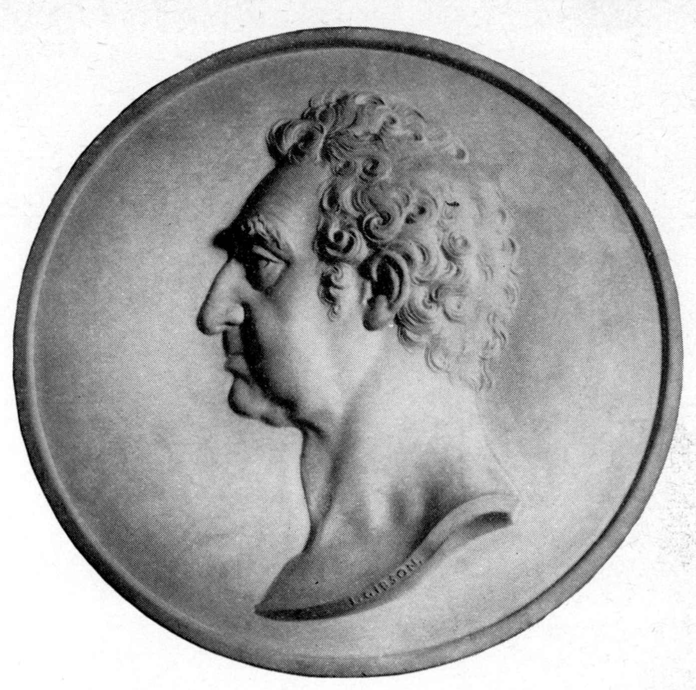

J. Gibson *William Roscoe* 1813
Private collection

The romantic movement had little impact on English sculpture and nothing comparable in vitality to the best French products appeared in England until the career of Alfred Stevens. Little alternative was offered to the sterile academic realism of the artists of the Albert Memorial, who achieved a deadly competence of technique at the expense of artistic vitality. Fine portrait busts were occasionally produced, but the subtly deadening effect of mechanical reproduction and enlargement undermined the expression of artistic personality, while the development of artificial stone that could be cast and worked easily, such as Coade stone, meant that even large-scale monuments could be treated as commodities for mass production. John Gibson (1791–1866), who was discovered by the Liverpool connoisseur William

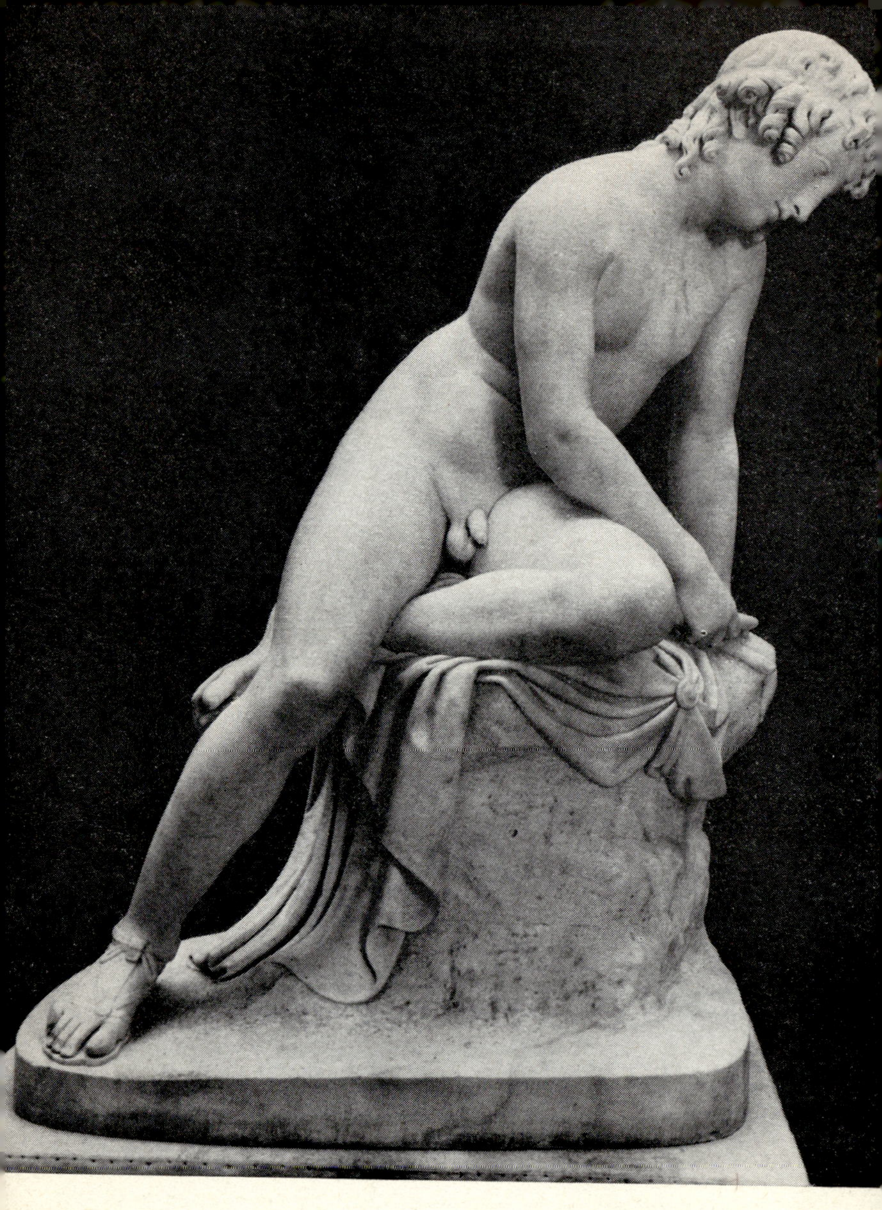

J. Gibson *Narcissus* 1838
Royal Academy, London

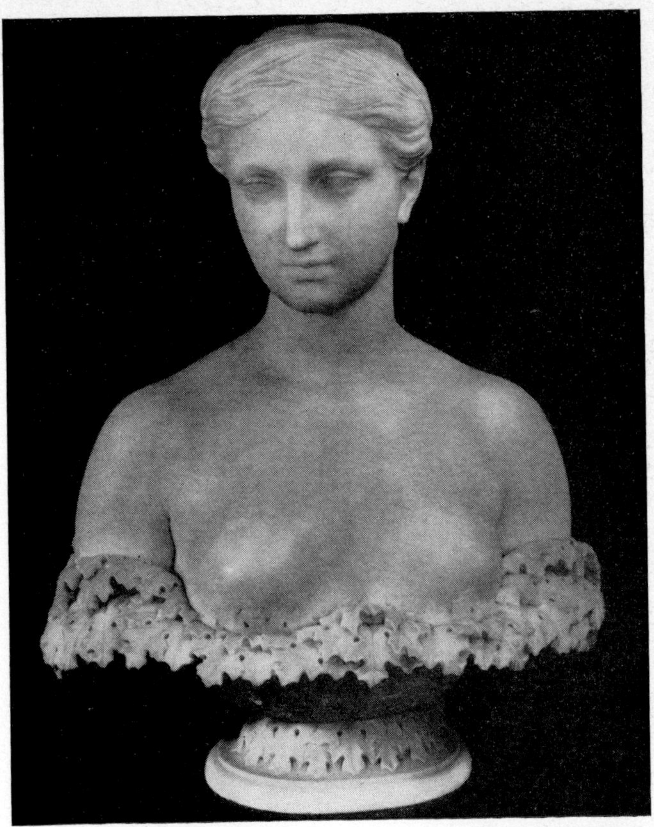

Hiram Powers *Proserpine* 1850–60
Heim Gallery, London

Roscoe, tried to preserve into the second half of the century the integrity of neoclassicism that he had learned from his masters Canova and Thorwaldsen but he succeeded only by working for most of his life in Rome. The severity of his work is tempered by a close study of the human body, but the work of the American Hiram Powers (1805–73) shows a striving after purity of form that all too frequently becomes merely insipid. The classicists of the nineteenth century should not, however, be seen only as *retardataire* in style; they preserved the ideal of purity of form that was to flower again in the work of Maillol and Brancusi, who sought, at the end of the century, an alternative to the 'beefsteak' art of Rodin. Alfred Stevens was the only sculptor before Sir Alfred Gilbert to possess the gifts that might have brought English sculpture out of its provincialism, but his career was one of perpetual frustration and only his powerful maquettes give a true idea of his Michelangelesque qualities and ambitions.

A. Stevens *Valour and Cowardice* 1857
Victoria and Albert Museum, London

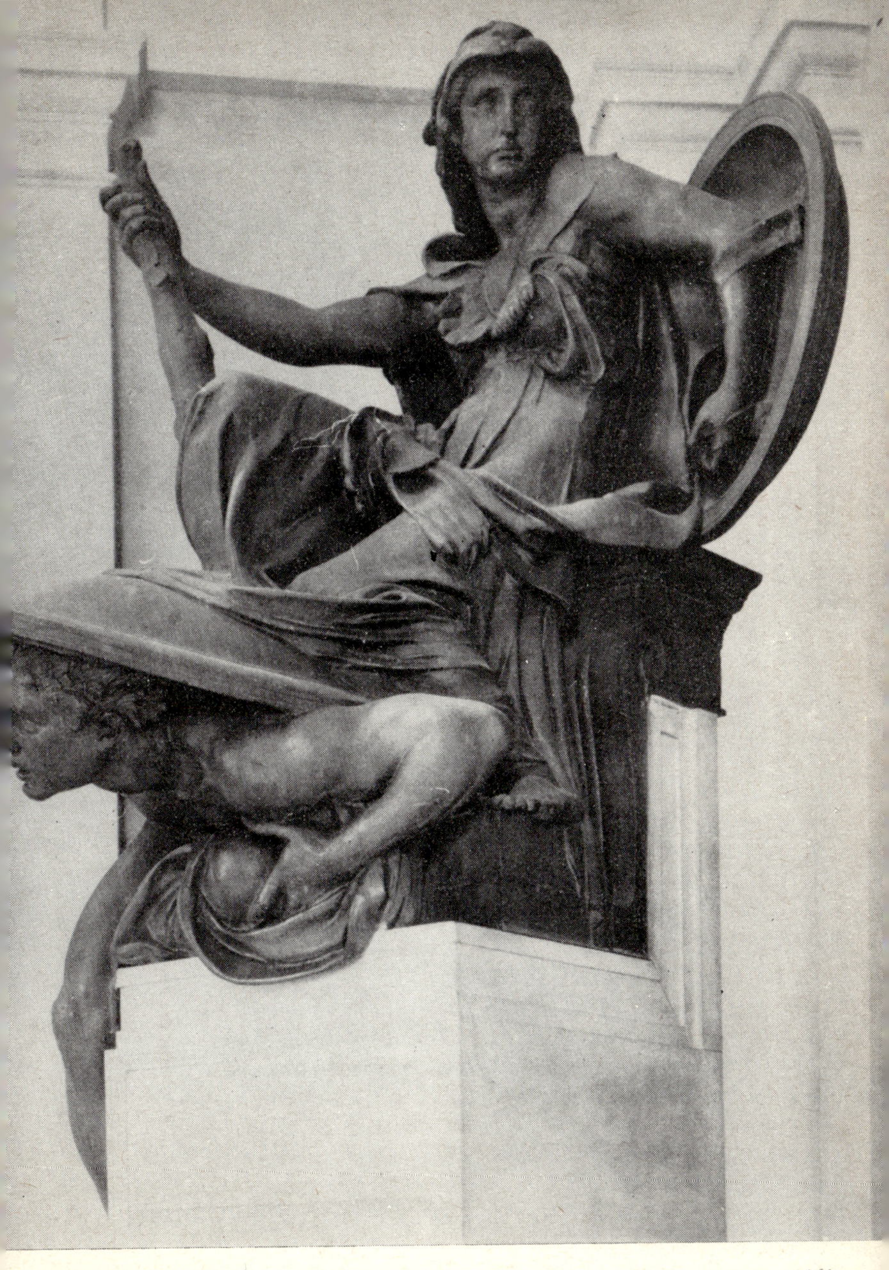

Rodin

Rodin inherited the contradictions that were implicit in the situation of the nineteenth-century sculptor: he was the last major artist to try to create a style out of the synthesis of other styles. He sought the vivacity of Carpeaux, but also the seriousness of Rude, the inward anguish of the gothic combined with the open sensuality of the Greeks. As a realist he wanted an art that would be immediately comprehensible to everybody, but as an admirer of Baudelaire he wished to create a form that would express man's intangible desires. No one was more aware of this conflict than he himself, but he repeatedly sought after public commissions in an attempt to revive the public monument as an art form.

Rodin was born in Paris in 1840, and in 1854 he enrolled at the 'Petite Ecole', which was an official preparatory drawing school for entry into the 'Grande Ecole' or Ecole des Beaux-Arts. At the Petite Ecole he was taught by Horace Lecoq de Bois-baudran, an inspiring teacher, who made his pupils draw from memory and copy eighteenth-century drawings. Rodin was only too good a pupil, and he absorbed the rococo style so well that he was unable to satisfy the examiners at the Grande Ecole, who demanded a more academic approach. Dalou told him later that he was lucky to have avoided the Grande Ecole, but the consequence of failure was to cut Rodin off from the normal process of an academic training which was an almost indispensable requirement for official commissions. He was obliged to support himself by work for decorative sculptors while working for himself in the evenings. His menial work helped him to achieve great facility, but he regarded its purpose as too trivial, and his monumental ambitions had been stimulated by his work on the Loos Monument in Belgium in 1874. In 1875 he went to Italy for two months and was able to study Donatello and Michelangelo. The confrontation with those masters confirmed his interest in character rather than ideal beauty that had been foreshadowed in his *Man with a Broken Nose* of 1863, but more profoundly he absorbed Michelangelo's way of showing inner anguish and suffering through the gestures of the whole body. Rodin later

A. Rodin *Man with a Broken Nose* 1863
Fitzwilliam Museum, Cambridge

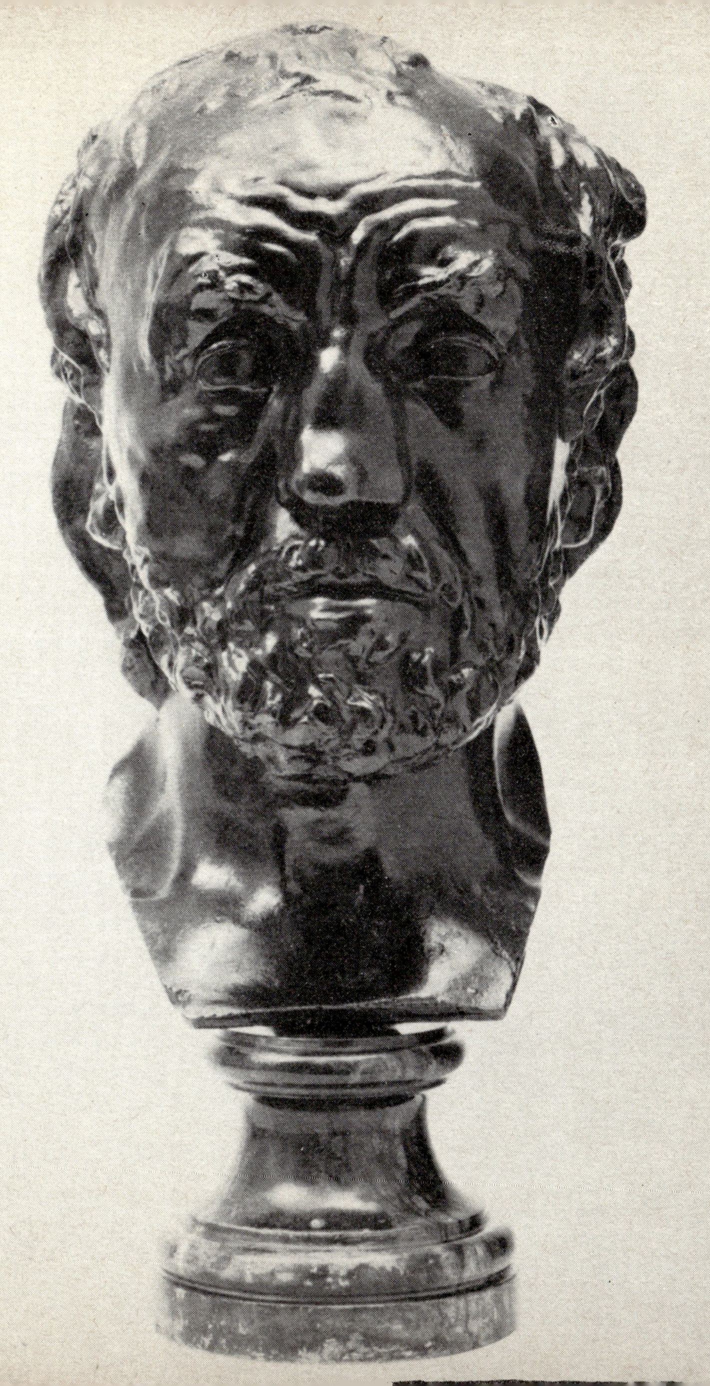

described Michelangelo as the last of the gothic artists whom he contrasted with the serenity of the Greeks. Michelangelo 'was only the last and greatest of the Gothics. The turning-in of the soul upon itself, suffering, a disgust with life, struggle against the chains of matter, such are the elements of his inspiration . . . he himself has been tortured by melancholy.'

Rodin's early work had been admired by a number of connoisseurs, but his public reputation sprang from the exhibition of the *Age of Bronze* in 1877. It was originally exhibited under the title of the *Vanquished*, but his contemporaries were baffled by its apparent lack of subject. None the less Rodin quite clearly intended it to represent a man in the process of awakening as symbolic of primitive man's incipient feelings of conscience, the first triumph of reason over bestiality. The beautiful unfolding movement of the figure is achieved by showing different phases of the action as if they were taking place at one moment. The transition from somnolence to wakeful readiness begins with the legs, which are still unsteady with sleep, and moves through the stretched torso to the head and arms, which show the sudden dawning of the idea. The *Age of Bronze* clearly owes a lot to the *Bound Slave* from Michelangelo's tomb of Julius II (in the Louvre), but Rodin himself cited Rude's *Maréchal Ney* as its true forebear, pointing to a comparable telescoping of the action from the moment that the Maréchal draws the sword out of the scabbard, to the point of waving it in the air while exhorting his troops to advance. The illusion that one is seeing the movement actually being accomplished is created by showing different parts of the statue at successive moments.

A. Rodin *Age of Bronze* 1877
Tate Gallery, London

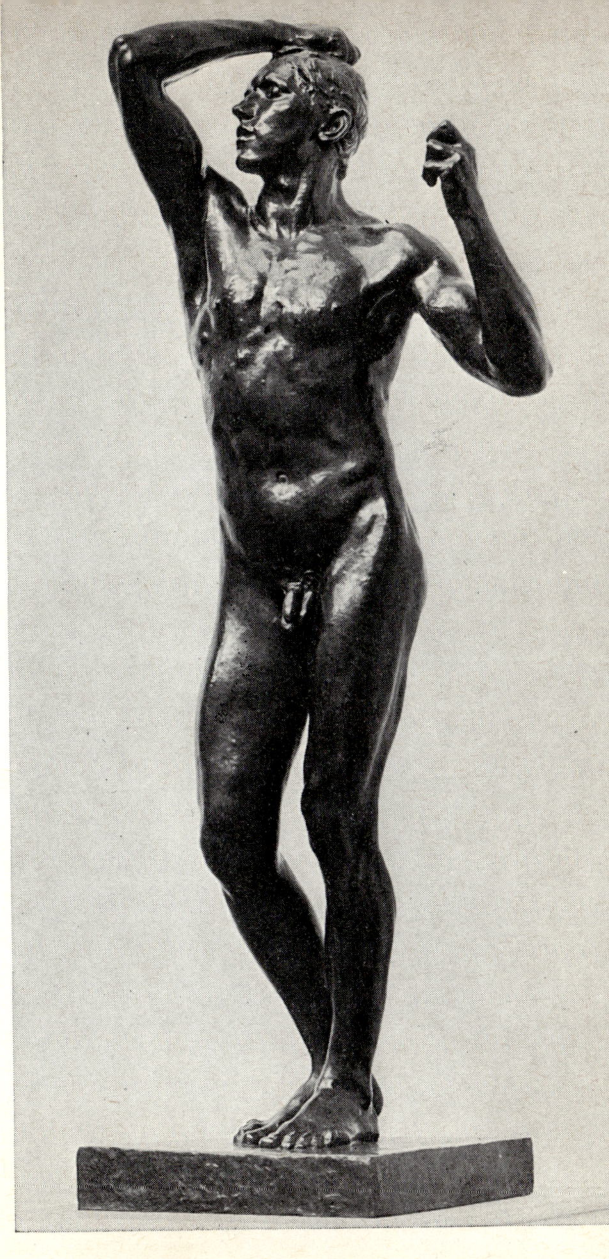

F. Rude *Le Maréchal Ney* 1852–3
Rue de l'Observatoire, Paris

Michelangelo *Bound Slave* c. 1513
Louvre, Paris

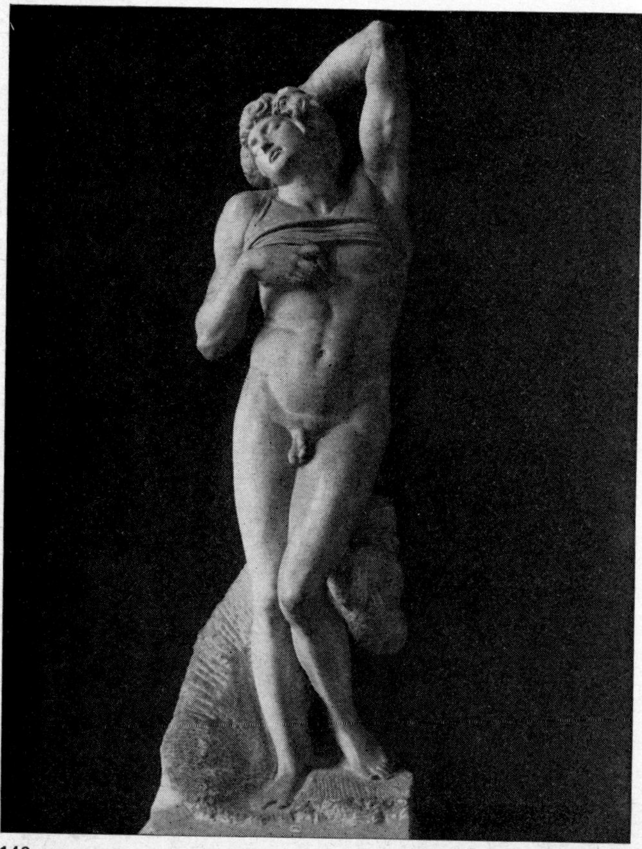

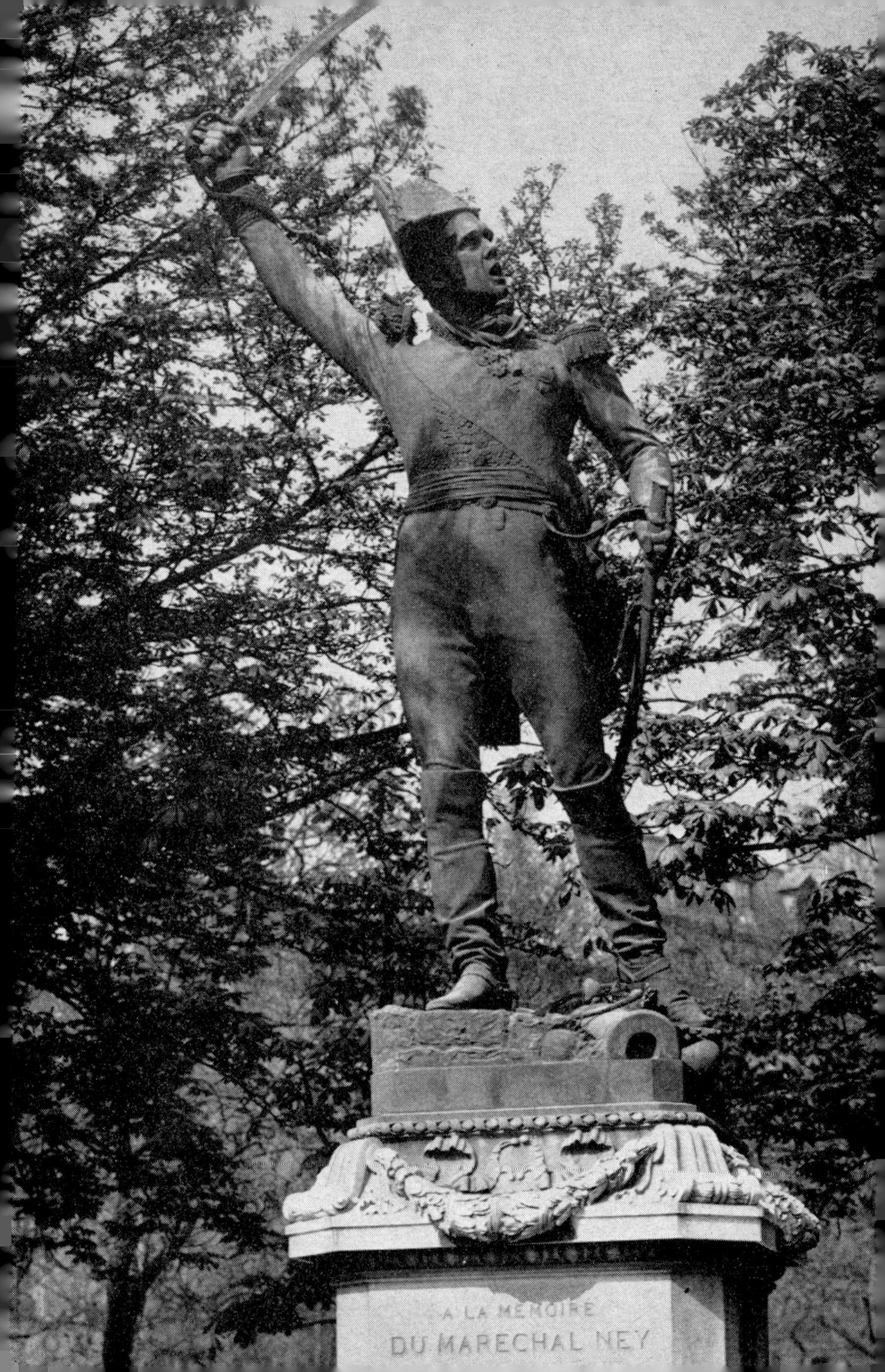
A LA MÉMOIRE
DU MARÉCHAL NEY

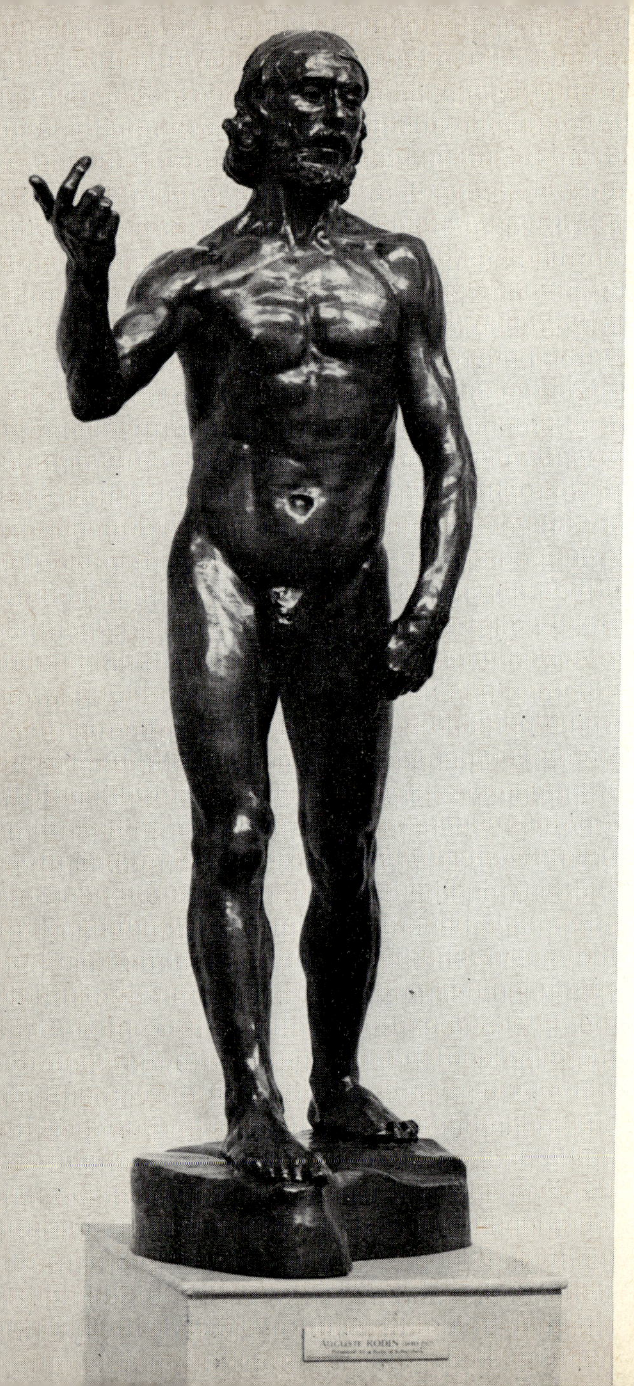

AUGUSTE RODIN (1840-1917)

A. Rodin *St John the Baptist Preaching* 1878
Tate Gallery, London

A. Rodin *Walking Man* c. 1877
Rodin Museum Paris

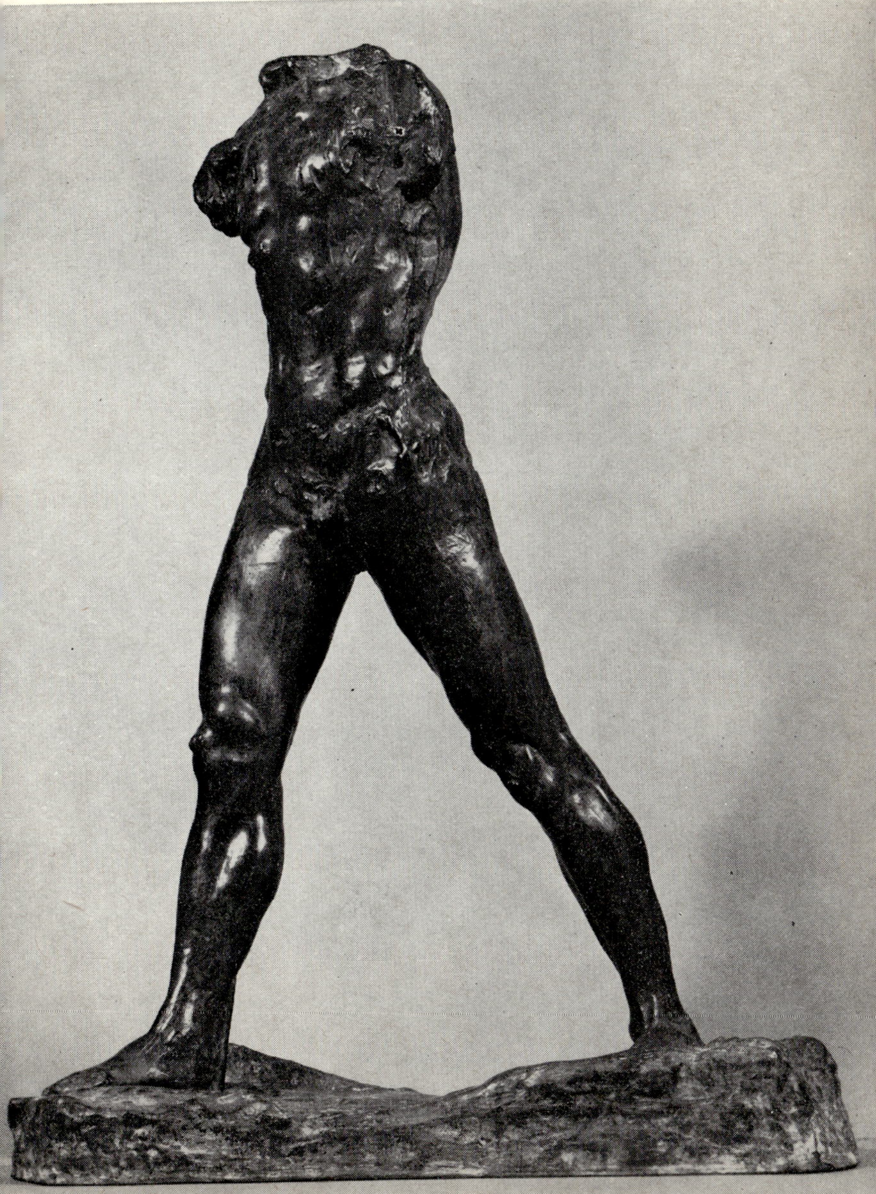

The same principle can be applied to his next major work, the *St John the Baptist Preaching* (1878), for which the *Walking Man* was originally a study. Rodin pointed out that if one took a photograph of a man in the process of walking, as Edward Muybridge had done, one would notice that at any given moment one foot or the other would be raised up from the ground. The *St John* has both feet placed firmly on the ground, while the torso leans forward; thus Rodin shows the forward movement in the process of being accomplished, while the strong arch formed by the legs gives the figure a powerful stability.

Rodin also applied the principle of simultaneity to groups of figures, and he explained it by reference to Rude's *Marseillaise* (see page 121). Here, instead of the parts of the body being in a different phase of the action at one time, the figures themselves carry out their actions at different moments but are still seen simultaneously. One looks first at the figure of La Patrie, who urges the troops to prepare for war. In the second phase the Gaul in uniform replies to the call by saluting her while his son asks to join him; the third phase shows an old man putting on his armour while another offers advice, and in the final phase an archer limbers up as the clarion is sounded to send the spears forward into battle. Similarly, in the *Burghers of Calais* (1885–95) each of the six burghers can be seen as representing the thoughts and gestures of one man at a moment of heroism. The group commemorates six citizens of Calais who offered themselves as hostages to Edward III to lift the siege of their town in 1447. The commission was originally for only one figure, of Eustache de Saint-Pierre their leader, but Rodin decided to show all six burghers so that the work would commemorate their communal heroism, and at the same time show true heroism as something that requires the overcoming of ordinary fears and regrets.

The principal figure is Eustache de Saint-Pierre, who is the first one to volunteer, and it is to his example that the others react. The man to his left, holding the key, expresses the humiliation of his city's surrender, while behind Saint-Pierre a man shows hesitancy and fear; behind the man with the key another has surrendered to despair. To the right of Saint-Pierre a man passes his hand over his eyes as if seeing the spectre of death, while behind him a young man is thinking of all he is about to leave behind. All the figures are indecisive as they contemplate their

A. Rodin *Burghers of Calais* 1885–95
Philadelphia Museum of Art

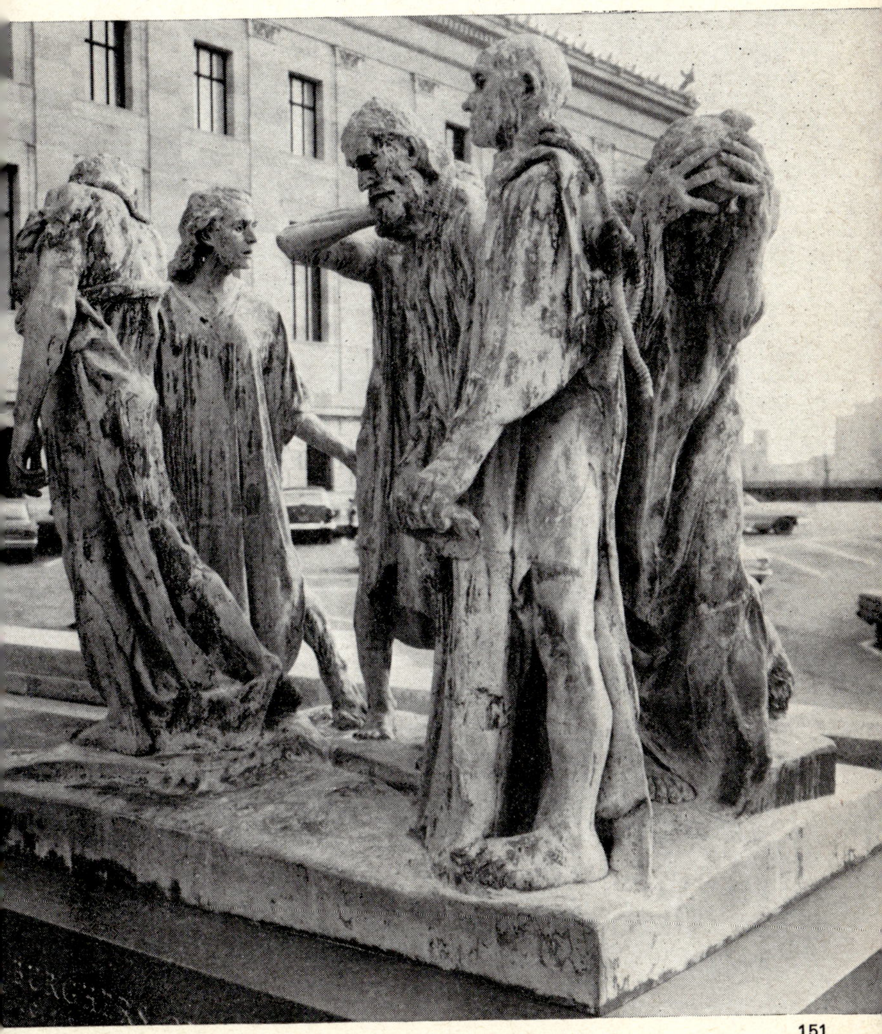

decision, except Saint-Pierre, who because of his age has the least to lose. The sequence of the action is circular because it begins with Saint-Pierre's resolute step forward, and passes through the varying emotions of the other figures and back again to him as they make their decision to go forward.

The *Gates of Hell* were commissioned in 1880, four years before the *Burghers of Calais*, but they were never completed, and Rodin used the groups that he designed for them as separate compositions in marble or bronze. The *Gates of Hell* express a more symbolic vision, which reflects the instability of modern man, his lack of absolutes and spiritual fixed points, and his eternal state of desire with no hope of fulfilment. The Poet or Thinker presides over this huge secular Last Judgment, which owes so much to Baudelaire's influence. He gradually lost interest in the

A. Rodin *Gates of Hell c.* 1880–1917
Philadelphia Museum of Art

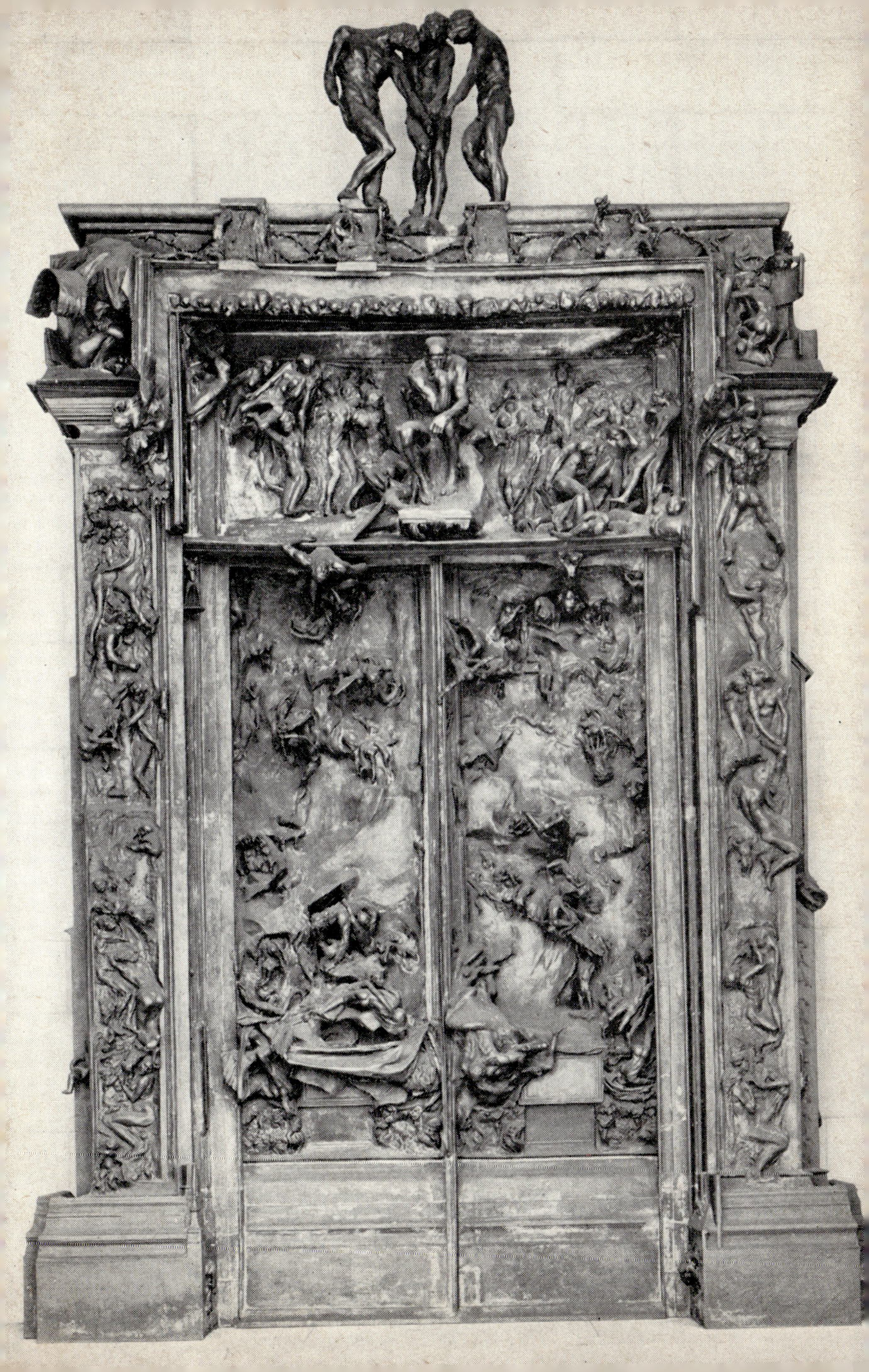

Gates, and in later years he began to adopt a more restrained 'Phidian' style, which superseded his earlier 'gothic' style. He continued to depict the human body in vivid studies in clay and outline drawing, but these works were rarely exhibited, although they are now much more to contemporary taste than his rather pretentious late marbles. He saw himself as a conservative up-holding the values of a decaying civilization, but the spontaneity of his late studies and his exploitation of the fragment made a vital contribution to the art of the twentieth century.

Book list

Blunt, A. F. *Art and Architecture in France, 1500–1700* Penguin, Harmondsworth, 1958

Elsen, A. E. *Rodin* Museum of Modern Art, New York, 1963

Elsen, A. E. (ed.) *Auguste Rodin: Readings on his Life and Work* Prentice-Hall, New Jersey, 1965

Hempel, E. *Baroque Art and Architecture in Central Europe* Penguin, Harmondsworth, 1965

Honour, H. *Neo-classicism* Penguin, Harmondsworth, 1968

Irwin, D. *English Neoclassical Art* Faber & Faber, London, 1966

Licht, F. *Sculpture in the 19th and 20th Centuries* Michael Joseph, London, 1967

Luc-Benoist *La Sculpture Française* Larousse, Paris, 1945

Luc-Benoist *La Sculpture Romantique* Larousse, Paris

Novotny, F. *Painting and Sculpture in Europe 1780–1880* Penguin, Harmondsworth, 1960

Pope-Hennessy, J. *Italian High Renaissance and Baroque Sculpture* Phaidon, London, 1963

Reau, L. *Pigalle* Pierre Pisné, Paris, 1950

Rilke, R. M. *Rodin* Grey Walls Press, London, 1946

Whinney, M. D. *English Sculpture, 1530–1830* Penguin, Harmondsworth, 1964

Wittkower, R. *Gian Lorenzo Bernini* Phaidon, London, 1955

Wittkower, R. *Art and Architecture in Italy 1600–1750* Penguin, Harmondsworth, 1958

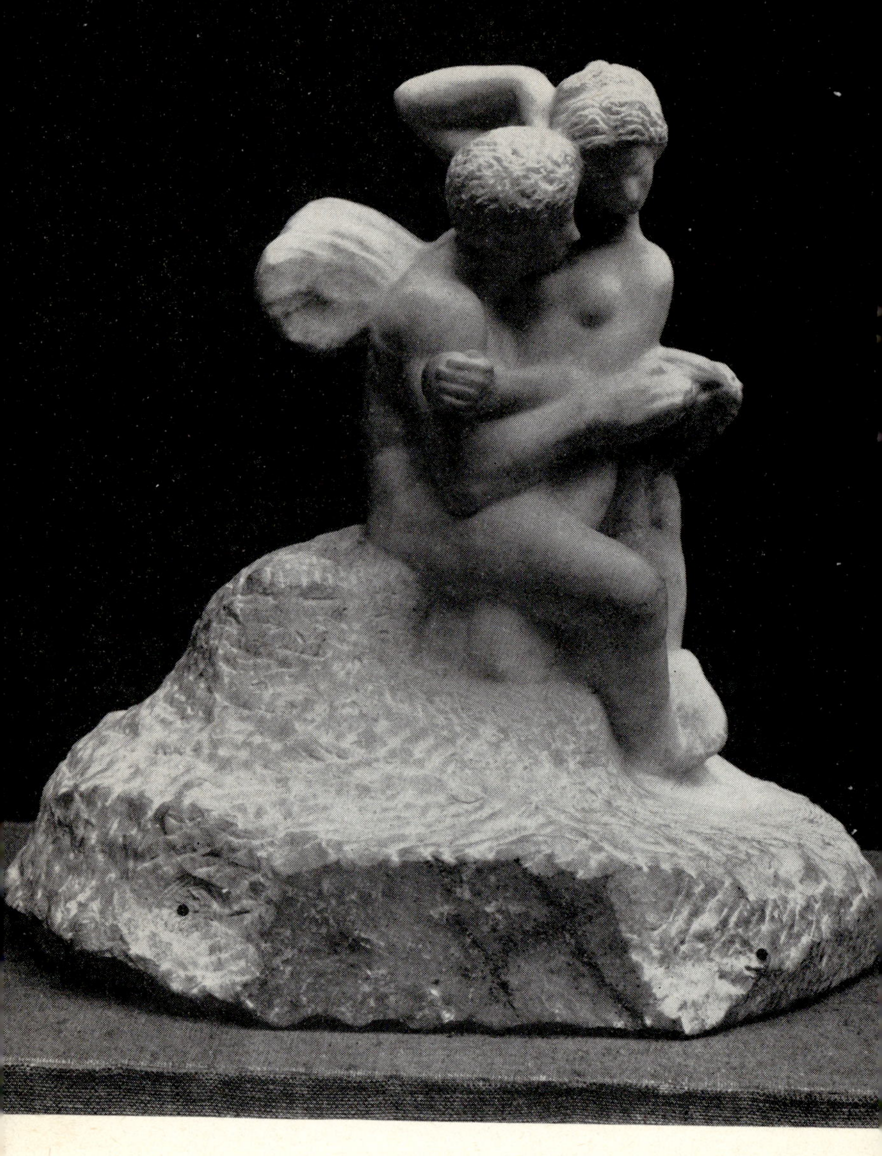

A. Rodin *Cupid and Psyche c.* 1908
Tate Gallery, London
156

Index

STUDIO VISTA/DUTTON PICTUREBACKS
edited by David Herbert

British churches by Edwin Smith and Olive Cook
European domestic architecture by Sherban Cantacuzino
Great modern architecture by Sherban Cantacuzino
Modern churches of the world
by Robert Maguire and Keith Murray
Modern houses of the world by Sherban Cantacuzino

African sculpture by William Fagg and Margaret Plass
European sculpture by David Bindman
Florentine sculpture by Anthony Bertram
Greek sculpture by John Barron
Indian sculpture by Philip Rawson
Michelangelo by Anthony Bertram
Modern sculpture by Alan Bowness

Art deco by Bevis Hillier
Art nouveau by Mario Amaya
The bauhaus by Gillian Naylor
De Stijl by Paul Overy
Modern graphics by Keith Murgatroyd
Modern prints by Pat Gilmour
Pop art: object and image by Christopher Finch
Surrealism by Roger Cardinal and Robert Stuart Short
1000 years of drawing by Anthony Bertram

Arms and armour by Howard L. Blackmore
The art of the garden by Miles Hadfield
Art in silver and gold by Gerald Taylor
Costume in pictures by Phillis Cunnington
Firearms by Howard L. Blackmore
Jewelry by Graham Hughes
Modern ballet by John Percival
Modern ceramics by Geoffrey Beard
Modern furniture by Ella Moody
Modern glass by Geoffrey Beard
Motoring history by L. T. C. Rolt
Railway history by C. Hamilton Ellis
Toys by Patrick Murray

Charlie Chaplin: early comedies by Isabel Quigly
The films of Alfred Hitchcock by George Perry
The great funnies by David Robinson
Greta Garbo by Raymond Durgnat and John Kobal
Marlene Dietrich by John Kobal
Movie monsters by Denis Gifford
New cinema in Britain by Roger Manvell
New cinema in Europe by Roger Manvell
New cinema in the USA by Roger Manvell
The silent cinema by Liam O'Leary